Microsoft®
Excel 97
Worksheet Function
Reference

Microsoft Press

PUBLISHED BY
Microsoft Press
A Division of Microsoft Corporation
One Microsoft Way
Redmond, Washington 98052-6399

Library of Congress Cataloging-in-Publication Data
Microsoft Excel 97 worksheet function reference : complete reference to
    the built-in functions and formulas in Microsoft Excel / Microsoft
    Corporation.
        p.   cm.
    Includes bibliographical references and index.
    ISBN 1-57231-341-2
    1. Microsoft Excel (Computer file)   2. Business--Computer
programs.   3. Electronic spreadsheets.   I. Microsoft Corporation.
HF5548.4.M523M543   1996
005.369--dc20   96-33464
                                                       CIP

Printed and bound in the United States of America.

1 2 3 4 5 6 7 8 9   MLML   2 1 0 9 8 7

Distributed to the book trade in Canada by Macmillan of Canada, a division of Canada Publishing Corporation.

A CIP catalogue record for this book is available from the British Library.

Microsoft Press books are available through booksellers and distributors worldwide. For further information about international editions, contact your local Microsoft Corporation office. Or contact Microsoft Press International directly at fax (206) 936-7329.

Acquisitions Editor: Casey D. Doyle
Project Editor: Maureen Williams Zimmerman

Contents

Introduction

This book explains the worksheet functions included in Microsoft® Excel 97. Except for a few differences, worksheet functions are identical for all operating systems supported by Microsoft Excel. Whenever information pertains to a specific operating system, such as the Apple® Macintosh®, the operating system is mentioned.

What Are Worksheet Functions?

Worksheet functions are the calculations built into Microsoft Excel for you. Each function calculates a different type of value. For example, you can use functions to calculate sums, averages, loan payments, and slopes of lines. Microsoft Excel includes hundreds of functions for financial, statistical, mathematical, trigonometric, and other types of calculations.

Using these functions saves you the time and effort of knowing, calculating, and recalculating many different mathematical equations. Functions can tell you whether a condition is true or false, whether one number is greater than another, or whether two words are exactly the same. Functions also help you to sort through data by identifying and calculating minimum, maximum, average, percentile, and rankings of values.

The Anatomy of a Function

Each function has two parts: the name of the function and its *arguments*. The name of a function always appears in uppercase letters and describes what the function does. For example, the AVERAGE function calculates the average of all the arguments included with the function.

Arguments are the numbers, cell references, worksheet names, or other information that a function needs to calculate a value for you. An argument can be any one of the following:

- Numbers, such as -5, 11, and 63.2.
- Text, such as "a", "Word", and "w/punc." If the text you want to use contains quotation marks, use two double quotation marks ("""text""") for each double quotation mark.

- Logical values, such as TRUE or FALSE, or a statement that creates a logical value when calculated, such as B10>20.

- Error values, such as #REF!.

- References, such as D12 or C4:C6.

Arguments follow the name of the function and are enclosed in parentheses. Multiple arguments are separated by commas. For example, if you wanted to find the average of the numbers 5, 11, and 63, plus the numbers included in the range C4:C6, you would enter the AVERAGE function and the following arguments into a cell:

`=AVERAGE(5, 11, 63, C4:C6)`

When you enter a function, you must precede it with an equal sign (=).

The functions, equal sign, and numbers, text, or references entered in a cell are referred to as a *formula*. After you enter a formula, Microsoft Excel calculates the formula and displays the resulting value in the cell. However, your formula isn't erased when a cell displays the value calculated from the formula. You can see your formula by selecting the cell and looking at the formula bar. Microsoft Excel recalculates the formula every time an argument changes.

Find Answers by Combining Functions

Functions can be used as arguments to other functions. Combining functions in this way helps you to make the most of the data entered on your worksheet. It also takes advantage of the ability of Microsoft Excel to quickly calculate and recalculate formulas. Remember to type an equal sign at the beginning of every formula, but not before functions used as arguments to other functions.

For example, suppose you want to estimate your income tax bill for the next year based on your last three years' worth of tax records. The cells A1:A3 on your worksheet contain your taxable income for the last three years and the cells B1:B3 contain your tax rates for those years. Without re-entering any data that is already on your worksheet, you can estimate the tax you will owe next year by using the formula:

`=PRODUCT(AVERAGE(A1:A3), AVERAGE(B1:B3))`

Conventions Used in This Book

Each function description in this book contains a section called Syntax, which shows the name of the function, the order of its arguments, and which arguments are required. Function names appear in uppercase letters without an equal sign (=). Required arguments are shown in **bold** and optional arguments are in plain text (not bold). Where functions and arguments are discussed in the text, all arguments are shown in plain text (not bold), whether they are required or optional.

Argument names use underline characters to separate the parts of the argument name. For example, num_chars is the name of an argument specifying the number of characters (letters) in a word or phrase.

In addition to the Syntax section, each function description might also include other information, such as:

- Explanation about a function and its use
- Examples showing how to use a function in a formula
- Related functions that are similar or complimentary to the one described
- Return values, the possible values calculated by the function

Learning More About Functions

The documentation included with Microsoft Excel contains additional information about using functions. For more information, including how to enter worksheet functions, how to use the Formula Palette, how Microsoft Excel calculates worksheet functions, and how to create your own worksheet functions, see Microsoft Excel 97 Help.

Worksheet Functions Listed by Category

Database & List Management Functions

DAVERAGE	Returns the average of selected database entries
DCOUNT	Counts the cells that contain numbers in a database
DCOUNTA	Counts nonblank cells in a database
DGET	Extracts from a database a single record that matches the specified criteria
DMAX	Returns the maximum value from selected database entries
DMIN	Returns the minimum value from selected database entries
DPRODUCT	Multiplies the values in a particular field of records that match the criteria in a database
DSTDEV	Estimates the standard deviation based on a sample of selected database entries
DSTDEVP	Calculates the standard deviation based on the entire population of selected database entries
DSUM	Adds the numbers in the field column of records in the database that match the criteria
DVAR	Estimates variance based on a sample from selected database entries
DVARP	Calculates variance based on the entire population of selected database entries
GETPIVOTDATA	Returns data stored in a PivotTable®

Date & Time Functions

DATE	Returns the serial number of a particular date
DATEVALUE	Converts a date in the form of text to a serial number
DAY	Converts a serial number to a day of the month
DAYS360	Calculates the number of days between two dates based on a 360-day year

EDATE	Returns the serial number of the date that is the indicated number of months before or after the start date
EOMONTH	Returns the serial number of the last day of the month before or after a specified number of months
HOUR	Converts a serial number to an hour
MINUTE	Converts a serial number to a minute
MONTH	Converts a serial number to a month
NETWORKDAYS	Returns the number of whole workdays between two dates
NOW	Returns the serial number of the current date and time
SECOND	Converts a serial number to a second
TIME	Returns the serial number of a particular time
TIMEVALUE	Converts a time in the form of text to a serial number
TODAY	Returns the serial number of today's date
WEEKDAY	Converts a serial number to a day of the week
WORKDAY	Returns the serial number of the date before or after a specified number of workdays
YEAR	Converts a serial number to a year
YEARFRAC	Returns the year fraction representing the number of whole days between start_date and end_date

DDE & External Functions

CALL	Calls a procedure in a dynamic link library or code resource
REGISTER.ID	Returns the register ID of the specified dynamic link library (DLL) or code resource that has been previously registered
SQLREQUEST	Connects with an external data source and runs a query from a worksheet, then returns the result as an array without the need for macro programming

Engineering Functions

BESSELI	Returns the modified Bessel function In(x)
BESSELJ	Returns the Bessel function Jn(x)
BESSELK	Returns the modified Bessel function Kn(x)
BESSELY	Returns the Bessel function Yn(x)
BIN2DEC	Converts a binary number to decimal
BIN2HEX	Converts a binary number to hexadecimal
BIN2OCT	Converts a binary number to octal
COMPLEX	Converts real and imaginary coefficients into a complex number

CONVERT	Converts a number from one measurement system to another
DEC2BIN	Converts a decimal number to binary
DEC2HEX	Converts a decimal number to hexadecimal
DEC2OCT	Converts a decimal number to octal
DELTA	Tests whether two values are equal
ERF	Returns the error function
ERFC	Returns the complementary error function
GESTEP	Tests whether a number is greater than a threshold value
HEX2BIN	Converts a hexadecimal number to binary
HEX2DEC	Converts a hexadecimal number to decimal
HEX2OCT	Converts a hexadecimal number to octal
IMABS	Returns the absolute value (modulus) of a complex number
IMAGINARY	Returns the imaginary coefficient of a complex number
IMARGUMENT	Returns the argument theta, an angle expressed in radians
IMCONJUGATE	Returns the complex conjugate of a complex number
IMCOS	Returns the cosine of a complex number
IMDIV	Returns the quotient of two complex numbers
IMEXP	Returns the exponential of a complex number
IMLN	Returns the natural logarithm of a complex number
IMLOG10	Returns the base-10 logarithm of a complex number
IMLOG2	Returns the base-2 logarithm of a complex number
IMPOWER	Returns a complex number raised to an integer power
IMPRODUCT	Returns the product of two complex numbers
IMREAL	Returns the real coefficient of a complex number
IMSIN	Returns the sine of a complex number
IMSQRT	Returns the square root of a complex number
IMSUB	Returns the difference of two complex numbers
IMSUM	Returns the sum of complex numbers
OCT2BIN	Converts an octal number to binary
OCT2DEC	Converts an octal number to decimal
OCT2HEX	Converts an octal number to hexadecimal
SQRTPI	Returns the square root of (number * PI)

Financial Functions

ACCRINT	Returns the accrued interest for a security that pays periodic interest
ACCRINTM	Returns the accrued interest for a security that pays interest at maturity
AMORDEGRC	Returns the depreciation for each accounting period
AMORLINC	Returns the depreciation for each accounting period
COUPDAYBS	Returns the number of days from the beginning of the coupon period to the settlement date
COUPDAYS	Returns the number of days in the coupon period that contains the settlement date
COUPDAYSNC	Returns the number of days from the settlement date to the next coupon date
COUPNCD	Returns the next coupon date after the settlement date
COUPNUM	Returns the number of coupons payable between the settlement date and maturity date
COUPPCD	Returns the previous coupon date before the settlement date
CUMIPMT	Returns the cumulative interest paid between two periods
CUMPRINC	Returns the cumulative principal paid on a loan between two periods
DB	Returns the depreciation of an asset for a specified period using the fixed-declining balance method
DDB	Returns the depreciation of an asset for a spcified period using the double-declining balance method or some other method you specify
DISC	Returns the discount rate for a security
DOLLARDE	Converts a dollar price, expressed as a fraction, into a dollar price, expressed as a decimal number
DOLLARFR	Converts a dollar price, expressed as a decimal number, into a dollar price, expressed as a fraction
DURATION	Returns the annual duration of a security with periodic interest payments
EFFECT	Returns the effective annual interest rate
FV	Returns the future value of an investment
FVSCHEDULE	Returns the future value of an initial principal after applying a series of compound interest rates
INTRATE	Returns the interest rate for a fully invested security
IPMT	Returns the interest payment for an investment for a given period
IRR	Returns the internal rate of return for a series of cash flows
MDURATION	Returns the Macauley modified duration for a security with an assumed par value of $100
MIRR	Returns the internal rate of return where positive and negative cash flows are financed at different rates
NOMINAL	Returns the annual nominal interest rate

NPER	Returns the number of periods for an investment
NPV	Returns the net present value of an investment based on a series of periodic cash flows and a discount rate
ODDFPRICE	Returns the price per $100 face value of a security with an odd first period
ODDFYIELD	Returns the yield of a security with an odd first period
ODDLPRICE	Returns the price per $100 face value of a security with an odd last period
ODDLYIELD	Returns the yield of a security with an odd last period
PMT	Returns the periodic payment for an annuity
PPMT	Returns the payment on the principal for an investment for a given period
PRICE	Returns the price per $100 face value of a security that pays periodic interest
PRICEDISC	Returns the price per $100 face value of a discounted security
PRICEMAT	Returns the price per $100 face value of a security that pays interest at maturity
PV	Returns the present value of an investment
RATE	Returns the interest rate per period of an annuity
RECEIVED	Returns the amount received at maturity for a fully invested security
SLN	Returns the straight-line depreciation of an asset for one period
SYD	Returns the sum-of-years' digits depreciation of an asset for a specified period
TBILLEQ	Returns the bond-equivalent yield for a Treasury bill
TBILLPRICE	Returns the price per $100 face value for a Treasury bill
TBILLYIELD	Returns the yield for a Treasury bill
VDB	Returns the depreciation of an asset for a specified or partial period using a declining balance method
XIRR	Returns the internal rate of return for a schedule of cash flows that is not necessarily periodic
XNPV	Returns the net present value for a schedule of cash flows that is not necessarily periodic
YIELD	Returns the yield on a security that pays periodic interest
YIELDDISC	Returns the annual yield for a discounted security. For example, a treasury bill
YIELDMAT	Returns the annual yield of a security that pays interest at maturity

Information Functions

CELL	Returns information about the formatting, location, or contents of a cell
COUNTBLANK	Counts the number of blank cells within a range
ERROR.TYPE	Returns a number corresponding to an error type
INFO	Returns information about the current operating environment
ISBLANK	Returns TRUE if the value is blank
ISERR	Returns TRUE if the value is any error value except #N/A
ISERROR	Returns TRUE if the value is any error value
ISEVEN	Returns TRUE if the number is even
ISLOGICAL	Returns TRUE if the value is a logical value
ISNA	Returns TRUE if the value is the #N/A error value
ISNONTEXT	Returns TRUE if the value is not text
ISNUMBER	Returns TRUE if the value is a number
ISODD	Returns TRUE if the number is odd
ISREF	Returns TRUE if the value is a reference
ISTEXT	Returns TRUE if the value is text
N	Returns a value converted to a number
NA	Returns the error value #N/A
TYPE	Returns a number indicating the data type of a value

Logical Functions

AND	Returns TRUE if all its arguments are TRUE
FALSE	Returns the logical value FALSE
IF	Specifies a logical test to perform
NOT	Reverses the logic of its argument
OR	Returns TRUE if any argument is TRUE
TRUE	Returns the logical value TRUE

Lookup & Reference Functions

ADDRESS	Returns a reference as text to a single cell in a worksheet
AREAS	Returns the number of areas in a reference
CHOOSE	Chooses a value from a list of values
COLUMN	Returns the column number of a reference
COLUMNS	Returns the number of columns in a reference
HLOOKUP	Looks in the top row of an array and returns the value of the indicated cell
HYPERLINK	Creates a shortcut or jump that opens a document stored on a network server, an intranet, or the Internet
INDEX	Uses an index to choose a value from a reference or array
INDIRECT	Returns a reference indicated by a text value
LOOKUP	Looks up values in a vector or array
MATCH	Looks up values in a reference or array
OFFSET	Returns a reference offset from a given reference
ROW	Returns the row number of a reference
ROWS	Returns the number of rows in a reference
TRANSPOSE	Returns the transpose of an array
VLOOKUP	Looks in the first column of an array and moves across the row to return the value of a cell

Math & Trigonometry Functions

ABS	Returns the absolute value of a number
ACOS	Returns the arccosine of a number
ACOSH	Returns the inverse hyperbolic cosine of a number
ASIN	Returns the arcsine of a number
ASINH	Returns the inverse hyperbolic sine of a number
ATAN	Returns the arctangent of a number
ATAN2	Returns the arctangent from x- and y- coordinates
ATANH	Returns the inverse hyperbolic tangent of a number
CEILING	Rounds a number to the nearest integer or to the nearest multiple of significance
COMBIN	Returns the number of combinations for a given number of objects
COS	Returns the cosine of a number
COSH	Returns the hyperbolic cosine of a number
COUNTIF	Counts the number of non-blank cells within a range which meet the given criteria

DEGREES	Converts radians to degrees
EVEN	Rounds a number up to the nearest even integer
EXP	Returns e raised to the power of a given number
FACT	Returns the factorial of a number
FACTDOUBLE	Returns the double factorial of a number
FLOOR	Rounds a number down, toward zero
GCD	Returns the greatest common divisor
INT	Rounds a number down to the nearest integer
LCM	Returns the least common multiple
LN	Returns the natural logarithm of a number
LOG	Returns the logarithm of a number to a specified base
LOG10	Returns the base-10 logarithm of a number
MDETERM	Returns the matrix determinant of an array
MINVERSE	Returns the matrix inverse of an array
MMULT	Returns the matrix product of two arrays
MOD	Returns the remainder from division
MROUND	Returns a number rounded to the desired multiple
MULTINOMIAL	Returns the multinomial of a set of numbers
ODD	Rounds a number up to the nearest odd integer
PI	Returns the value of Pi
POWER	Returns the result of a number raised to a power
PRODUCT	Multiplies its arguments
QUOTIENT	Returns the integer portion of a division
RADIANS	Converts degrees to radians
RAND	Returns a random number between 0 and 1
RANDBETWEEN	Returns a random number between the numbers you specify
ROMAN	Converts an Arabic numeral to Roman, as text
ROUND	Rounds a number to a specified number of digits
ROUNDDOWN	Rounds a number down, toward zero
ROUNDUP	Rounds a number up, away from zero
SERIESSUM	Returns the sum of a power series based on the formula
SIGN	Returns the sign of a number
SIN	Returns the sine of the given angle
SINH	Returns the hyperbolic sine of a number
SQRT	Returns a positive square root
SQRTPI	Returns the square root of (number * PI)
SUBTOTAL	Returns a subtotal in a list or database
SUM	Adds its arguments

SUMIF	Adds the cells specified by a given criteria
SUMPRODUCT	Returns the sum of the products of corresponding array components
SUMSQ	Returns the sum of the squares of the arguments
SUMX2MY2	Returns the sum of the difference of squares of corresponding values in two arrays
SUMX2PY2	Returns the sum of the sum of squares of corresponding values in two arrays
SUMXMY2	Returns the sum of squares of differences of corresponding values in two arrays
TAN	Returns the tangent of a number
TANH	Returns the hyperbolic tangent of a number
TRUNC	Truncates a number to an integer

Statistical Functions

AVEDEV	Returns the average of the absolute deviations of data points from their mean
AVERAGE	Returns the average of its arguments
AVERAGEA	Returns the average of its arguments, including numbers, text, and logical values
BETADIST	Returns the cumulative beta probability density function
BETAINV	Returns the inverse of the cumulative beta probability density function
BINOMDIST	Returns the individual term binomial distribution probability
CHIDIST	Returns the one-tailed probability of the chi-squared distribution
CHIINV	Returns the inverse of the one-tailed probability of the chi-squared distribution
CHITEST	Returns the test for independence
CONFIDENCE	Returns the confidence interval for a population mean
CORREL	Returns the correlation coefficient between two data sets
COUNT	Counts how many numbers are in the list of arguments
COUNTA	Counts how many values are in the list of arguments
COVAR	Returns covariance, the average of the products of paired deviations
CRITBINOM	Returns the smallest value for which the cumulative binomial distribution is less than or equal to a criterion value
DEVSQ	Returns the sum of squares of deviations
EXPONDIST	Returns the exponential distribution
FDIST	Returns the F probability distribution
FINV	Returns the inverse of the F probability distribution
FISHER	Returns the Fisher transformation
FISHERINV	Returns the inverse of the Fisher transformation

FORECAST	Returns a value along a linear trend
FREQUENCY	Returns a frequency distribution as a vertical array
FTEST	Returns the result of an F-test
GAMMADIST	Returns the gamma distribution
GAMMAINV	Returns the inverse of the gamma cumulative distribution
GAMMALN	Returns the natural logarithm of the gamma function, $G(x)$
GEOMEAN	Returns the geometric mean
GROWTH	Returns values along an exponential trend
HARMEAN	Returns the harmonic mean
HYPGEOMDIST	Returns the hypergeometric distribution
INTERCEPT	Returns the intercept of the linear regression line
KURT	Returns the kurtosis of a data set
LARGE	Returns the k-th largest value in a data set
LINEST	Returns the parameters of a linear trend
LOGEST	Returns the parameters of an exponential trend
LOGINV	Returns the inverse of the lognormal distribution
LOGNORMDIST	Returns the cumulative lognormal distribution
MAX	Returns the maximum value in a list of arguments
MAXA	Returns the maximum value in a list of arguments, including numbers, text, and logical values
MEDIAN	Returns the median of the given numbers
MIN	Returns the minimum value in a list of arguments
MINA	Returns the smallest value in a list of arguments, including numbers, text, and logical values
MODE	Returns the most common value in a data set
NEGBINOMDIST	Returns the negative binomial distribution
NORMDIST	Returns the normal cumulative distribution
NORMINV	Returns the inverse of the normal cumulative distribution
NORMSDIST	Returns the standard normal cumulative distribution
NORMSINV	Returns the inverse of the standard normal cumulative distribution
PEARSON	Returns the Pearson product moment correlation coefficient
PERCENTILE	Returns the k-th percentile of values in a range
PERCENTRANK	Returns the percentage rank of a value in a data set
PERMUT	Returns the number of permutations for a given number of objects
POISSON	Returns the Poisson distribution
PROB	Returns the probability that values in a range are between two limits
QUARTILE	Returns the quartile of a data set
RANK	Returns the rank of a number in a list of numbers
RSQ	Returns the square of the Pearson product moment correlatin coefficient

SKEW	Returns the skewness of a distribution
SLOPE	Returns the slope of the linear regression line
SMALL	Returns the k-th smallest value in a data set
STANDARDIZE	Returns a normalized value
STDEV	Estimates standard deviation based on a sample
STDEVA	Estimates standard deviation based on a sample, including numbers, text, and logical values
STDEVP	Calculates standard deviation based on the entire population
STDEVPA	Calculates standard deviation based on the entire population, including numbers, text, and logical values
STEYX	Returns the standard error of the predicted y-value for each x in the regression
TDIST	Returns the Student's t-distribution
TINV	Returns the inverse of the Student's t-distribution
TREND	Returns values along a linear trend
TRIMMEAN	Returns the mean of the interior of a data set
TTEST	Returns the probability associated with a Student's t-Test
VAR	Estimates variance based on a sample
VARA	Estimates variance based on a sample, including numbers, text, and logical values
VARP	Calculates variance based on the entire population
VARPA	Calculates variance based on the entire population, including numbers, text, and logical values
WEIBULL	Returns the Weibull distribution
ZTEST	Returns the two-tailed P-value of a z-test

Text Functions

CHAR	Returns the character specified by the code number
CLEAN	Removes all nonprintable characters from text
CODE	Returns a numeric code for the first character in a text string
CONCATENATE	Joins several text items into one text item
DOLLAR	Converts a number to text, using currency format
EXACT	Checks to see if two text values are identical
FIND	Finds one text value within another (case-sensitive)
FIXED	Formats a number as text with a fixed number of decimals
LEFT	Returns the leftmost characters from a text value
LEN	Returns the number of characters in a text string
LOWER	Converts text to lowercase

MID	Returns a specific number of characters from a text string starting at the position you specify
PROPER	Capitalizes the first letter in each word of a text value
REPLACE	Replaces characters within text
REPT	Repeats text a given number of times
RIGHT	Returns the rightmost characters from a text value
SEARCH	Finds one text value within another (not case-sensitive)
SUBSTITUTE	Substitutes new text for old text in a text string
T	Converts its arguments to text
TEXT	Formats a number and converts it to text
TRIM	Removes spaces from text
UPPER	Converts text to uppercase
VALUE	Converts a text argument to a number

ABS

Returns the absolute value of a number. The absolute value of a number is the number without its sign.

Syntax

ABS(number)

Number   is the real number of which you want the absolute value.

Examples

ABS(2) equals 2

ABS(-2) equals 2

If A1 contains -16, then:

SQRT(ABS(A1)) equals 4

ACCRINT

Returns the accrued interest for a security that pays periodic interest.

If this function is not available, run the Setup program to install the Analysis ToolPak. After you install the Analysis ToolPak, you must enable it by using the **Add-Ins** command on the **Tools** menu.

Syntax

ACCRINT(issue,first_interest,settlement,rate,par,frequency,basis)

Issue   is the security's issue date.

First_interest   is the security's first interest date.

Settlement   is the security's settlement date. The security settlement date is the date after the issue date when the security is traded to the buyer.

Rate   is the security's annual coupon rate.

Par   is the security's par value. If you omit par, ACCRINT uses $1,000.

Frequency   is the number of coupon payments per year. For annual payments, frequency = 1; for semiannual, frequency = 2; for quarterly, frequency = 4.

Basis   is the type of day count basis to use.

Basis	Day count basis
0 or omitted	US (NASD) 30/360
1	Actual/actual
2	Actual/360
3	Actual/365
4	European 30/360

Remarks

- If any argument is nonnumeric, ACCRINT returns the #VALUE! error value.
- Issue, first_interest, settlement, frequency, and basis are truncated to integers.
- If issue, first_interest, or settlement is not a valid date, ACCRINT returns the #NUM! error value.
- If coupon ≤ 0 or if par ≤ 0, ACCRINT returns the #NUM! error value.
- If frequency is any number other than 1, 2, or 4, ACCRINT returns the #NUM! error value.
- If basis < 0 or if basis > 4, ACCRINT returns the #NUM! error value.
- If issue ≥ settlement, ACCRINT returns the #NUM! error value.
- ACCRINT is calculated as follows:

$$ACCRINT = par \times \frac{rate}{frequency} \times \sum_{i=1}^{NC} \frac{A_i}{NL_i}$$

where:

A_i = number of accrued days for the ith quasi-coupon period within odd period.

NC = number of quasi-coupon periods that fit in odd period. If this number contains a fraction, raise it to the next whole number.

NL_i = normal length in days of the ith quasi-coupon period within odd period.

Example

A treasury bond has the following terms:

February 28, 1993, issue date
August 31, 1993, first interest date
May 1, 1993, settlement date
10.0 percent coupon
$1,000 par value
Frequency is semiannual
30/360 basis

The accrued interest (in the 1900 date system) is:

```
ACCRINT("2/28/93","8/31/93","5/1/93",0.1,1000,2,0) equals 16.94444
```

ACCRINTM

Returns the accrued interest for a security that pays interest at maturity.

If this function is not available, run the Setup program to install the Analysis ToolPak. After you install the Analysis ToolPak, you must enable it by using the **Add-Ins** command on the **Tools** menu.

Syntax

ACCRINTM(issue,maturity,rate,par,basis)

Issue   is the security's issue date.

Maturity   is the security's maturity date.

Rate   is the security's annual coupon rate.

Par   is the security's par value. If you omit par, ACCRINTM uses $1,000.

Basis   is the type of day count basis to use.

Basis	Day count basis
0 or omitted	US (NASD) 30/360
1	Actual/actual
2	Actual/360
3	Actual/365
4	European 30/360

Remarks

- Issue, settlement, and basis are truncated to integers.
- If any argument is nonnumeric, ACCRINTM returns the #VALUE! error value.
- If issue or settlement is not a valid date, ACCRINTM returns the #NUM! error value.
- If rate ≤ 0 or if par ≤ 0, ACCRINTM returns the #NUM! error value.
- If basis < 0 or if basis > 4, ACCRINTM returns the #NUM! error value.
- If issue ≥ settlement, ACCRINTM returns the #NUM! error value.
- ACCRINTM is calculated as follows:

$$ACCRINTM = par \times rate \times \frac{A}{D}$$

where:

A = Number of accrued days counted according to a monthly basis. For interest at maturity items, the number of days from the issue date to the maturity date is used.

D = Annual Year Basis.

Example

A note has the following terms:

April 1, 1993, issue date
June 15, 1993, maturity date
10.0 percent coupon
$1,000 par value
Actual/365 basis

The accrued interest (in the 1900 date system) is:

ACCRINTM("4/1/93","6/15/93",0.1,1000,3) equals 20.54795

ACOS

Returns the arccosine of a number. The arccosine is the angle whose cosine is number. The returned angle is given in radians in the range 0 (zero) to π (pi).

Syntax

ACOS(number)

Number   is the cosine of the angle you want and must be from -1 to 1.

If you want to convert the result from radians to degrees, multiply it by 180/PI().

Examples

ACOS(-0.5) equals 2.094395 ($2\pi/3$ radians)

ACOS(-0.5)*180/PI() equals 120 (degrees)

ACOSH

Returns the inverse hyperbolic cosine of a number. Number must be greater than or equal to 1. The inverse hyperbolic cosine is the value whose hyperbolic cosine is number, so ACOSH(COSH(number)) equals number.

Syntax

ACOSH(number)

Number   is any real number equal to or greater than 1.

Examples

ACOSH(1) equals 0

ACOSH(10) equals 2.993223

ADDRESS

Creates a cell address as text, given specified row and column numbers.

Syntax

ADDRESS(row_num,column_num,abs_num,a1,sheet_text)

Row_num   is the row number to use in the cell reference.

Column_num   is the column number to use in the cell reference.

Abs_num   specifies the type of reference to return.

Abs_num	Returns this type of reference
1 or omitted	Absolute
2	Absolute row; relative column
3	Relative row; absolute column
4	Relative

A1   is a logical value that specifies the A1 or R1C1 reference style. If a1 is TRUE or omitted, ADDRESS returns an A1-style reference; if FALSE, ADDRESS returns an R1C1-style reference.

Sheet_text   is text specifying the name of the worksheet to be used as the external reference. If sheet_text is omitted, no sheet name is used.

Examples

ADDRESS(2,3) equals "$C$2"

ADDRESS(2,3,2) equals "C$2"

ADDRESS(2,3,2,FALSE) equals "R2C[3]"

ADDRESS(2,3,1,FALSE,"[Book1]Sheet1") equals "[Book1]Sheet1!R2C3"

ADDRESS(2,3,1,FALSE,"EXCEL SHEET") equals "'EXCEL SHEET'!R2C3"

AMORDEGRC

Returns the depreciation for each accounting period. This function is provide for the French accounting system. If an asset is purchased in the middle of the accounting period, then the prorated depreciation is taken into account. The function is similar to AMORLINC, except that a depreciation coefficient is applied in the calculation depending on the life of the assets.

If this function is not available, run the Setup program to install the Analysis ToolPak. After you install the Analysis ToolPak, you must enable it by using the **Add-Ins** command on the **Tools** menu.

Syntax

AMORDEGRC(cost,date_purchased,first_period,salvage,period,rate,basis)

Cost   is the cost of the asset.

Date_purchased   is the date of the purchase of the asset.

First_period   is the date of the end of the first period.

Salvage   is the salvage value at the end of the life of the asset.

Period   is the period.

Rate   is the rate of depreciation.

Basis   is the year_basis to be used.

Basis	Date system
0	360 days (NASD method)
1	Actual
3	365 days in a year
4	360 days in a year (European method)

Remarks

- This function will return the depreciation until the last period of the life of the assets or until the cumulated value of depreciation is greater than the cost of the assets minus the salvage value.

- The depreciation coefficients are:

Life of assets (1/rate)	Depreciation coefficient
Between 3 and 4 years	1.5
Between 5 and 6 years	2
More than 6 years	2.5

- The depreciation rate will grow to 50 percent for the period preceding the last period and will grow to 100 percent for the last period.

- If the life of assets is between 0 (zero) and 1, 1 and 2, 2 and 3, or 4 and 5, the #NUM! error value is returned.

Example

Suppose a machine bought on August 19, 1993, costs $2,400 and has a salvage value of $300, with a 15 percent depreciation rate. December 31, 1993, is the end of the first period.

`AMORDEGRC(2400,34199,34334,300,1,0.15,1)` equals a first period depreciation of $775

AMORLINC

Returns the depreciation for each accounting period. This function is provided for the French accounting system. If an asset is purchased in the middle of the accounting period, then the prorated depreciation is taken into account.

If this function is not available, run the Setup program to install the Analysis ToolPak. After you install the Analysis ToolPak, you must enable it by using the **Add-Ins** command on the **Tools** menu.

Syntax

AMORLINC(cost,date_purchased,first_period,salvage,period,rate,basis)

Cost   is the cost of the asset.

Date_purchased   is the date of the purchase of the asset.

First_period   is the date of the end of the first period.

Salvage   is the salvage value at the end of the life of the asset.

Period   is the period.

Rate   is the rate of depreciation.

Basis   is the year_basis to be used.

Basis	Date system
0	360 days (NASD method)
1	Actual
3	365 days in a year
4	360 days in a year (European method)

Example

Suppose a machine bought on August 19, 1993, costs $2,400 and has a salvage value of $300, with a 15 percent depreciation rate. December 31, 1993, is the end of the first period.

AMORLINC(2400,34199,34334,300,1,0.15,1) equals a first period depreciation of $360

AND

Returns TRUE if all its arguments are TRUE; returns FALSE if one or more arguments is FALSE.

Syntax

AND(logical1,logical2, ...)

Logical1, logical2, ... are 1 to 30 conditions you want to test that can be either TRUE or FALSE.

- The arguments must evaluate to logical values such as TRUE or FALSE, or the arguments must be arrays or references that contain logical values.

- If an array or reference argument contains text or empty cells, those values are ignored.

- If the specified range contains no logical values, AND returns the #VALUE! error value.

Examples

AND(TRUE, TRUE) equals TRUE

AND(TRUE, FALSE) equals FALSE

AND(2+2=4, 2+3=5) equals TRUE

If B1:B3 contains the values TRUE, FALSE, and TRUE, then:

AND(B1:B3) equals FALSE

If B4 contains a number between 1 and 100, then:

AND(1<B4, B4<100) equals TRUE

Suppose you want to display B4 if it contains a number strictly between 1 and 100, and you want to display a message if it is not. If B4 contains 104, then:

IF(AND(1<B4, B4<100), B4, "The value is out of range.") equals "The value is out of range."

If B4 contains 50, then:

IF(AND(1<B4, B4<100), B4, "The value is out of range.") equals 50

AREAS

Returns the number of areas in a reference. An area is a range of contiguous cells or a single cell.

Syntax

AREAS(reference)

Reference   is a reference to a cell or range of cells and can refer to multiple areas. If you want to specify several references as a single argument, then you must include extra sets of parentheses so that Microsoft Excel will not interpret the comma as a field separator. See the second example following.

Examples

AREAS(B2:D4) equals 1

AREAS((B2:D4,E5,F6:I9)) equals 3

If the name Prices refers to the areas B1:D4, B2, and E1:E10, then:

AREAS(Prices) equals 3

ASIN

Returns the arcsine of a number. The arcsine is the angle whose sine is number. The returned angle is given in radians in the range $-\pi/2$ to $\pi/2$.

Syntax

ASIN(number)

Number   is the sine of the angle you want and must be from -1 to 1.

Remarks

To express the arcsine in degrees, multiply the result by 180/PI().

Examples

ASIN(-0.5) equals -0.5236 ($-\pi/6$ radians)

ASIN(-0.5)*180/PI() equals -30 (degrees)

ASINH

Returns the inverse hyperbolic sine of a number. The inverse hyperbolic sine is the value whose hyperbolic sine is number, so ASINH(SINH(number)) equals number.

Syntax

ASINH(number)

Number is any real number.

Examples

ASINH(-2.5) equals -1.64723

ASINH(10) equals 2.998223

ATAN

Returns the arctangent of a number. The arctangent is the angle whose tangent is number. The returned angle is given in radians in the range $-\pi/2$ to $\pi/2$.

Syntax

ATAN(number)

Number is the tangent of the angle you want.

Remarks

To express the arctangent in degrees, multiply the result by 180/PI( ).

Examples

ATAN(1) equals 0.785398 ($\pi/4$ radians)

ATAN(1)*180/PI() equals 45 (degrees)

ATAN2

Returns the arctangent of the specified x- and y- coordinates. The arctangent is the angle from the x-axis to a line containing the origin (0, 0) and a point with coordinates (x_num, y_num). The angle is given in radians between $-\pi$ and π, excluding $-\pi$.

Syntax

ATAN2(x_num,y_num)

X_num is the x-coordinate of the point.

Y_num is the y-coordinate of the point.

Remarks

- A positive result represents a counterclockwise angle from the x-axis; a negative result represents a clockwise angle.
- ATAN2(a,b) equals ATAN(b/a), except that a can equal 0 in ATAN2.
- If both x_num and y_num are 0, ATAN2 returns the #DIV/0! error value.
- To express the arctangent in degrees, multiply the result by 180/PI( ).

Examples

ATAN2(1, 1) equals 0.785398 (π/4 radians)

ATAN2(-1, -1) equals -2.35619 (-3π/4 radians)

ATAN2(-1, -1)*180/PI( ) equals -135 (degrees)

ATANH

Returns the inverse hyperbolic tangent of a number. Number must be between -1 and 1 (excluding -1 and 1). The inverse hyperbolic tangent is the value whose hyperbolic tangent is number, so ATANH(TANH(number)) equals number.

Syntax

ATANH(number)

Number   is any real number between 1 and -1.

Examples

ATANH(0.76159416) equals 1, approximately

ATANH(-0.1) equals -0.10034

AVEDEV

Returns the average of the absolute deviations of data points from their mean. AVEDEV is a measure of the variability in a data set.

Syntax

AVEDEV(number1,number2, ...)

Number1, number2, ...   are 1 to 30 arguments for which you want the average of the absolute deviations. You can also use a single array or a reference to an array instead of arguments separated by commas.

Remarks

- The arguments must be either numbers or names, arrays, or references that contain numbers.
- If an array or reference argument contains text, logical values, or empty cells, those values are ignored; however, cells with the value zero are included.
- The equation for average deviation is:

$$\frac{1}{n} \sum x - \bar{x}$$

AVEDEV is influenced by the unit of measurement in the input data.

Example

AVEDEV(4, 5, 6, 7, 5, 4, 3) equals 1.020408

AVERAGE

Returns the average (arithmetic mean) of the arguments.

Syntax

AVERAGE(number1,number2, ...)

Number1, number2, ...   are 1 to 30 numeric arguments for which you want the average.

Remarks

- The arguments must be either numbers or names, arrays, or references that contain numbers.
- If an array or reference argument contains text, logical values, or empty cells, those values are ignored; however, cells with the value zero are included.

Tip   When averaging cells, keep in mind the difference between empty cells and those containing the value zero, especially if you have cleared the **Zero values** check box on the **View** tab (**Options** command, **Tools** menu). Empty cells are not counted, but zero values are.

Examples

If A1:A5 is named Scores and contains the numbers 10, 7, 9, 27, and 2, then:

AVERAGE(A1:A5) equals 11

AVERAGE(Scores) equals 11

AVERAGE(A1:A5, 5) equals 10

AVERAGE(A1:A5) equals SUM(A1:A5)/COUNT(A1:A5) equals 11

If C1:C3 is named OtherScores and contains the numbers 4, 18, and 7, then:

AVERAGE(Scores, OtherScores) equals 10.5

AVERAGEA

Calculates the average (arithmetic mean) of the values in the list of arguments. In addition to numbers, text and logical values such as TRUE and FALSE are included in the calculation.

Syntax

AVERAGEA(value1,value2, ...)

Value1, value2, ... are 1 to 30 cells, ranges of cells, or values for which you want the average.

Remarks

- The arguments must be numbers, names, arrays, or references.

- Array or reference arguments that contain text evaluate as 0 (zero). Empty text ("") evaluates as 0 (zero). If the calculation must not include text values in the average, use the AVERAGE function.

- Arguments that contain TRUE evaluate as 1; arguments that contain FALSE evaluate as 0 (zero).

Tip When averaging cells, keep in mind the difference between empty cells and those containing the value zero, especially if you have cleared the **Zero values** check box on the **View** tab (**Options** command, **Tools** menu). Empty cells are not counted, but zero values are.

Examples

If A1:A5 is named Scores and contains the values 10, 7, 9, 2, and "Not available", then:

AVERAGEA(A1:A5) equals 5.6

AVERAGEA(Scores) equals 5.6

AVERAGEA(A1:A5) equals SUM(A1:A5)/COUNTA(A1:A5) equals 5.6

If A1:A4 contains the values 10, 7, 9, and 2, and A5 is empty, then:

AVERAGEA(A1:A5) equals 7

BESSELI

Returns the modified Bessel function, which is equivalent to the Bessel function evaluated for purely imaginary arguments.

If this function is not available, run the Setup program to install the Analysis ToolPak. After you install the Analysis ToolPak, you must enable it by using the **Add-Ins** command on the **Tools** menu.

Syntax

BESSELI(x,n)

X   is the value at which to evaluate the function.

N   is the order of the Bessel function. If n is not an integer, it is truncated.

Remarks

- If x is nonnumeric, BESSELI returns the #VALUE! error value.
- If n is nonnumeric, BESSELI returns the #VALUE! error value.
- If n < 0, BESSELI returns the #NUM! error value.
- The n-th order modified Bessel function of the variable x is:

$$I_n(x) = (i)^{-n} J_n(ix)$$

Example

BESSELI(1.5, 1) equals 0.981666

BESSELJ

Returns the Bessel function.

If this function is not available, run the Setup program to install the Analysis ToolPak. After you install the Analysis ToolPak, you must enable it by using the **Add-Ins** command on the **Tools** menu.

Syntax

BESSELJ(x,n)

X   is the value at which to evaluate the function.

N   is the order of the Bessel function. If n is not an integer, it is truncated.

Remarks

- If x is nonnumeric, BESSELJ returns the #VALUE! error value.
- If n is nonnumeric, BESSELJ returns the #VALUE! error value.
- If n < 0, BESSELJ returns the #NUM! error value.

- The n-th order Bessel function of the variable x is:

$$J_n(x) = \sum_{k=0}^{\infty} \frac{(-1)^k}{k!\,\Gamma(n+k+1)}\left(\frac{x}{2}\right)^{n+2k}$$

where:

$$\Gamma(n+k+1) = \int_0^{\infty} e^{-x} x^{n+k}\,dx$$

is the Gamma function.

Example

BESSELJ(1.9, 2) equals 0.329926

BESSELK

Returns the modified Bessel function, which is equivalent to the Bessel functions evaluated for purely imaginary arguments.

If this function is not available, run the Setup program to install the Analysis ToolPak. After you install the Analysis ToolPak, you must enable it by using the **Add-Ins** command on the **Tools** menu.

Syntax

BESSELK(x,n)

X   is the value at which to evaluate the function.

N   is the order of the function. If n is not an integer, it is truncated.

Remarks

- If x is nonnumeric, BESSELK returns the #VALUE! error value.
- If n is nonnumeric, BESSELK returns the #VALUE! error value.
- If n < 0, BESSELK returns the #NUM! error value.
- The n-th order modified Bessel function of the variable x is:

$$K_n(x) = \frac{p}{2} i^{n+1} [J_n(ix) + iY_n(ix)]$$

where Jn and Yn are the J and Y Bessel functions, respectively.

Example

BESSELK(1.5, 1) equals 0.277388

BESSELY

Returns the Bessel function, which is also called the Weber function or the Neumann function.

If this function is not available, run the Setup program to install the Analysis ToolPak. After you install the Analysis ToolPak, you must enable it by using the **Add-Ins** command on the **Tools** menu.

Syntax

BESSELY(x,n)

X   is the value at which to evaluate the function.

N   is the order of the function. If n is not an integer, it is truncated.

Remarks

- If x is nonnumeric, BESSELY returns the #VALUE! error value.
- If n is nonnumeric, BESSELY returns the #VALUE! error value.
- If n < 0, BESSELY returns the #NUM! error value.
- The n-th order Bessel function of the variable x is:

$$Y_n(x) = \lim_{v \to n} \frac{J_v(x)\cos(v\,\pi) - J_{-v}(x)}{\sin(v\,\pi)}$$

where:

$$ERF(z) = \frac{2}{\sqrt{\pi}} \int_0^z e^{-t^2}\,dt$$

Example

BESSELY(2.5, 1) equals 0.145918

BETADIST

Returns the cumulative beta probability density function. The cumulative beta probability density function is commonly used to study variation in the percentage of something across samples, such as the fraction of the day people spend watching television.

Syntax

BETADIST(x,alpha,beta,A,B)

X   is the value between A and B at which to evaluate the function.

Alpha   is a parameter to the distribution.

Beta   is a parameter to the distribution.

A   is an optional lower bound to the interval of x.

B   is an optional upper bound to the interval of x.

Remarks

- If any argument is nonnumeric, BETADIST returns the #VALUE! error value.
- If alpha ≤ 0 or beta ≤ 0, BETADIST returns the #NUM! error value.
- If x < A, x > B, or A = B, BETADIST returns the #NUM! error value.
- If you omit values for A and B, BETADIST uses the standard cumulative beta distribution, so that A = 0 and B = 1.

Example

`BETADIST(2,8,10,1,3)` equals 0.685470581

BETAINV

Returns the inverse of the cumulative beta probability density function. That is, if probability = BETADIST(x,...), then BETAINV(probability,...) = x. The cumulative beta distribution can be used in project planning to model probable completion times given an expected completion time and variability.

Syntax

BETAINV(probability,alpha,beta,A,B)

Probability   is a probability associated with the beta distribution.

Alpha   is a parameter to the distribution.

Beta   is a parameter to the distribution.

A   is an optional lower bound to the interval of x.

B   is an optional upper bound to the interval of x.

Remarks

- If any argument is nonnumeric, BETAINV returns the #VALUE! error value.

- If alpha ≤ 0 or beta ≤ 0, BETAINV returns the #NUM! error value.

- If probability ≤ 0 or probability > 1, BETAINV returns the #NUM! error value.

- If you omit values for A and B, BETAINV uses the standard cumulative beta distribution, so that A = 0 and B = 1.

- BETAINV uses an iterative technique for calculating the function. Given a probability value, BETAINV iterates until the result is accurate to within $\pm 3 \times 10^{-7}$. If BETAINV does not converge after 100 iterations, the function returns the #N/A error value.

Example

BETAINV(0.685470581,8,10,1,3) equals 2

BIN2DEC

Converts a binary number to decimal.

If this function is not available, run the Setup program to install the Analysis ToolPak. After you install the Analysis ToolPak, you must enable it by using the **Add-Ins** command on the **Tools** menu.

Syntax

BIN2DEC(number)

Number   is the binary number you want to convert. Number cannot contain more than 10 characters (10 bits). The most significant bit of number is the sign bit. The remaining 9 bits are magnitude bits. Negative numbers are represented using two's-complement notation.

Remarks

- If number is not a valid binary number, or if number contains more than 10 characters (10 bits), BIN2DEC returns the #NUM! error value.

Examples

BIN2DEC(1100100) equals 100

BIN2DEC(1111111111) equals -1

BIN2HEX

Converts a binary number to hexadecimal.

If this function is not available, run the Setup program to install the Analysis ToolPak. After you install the Analysis ToolPak, you must enable it by using the **Add-Ins** command on the **Tools** menu.

Syntax

BIN2HEX(number,places)

Number   is the binary number you want to convert. Number cannot contain more than 10 characters (10 bits). The most significant bit of number is the sign bit. The remaining 9 bits are magnitude bits. Negative numbers are represented using two's-complement notation.

Places   is the number of characters to use. If places is omitted, BIN2HEX uses the minimum number of characters necessary. Places is useful for padding the return value with leading 0s (zeros).

Remarks

- If number is not a valid binary number, or if number contains more than 10 characters (10 bits), BIN2HEX returns the #NUM! error value.
- If number is negative, BIN2HEX ignores places and returns a 10-character hexadecimal number.
- If BIN2HEX requires more than places characters, it returns the #NUM! error value.
- If places is not an integer, it is truncated.
- If places is nonnumeric, BIN2HEX returns the #VALUE! error value.
- If places is negative, BIN2HEX returns the #NUM! error value.

Examples

BIN2HEX(11111011, 4) equals 00FB

BIN2HEX(1110) equals E

BIN2HEX(1111111111) equals FFFFFFFFFF

BIN2OCT

Converts a binary number to octal.

If this function is not available, run the Setup program to install the Analysis ToolPak. After you install the Analysis ToolPak, you must enable it by using the **Add-Ins** command on the **Tools** menu.

Syntax

BIN2OCT(number,places)

Number   is the binary number you want to convert. Number cannot contain more than 10 characters (10 bits). The most significant bit of number is the sign bit. The remaining 9 bits are magnitude bits. Negative numbers are represented using two's-complement notation.

Places   is the number of characters to use. If places is omitted, BIN2OCT uses the minimum number of characters necessary. Places is useful for padding the return value with leading 0s (zeros).

Remarks

- If number is not a valid binary number, or if number contains more than 10 characters (10 bits), BIN2OCT returns the #NUM! error value.

- If number is negative, BIN2OCT ignores places and returns a 10-character octal number.

- If BIN2OCT requires more than places characters, it returns the #NUM! error value.

- If places is not an integer, it is truncated.

- If places is nonnumeric, BIN2OCT returns the #VALUE! error value.

- If places is negative, BIN2OCT returns the #NUM! error value.

Examples

BIN2OCT(1001, 3) equals 011

BIN2OCT(01100100) equals 144

BIN2OCT(1111111111) equals 7777777777

BINOMDIST

Returns the individual term binomial distribution probability. Use BINOMDIST in problems with a fixed number of tests or trials, when the outcomes of any trial are only success or failure, when trials are independent, and when the probability of success is constant throughout the experiment. For example, BINOMDIST can calculate the probability that two of the next three babies born are male.

Syntax

BINOMDIST(number_s,trials,probability_s,cumulative)

Number_s   is the number of successes in trials.

Trials   is the number of independent trials.

Probability_s   is the probability of success on each trial.

Cumulative   is a logical value that determines the form of the function. If cumulative is TRUE, then BINOMDIST returns the cumulative distribution function, which is the probability that there are at most number_s successes; if FALSE, it returns the probability mass function, which is the probability that there are number_s successes.

Remarks

- Number_s and trials are truncated to integers.
- If number_s, trials, or probability_s is nonnumeric, BINOMDIST returns the #VALUE! error value.
- If number_s < 0 or number_s > trials, BINOMDIST returns the #NUM! error value.
- If probability_s < 0 or probability_s > 1, BINOMDIST returns the #NUM! error value.

- The binomial probability mass function is:

$$b(x;n,p) = \binom{n}{x} p^x (1-p)^{n-x}$$

where:

$$\binom{n}{x}$$

is COMBIN(n,x).

The cumulative binomial distribution is:

$$B(x;n,p) = \sum_{y=0}^{x} b(y;n,p)$$

Example

The flip of a coin can only result in heads or tails. The probability of the first flip being heads is 0.5, and the probability of exactly 6 of 10 flips being heads is:

BINOMDIST(6,10,0.5,FALSE) equals 0.205078

CALL

Calls a procedure in a dynamic link library or code resource. There are two syntax forms of this function. Use syntax 1 only with a previously registered code resource, which uses arguments from the REGISTER function. Use syntax 2a or 2b to simultaneously register and call a code resource.

Important   This function is provided for advanced users only. If you use the CALL function incorrectly, you may cause errors that will require you to restart your computer.

Syntax 1

Used with REGISTER

CALL(register_id,argument1, ...)

Syntax 2a

Used alone (in Microsoft Excel for Windows®)

CALL(module_text,procedure,type_text,argument1, ...)

Syntax 2b

Used alone (in Microsoft Excel for the Macintosh)

CALL(file_text,resource,type_text,argument1, ...)

Register_id is the value returned by a previously executed REGISTER or REGISTER.ID function.

Argument1, ... are the arguments to be passed to the procedure.

Module_text is quoted text specifying the name of the dynamic link library (DLL) that contains the procedure in Microsoft Excel for Windows.

File_text is the name of the file that contains the code resource in Microsoft Excel for the Macintosh.

Procedure is text specifying the name of the function in the DLL in Microsoft Excel for Windows. You can also use the ordinal value of the function from the EXPORTS statement in the module-definition file (.DEF). The ordinal value must not be in the form of text.

Resource is the name of the code resource in Microsoft Excel for the Macintosh. You can also use the resource ID number. The resource ID number must not be in the form of text.

Type_text is text specifying the data type of the return value and the data types of all arguments to the DLL or code resource. The first letter of type_text specifies the return value. The codes you use for type_text are described in detail in For stand-alone DLLs or code resources (XLLs), you can omit this argument.

Example
Syntax 1 (32-Bit Microsoft Excel)

IN 32-bit Microsoft Excel for Windows 95 and Microsoft Excel for Windows NT®, the following macro formula registers the GetTickCount function from 32-bit Microsoft Windows. GetTickCount returns the number of milliseconds that have elapsed since Microsoft Windows was started.

```
REGISTER("Kernel32","GetTickCount","J")
```

Assuming that this REGISTER function is in cell A5, after your macro registers GetTickCount, you can use the CALL function to return the number of milliseconds that have elapsed:

```
CALL(A5)
```

Syntax 1 (16-Bit Microsoft Excel)

In 16-bit Microsoft Excel for Windows, the following macro formula registers the GetTickCount function from 16-bit Microsoft Windows. GetTickCount returns the number of milliseconds that have elapsed since Microsoft Windows was started.

```
REGISTER("User","GetTickCount","J")
```

Assuming that this REGISTER function is in cell A5, after your macro registers GetTickCount, you can use the CALL function to return the number of milliseconds that have elapsed:

```
CALL(A5)
```

Example
Syntax 2a (32-Bit Microsoft Excel)

On a worksheet, you can use the following CALL formula (syntax 2a) to call the GetTickCount function:

```
CALL("Kernel32","GetTickCount","J!")
```

The ! in the type_text argument forces Microsoft Excel to recalculate the CALL function every time the worksheet recalculates. This updates the elapsed time whenever the worksheet recalculates.

Syntax 2a (16-Bit Microsoft Excel)

On a worksheet, you can use the following CALL formula (syntax 2a) to call the GetTickCount function:

```
CALL("User","GetTickCount","J!")
```

The ! in the type_text argument forces Microsoft Excel to recalculate the CALL function every time the worksheet recalculates. This updates the elapsed time whenever the worksheet recalculates.

Tip   You can use optional arguments to the REGISTER function to assign a custom name to a function. This name will appear in the **Paste Function** dialog box, and you can call the function by using its custom name in a formula. For more information, see REGISTER.

CEILING

Returns number rounded up, away from zero, to the nearest multiple of significance. For example, if you want to avoid using pennies in your prices and your product is priced at $4.42, use the formula =CEILING(4.42,0.05) to round prices up to the nearest nickel.

Syntax

CEILING(number,significance)

Number   is the value you want to round.

Significance   is the multiple to which you want to round.

Remarks

- If either argument is nonnumeric, CEILING returns the #VALUE! error value.
- Regardless of the sign of number, a value is rounded up when adjusted away from zero. If number is an exact multiple of significance, no rounding occurs.
- If number and significance have different signs, CEILING returns the #NUM! error value.

Examples

CEILING(2.5, 1) equals 3

CEILING(-2.5, -2) equals -4

CEILING(-2.5, 2) equals #NUM!

CEILING(1.5, 0.1) equals 1.5

CEILING(0.234, 0.01) equals 0.24

CELL

Returns information about the formatting, location, or contents of the upper-left cell in a reference.

Syntax

CELL(info_type,reference)

Info_type   is a text value that specifies what type of cell information you want. The following list shows the possible values of info_type and the corresponding results.

Info_type	Returns
"address"	Reference of the first cell in reference, as text.
"col"	Column number of the cell in reference.
"color"	1 if the cell is formatted in color for negative values; otherwise returns 0 (zero).
"contents"	Contents of the upper-left cell in reference.
"filename"	Filename (including full path) of the file that contains reference, as text. Returns empty text ("") if the worksheet that contains reference has not yet been saved.
"format"	Text value corresponding to the number format of the cell. The text values for the various formats are shown in the following table. Returns "-" at the end of the text value if the cell is formatted in color for negative values. Returns "()" at the end of the text value if the cell is formatted with parentheses for positive or all values.
"parentheses"	1 if the cell is formatted with parentheses for positive or all values; otherwise returns 0.

Info_type	Returns
"prefix"	Text value corresponding to the "label prefix" of the cell. Returns single quotation mark (') if the cell contains left-aligned text, double quotation mark (") if the cell contains right-aligned text, caret (^) if the cell contains centered text, backslash (\) if the cell contains fill-aligned text, and empty text ("") if the cell contains anything else.
"protect"	0 if the cell is not locked, and 1 if the cell is locked.
"row"	Row number of the cell in reference.
"type"	Text value corresponding to the type of data in the cell. Returns "b" for blank if the cell is empty, "l" for label if the cell contains a text constant, and "v" for value if the cell contains anything else.
"width"	Column width of the cell rounded off to an integer. Each unit of column width is equal to the width of one character in the default font size.

Reference   is the cell that you want information about.

The following list describes the text values CELL returns when info_type is "format", and reference is a cell formatted with a built-in number format.

If the Microsoft Excel format is	CELL returns
General	"G"
0	"F0"
#,##0	",0"
0.00	"F2"
#,##0.00	",2"
$#,##0_);($#,##0)	"C0'
$#,##0_);[Red]($#,##0)	"C0-"
$#,##0.00_);($#,##0.00)	"C2"
$#,##0.00_);[Red]($#,##0.00)	"C2-"
0%	"P0"
0.00%	"P2"
0.00E+00	"S2"
# ?/? or # ??/??	"G"
m/d/yy or m/d/yy h:mm or mm/dd/yy	"D4"
d-mmm-yy or dd-mmm-yy	"D1"
d-mmm or dd-mmm	"D2"
mmm-yy	"D3"
mm/dd	"D5"
h:mm AM/PM	"D7"
h:mm:ss AM/PM	"D6"
h:mm	"D9"
h:mm:ss	"D8"

If the info_type argument in the CELL formula is "format", and if the cell is formatted later with a custom format, then you must recalculate the worksheet to update the CELL formula.

Remarks

The CELL function is provided for compatibility with other spreadsheet programs.

Examples

CELL("row",A20) equals 20

If B12 has the format "d-mmm", then:

CELL("format",B12) equals "D2"

If A3 contains TOTAL, then:

CELL("contents", A3) equals "TOTAL"

CHAR

Returns the character specified by a number. Use CHAR to translate code page numbers you might get from files on other types of computers into characters.

Operating environment	Character set
Macintosh	Macintosh character set
Windows	ANSI

Syntax

CHAR(number)

Number is a number between 1 and 255 specifying which character you want. The character is from the character set used by your computer.

Examples

CHAR(65) equals "A"

CHAR(33) equals "!"

CHIDIST

Returns the one-tailed probability of the chi-squared distribution. The χ^2 distribution is associated with a χ^2 test. Use the χ^2 test to compare observed and expected values. For example, a genetic experiment might hypothesize that the next generation of plants will exhibit a certain set of colors. By comparing the observed results with the expected ones, you can decide whether your original hypothesis is valid.

Syntax

CHIDIST(x,degrees_freedom)

X   is the value at which you want to evaluate the distribution.

Degrees_freedom   is the number of degrees of freedom.

Remarks

- If either argument is nonnumeric, CHIDIST returns the #VALUE! error value.

- If x is negative, CHIDIST returns the #NUM! error value.

- If degrees_freedom is not an integer, it is truncated.

- If degrees_freedom < 1 or degrees_freedom $\geq 10^{10}$, CHIDIST returns the #NUM! error value.

- CHIDIST * mergeformat is calculated as cHIDIST = P(X>x), where X is a χ^2 random variable.

Example

CHIDIST(18.307,10) equals 0.050001

CHIINV

Returns the inverse of the one-tailed probability of the chi-squared distribution. If probability = CHIDIST(x, …), then CHIINV(probability, …) = x. Use this function to compare observed results with expected ones to decide whether your original hypothesis is valid.

Syntax

CHIINV(probability,degrees_freedom)

Probability   is a probability associated with the chi-squared distribution.

Degrees_freedom   is the number of degrees of freedom.

Remarks

- If either argument is nonnumeric, CHIINV returns the #VALUE! error value.

- If probability < 0 or probability > 1, CHIINV returns the #NUM! error value.

- If degrees_freedom is not an integer, it is truncated.

- If degrees_freedom < 1 or degrees_freedom $\geq 10^{10}$, CHIINV returns the #NUM! error value.

CHIINV uses an iterative technique for calculating the function. Given a probability value, CHIINV iterates until the result is accurate to within $\pm 3\times10^{-7}$. If CHIINV does not converge after 100 iterations, the function returns the #N/A error value.

Example

CHIINV(0.05,10) equals 18.30703

CHITEST

Returns the test for independence. CHITEST returns the value from the chi-squared ($\chi 2$) distribution for the statistic and the appropriate degrees of freedom. You can use $\chi 2$ tests to determine whether hypothesized results are verified by an experiment.

Syntax

CHITEST(actual_range,expected_range)

Actual_range   is the range of data that contains observations to test against expected values.

Expected_range   is the range of data that contains the ratio of the product of row totals and column totals to the grand total.

Remarks

- If actual_range and expected_range have a different number of data points, CHITEST returns the #N/A error value.

- The $\chi 2$ test first calculates a $\chi 2$ statistic and then sums the differences of actual values from the expected values. The equation for this function is CHITEST=p(X>$\chi 2$), where:

$$\chi^2 = \sum_{i=1}^{r} \sum_{j=1}^{c} \frac{\left(A_{ij} - E_{ij}\right)^2}{E_{ij}}$$

and where:

Aij = actual frequency in the i-th row, j-th column

Eij = expected frequency in the i-th row, j-th column

r = number or rows

c = number of columns

CHITEST returns the probability for a $\chi 2$ statistic and degrees of freedom, df, where df = (r - 1)(c - 1).

Example

	A	B	C
1	Actual		
2		Men	Women
3	Agree	58	35
4	Neutral	11	25
5	Disagree	10	23
6			
7	Expected		
8		Men	Women
9	Agree	45.35	47.65
10	Neutral	17.56	18.44
11	Disagree	16.09	16.91

The $\chi 2$ statistic for the data above is 16.16957 with 2 degrees of freedom.

`CHITEST(B3:C5,B9:C11)` equals 0.000308

CHOOSE

Uses index_num to return a value from the list of value arguments. Use CHOOSE to select one of up to 29 values based on the index number. For example, if value1 through value7 are the days of the week, CHOOSE returns one of the days when a number between 1 and 7 is used as index_num.

Syntax

CHOOSE(index_num,value1,value2, …)

Index_num   specifies which value argument is selected. Index_num must be a number between 1 and 29, or a formula or reference to a cell containing a number between 1 and 29.

- If index_num is 1, CHOOSE returns value1; if it is 2, CHOOSE returns value2; and so on.

- If index_num is less than 1 or greater than the number of the last value in the list, CHOOSE returns the #VALUE! error value.

- If index_num is a fraction, it is truncated to the lowest integer before being used.

Value1, value2, …   are 1 to 29 value arguments from which CHOOSE selects a value or an action to perform based on index_num. The arguments can be numbers, cell references, defined names, formulas, functions, or text.

Remarks

- If index_num is an array, every value is evaluated when CHOOSE is evaluated.
- The value arguments to CHOOSE can be range references as well as single values. For example, the formula:

SUM(CHOOSE(2,A1:A10,B1:B10,C1:C10))

evaluates to:

SUM(B1:B10)

which then returns a value based on the values in the range B1:B10.

The CHOOSE function is evaluated first, returning the reference B1:B10. The SUM function is then evaluated using B1:B10, the result of the CHOOSE function, as its argument.

Examples

CHOOSE(2,"1st","2nd","3rd","Finished") equals "2nd"

SUM(A1:CHOOSE(3,A10,A20,A30)) equals SUM(A1:A30)

If A10 contains 4, then:

CHOOSE(A10,"Nails","Screws","Nuts","Bolts") equals "Bolts"

If A10-3 equals 3, then:

CHOOSE(A10-3,"1st","2nd","3rd","Finished") equals "3rd"

If SalesOld is a name defined to refer to the value 10,000, then:

CHOOSE(2,SalesNew,SalesOld,SalesBudget) equals 10,000

CLEAN

Removes all nonprintable characters from text. Use CLEAN on text imported from other applications that contains characters that may not print with your operating system. For example, you can use CLEAN to remove some low-level computer code that is frequently at the beginning and end of data files and cannot be printed.

Syntax

CLEAN(text)

Text is any worksheet information from which you want to remove nonprintable characters.

Example

Because CHAR(7) returns a nonprintable character:

CLEAN(CHAR(7)&"text"&CHAR(7)) equals "text"

CODE

Returns a numeric code for the first character in a text string. The returned code corresponds to the character set used by your computer.

Operating environment	Character set
Macintosh	Macintosh character set
Windows	ANSI

Syntax

CODE(text)

Text   is the text for which you want the code of the first character.

Examples

CODE("A") equals 65

CODE("Alphabet") equals 65

COLUMN

Returns the column number of the given reference.

Syntax

COLUMN(reference)

Reference   is the cell or range of cells for which you want the column number.

- If reference is omitted, it is assumed to be the reference of the cell in which the COLUMN function appears.
- If reference is a range of cells, and if COLUMN is entered as a horizontal array, COLUMN returns the column numbers of reference as a horizontal array.
- Reference cannot refer to multiple areas.

Examples

COLUMN(A3) equals 1

When entered as an array in any three horizontally contiguous cells:

COLUMN(A3:C5) equals {1,2,3}

If COLUMN is entered in C5, then:

COLUMN() equals COLUMN(C5) equals 3

COLUMNS

Returns the number of columns in an array or reference.

Syntax

COLUMNS(array)

Array   is an array or array formula, or a reference to a range of cells for which you want the number of columns.

Examples

COLUMNS(A1:C4) equals 3

COLUMNS({1,2,3;4,5,6}) equals 3

COMBIN

Returns the number of combinations for a given number of items. Use COMBIN to determine the total possible number of groups for a given number of items.

Syntax

COMBIN(number,number_chosen)

Number   is the number of items.

Number_chosen   is the number of items in each combination.

Remarks

- Numeric arguments are truncated to integers.

- If either argument is nonnumeric, COMBIN returns the #NAME? error value.

- If number < 0, number_chosen < 0, or number < number_chosen, COMBIN returns the #NUM! error value.

- A combination is any set or subset of items, regardless of their internal order. Combinations are distinct from permutations, for which the internal order is significant.

- The number of combinations is as follows, where number = n and number_chosen = k:

$$\binom{n}{k} = \frac{P_{k,n}}{k!} = \frac{n!}{k!(n-k)!}$$

where:

$$P_{k,n} = \frac{n!}{(n-k)!}$$

Example

Suppose you want to form a two-person team from eight candidates, and you want to know how many possible teams can be formed. COMBIN(8, 2) equals 28 teams.

COMPLEX

Converts real and imaginary coefficients into a complex number of the form x + yi or x + yj.

If this function is not available, run the Setup program to install the Analysis ToolPak. After you install the Analysis ToolPak, you must enable it by using the **Add-Ins** command on the **Tools** menu.

Syntax

COMPLEX(real_num,i_num,suffix)

Real_num is the real coefficient of the complex number.

I_num is the imaginary coefficient of the complex number.

Suffix is the suffix for the imaginary component of the complex number. If omitted, suffix is assumed to be "i".

Note All complex number functions accept "i" and "j" for suffix, but neither "I" nor "J". Using uppercase results in the #VALUE! error value. All functions that accept two or more complex numbers require that all suffixes match.

Remarks

- If real_num is nonnumeric, COMPLEX returns the #VALUE! error value.
- If i_num is nonnumeric, COMPLEX returns the #VALUE! error value.
- If suffix is neither "i" nor "j", COMPLEX returns the #VALUE! error value.

Examples

COMPLEX(3,4) equals 3 + 4i

COMPLEX(3,4,"j") equals 3 + 4j

COMPLEX(0,1) equals i

COMPLEX(1,0) equals 1

CONCATENATE

Joins several text strings into one text string.

Syntax

CONCATENATE (text1,text2, ...)

Text1, **text2**, ... are 1 to 30 text items to be joined into a single text item. The text items can be text strings, numbers, or single-cell references.

Remarks

The "&" operator can be used instead of CONCATENATE to join text items.

Examples

CONCATENATE("Total ", "Value") equals "Total Value". This is equivalent to typing
"Total"&" "&"Value"

Suppose in a stream survey worksheet, C2 contains "species", C5 contains "brook trout", and C8 contains the total 32.

CONCATENATE("Stream population for ",C5," ",C2," is
",C8,"/mile") equals "Stream population for brook trout species is 32/mile"

CONFIDENCE

Returns the confidence interval for a population mean. The confidence interval is a range on either side of a sample mean. For example, if you order a product through the mail, you can determine, with a particular level of confidence, the earliest and latest the product will arrive.

Syntax

CONFIDENCE(alpha,standard_dev,size)

Alpha is the significance level used to compute the confidence level. The confidence level equals 100*(1 - alpha)%, or in other words, an alpha of 0.05 indicates a 95 percent confidence level.

Standard_dev   is the population standard deviation for the data range and is assumed to be known.

Size   is the sample size.

Remarks

- If any argument is nonnumeric, CONFIDENCE returns the #VALUE! error value.
- If alpha ≤ 0 or alpha ≥ 1, CONFIDENCE returns the #NUM! error value.
- If standard_dev ≤ 0, CONFIDENCE returns the #NUM! error value.
- If size is not an integer, it is truncated.
- If size < 1, CONFIDENCE returns the #NUM! error value.
- If we assume alpha equals 0.05, we need to calculate the area under the standard normal curve that equals (1 - alpha), or 95 percent. This value is ± 1.96. The confidence interval is therefore:

$$\bar{x} \pm 1.96 \left(\frac{\sigma}{\sqrt{n}} \right)$$

Example

Suppose we observe that, in our sample of 50 commuters, the average length of travel to work is 30 minutes with a population standard deviation of 2.5. We can be 95 percent confident that the population mean is in the interval:

$$30 \pm 1.96 \left(\frac{2.5}{\sqrt{50}} \right)$$

or:

CONFIDENCE(0.05,2.5,50) equals 0.692951. In other words, the average length of travel to work equals 30 ± 0.692951 minutes, or 29.3 to 30.7 minutes.

CONVERT

Converts a number from one measurement system to another. For example, CONVERT can translate a table of distances in miles to a table of distances in kilometers.

If this function is not available, run the Setup program to install the Analysis ToolPak. After you install the Analysis ToolPak, you must enable it by using **Add-Ins** on the **Tools** menu.

Syntax

CONVERT(number,from_unit,to_unit)

Number   is the value in from_units to convert.

From_unit   is the units for number.

To_unit   is the units for the result. CONVERT accepts the following text values for from_unit and to_unit.

Weight and mass	From_unit or to_unit
Gram	"g"
Slug	"sg"
Pound mass (avoirdupois)	"lbm"
U (atomic mass unit)	"u"
Ounce mass (avoirdupois)	"ozm"

Distance	From_unit or to_unit
Meter	"m"
Statute mile	"mi"
Nautical mile	"Nmi"
Inch	"in"
Foot	"ft"
Yard	"yd"
Angstrom	"ang"
Pica (1/72 in.)	"Pica"

Time	From_unit or to_unit
Year	"yr"
Day	"day"
Hour	"hr"
Minute	"mn"
Second	"sec"

Pressure	From_unit or to_unit
Pascal	"Pa"
Atmosphere	"atm"
mm of Mercury	"mmHg"

Force	From_unit or to_unit
Newton	"N"
Dyne	"dyn"
Pound force	"lbf"

Energy	From_unit or to_unit
Joule	"J"
Erg	"e"
Thermodynamic calorie	"c"
IT calorie	"cal"
Electron volt	"eV"
Horsepower-hour	"HPh"
Watt-hour	"Wh"
Foot-pound	"flb"
BTU	"BTU"

Power	From_unit or to_unit
Horsepower	"HP"
Watt	"W"

Magnetism	From_unit or to_unit
Tesla	"T"
Gauss	"ga"

Temperature	From_unit or to_unit
Degree Celsius	"C"
Degree Fahrenheit	"F"
Degree Kelvin	"K"

Liquid measure	From_unit or to_unit
Teaspoon	"tsp"
Tablespoon	"tbs"
Fluid ounce	"oz"
Cup	"cup"
Pint	"pt"
Quart	"qt"
Gallon	"gal"
Liter	"l"

The following abbreviated unit prefixes can be prepended to any metric from_unit or to_unit.

Prefix	Multiplier	Abbreviation
exa	1E+18	"E"
peta	1E+15	"P"
tera	1E+12	"T"
giga	1E+09	"G"
mega	1E+06	"M"
kilo	1E+03	"k"
hecto	1E+02	"h"
dekao	1E+01	"e"
deci	1E-01	"d"
centi	1E-02	"c"
milli	1E-03	"m"
micro	1E-06	"u"
nano	1E-09	"n"
pico	1E-12	"p"
femto	1E-15	"f"
atto	1E-18	"a"

Remarks

- If the input data types are incorrect, CONVERT returns the #VALUE! error value.
- If the unit does not exist, CONVERT returns the #N/A error value.
- If the unit does not support an abbreviated unit prefix, CONVERT returns the #N/A error value.
- If the units are in different groups, CONVERT returns the #N/A error value.
- Unit names and prefixes are case-sensitive.

Examples

CONVERT(1.0, "lbm", "kg") equals 0.453592

CONVERT(68, "F", "C") equals 20

CONVERT(2.5, "ft", "sec") equals #N/A

CORREL

Returns the correlation coefficient of the array1 and array2 cell ranges. Use the correlation coefficient to determine the relationship between two properties. For example, you can examine the relationship between a location's average temperature and the use of air conditioners.

Syntax

CORREL(array1,array2)

Array1   is a cell range of values.

Array2   is a second cell range of values.

Remarks

- The arguments must be numbers, or names, arrays, or references that contain numbers.

- If an array or reference argument contains text, logical values, or empty cells, those values are ignored; however, cells with the value zero are included.

- If array1 and array2 have a different number of data points, CORREL returns the #N/A error value.

- If either array1 or array2 is empty, or if s (the standard deviation) of their values equals zero, CORREL returns the #DIV/0! error value.

- The equation for the correlation coefficient is:

$$\rho_{x,y} = \frac{Cov(X,Y)}{\sigma_x \cdot \sigma_y}$$

where:

$$-1 \le \rho_{xy} \le 1$$

and:

$$Cov(X,Y) = \frac{1}{n}\sum_{i=1}^{n}(x_i - \mu_x)(y_i - \mu_y)$$

Example

CORREL({3,2,4,5,6},{9,7,12,15,17}) equals 0.997054

COS

Returns the cosine of the given angle.

Syntax

COS(number)

Number   is the angle in radians for which you want the cosine. If the angle is in degrees, multiply it by PI()/180 to convert it to radians.

Examples

COS(1.047) equals 0.500171

COS(60*PI()/180) equals 0.5, the cosine of 60 degrees

COSH

Returns the hyperbolic cosine of a number.

Syntax

COSH(number)

The formula for the hyperbolic cosine is:

$$\mathrm{COSH}(z) = \frac{e^z + e^{-z}}{2}$$

Examples

COSH(4) equals 27.30823

COSH(EXP(1)) equals 7.610125, where EXP(1) is e, the base of the natural logarithm.

COUNT

Counts the number of cells that contain numbers and numbers within the list of arguments. Use COUNT to get the number of entries in a number field in a range or array of numbers.

Syntax

COUNT(value1,value2, ...)

Value1, value2, ... are 1 to 30 arguments that can contain or refer to a variety of different types of data, but only numbers are counted.

- Arguments that are numbers, dates, or text representations of numbers are counted; arguments that are error values or text that cannot be translated into numbers are ignored.

- If an argument is an array or reference, only numbers in that array or reference are counted. Empty cells, logical values, text, or error values in the array or reference are ignored. If you need to count logical values, text, or error values, use the COUNTA function.

Examples

In the following example,

	A
1	Sales
2	12/8/90
3	
4	19
5	22/24
6	TRUE
7	#DIV/0!

COUNT(A1:A7) equals 3

COUNT(A4:A7) equals 2

COUNT(A1:A7, 2) equals 4

COUNTA

Counts the number of cells that are not empty and the values within the list of arguments. Use COUNTA to count the number of cells that contain data in a range or array.

Syntax

COUNTA(value1,value2, ...)

Value1, value2, ... are 1 to 30 arguments representing the values you want to count. In this case, a value is any type of information, including empty text ("") but not including empty cells. If an argument is an array or reference, empty cells within the array or reference are ignored. If you do not need to count logical values, text, or error values, use the COUNT function.

Examples

In the following example,

	A
1	Sales
2	12/8/90
3	
4	19
5	22/24
6	TRUE
7	#DIV/0!

COUNTA(A1:A7) equals 6

COUNTA(A4:A7) equals 4

COUNTA(A1:A7, 2) equals 7

COUNTA(A1:A7, "Two") equals 7

COUNTBLANK

Counts empty cells in a specified range of cells.

Syntax

COUNTBLANK(range)

Range   is the range from which you want to count the blank cells.

Remarks

Cells with formulas that return "" (empty text) are also counted. Cells with zero values are not counted.

Example

	A	Bc	C	D
1				
2		6		
3			27	
4		4	34	
5		4	0	
6				

Suppose in the above worksheet, B3 contains the following formula:
IF(C3<30,"",C3), which returns "" (empty text).

COUNTBLANK(B2:C5) equals 2

COUNTIF

Counts the number of cells within a range that meet the given criteria.

Syntax

COUNTIF(range,criteria)

Range   is the range of cells from which you want to count cells.

Criteria   is the criteria in the form of a number, expression, or text that defines which cells will be counted. For example, criteria can be expressed as 32, "32", ">32", "apples".

Examples

Suppose A3:A6 contain "apples", "oranges", "peaches", "apples", respectively:

COUNTIF(A3:A6,"apples") equals 2

Suppose B3:B6 contain 32, 54, 75, 86, respectively:

COUNTIF(B3:B6,">55") equals 2

COUPDAYBS

Returns the number of days from the beginning of the coupon period to the settlement date.

If this function is not available, run the Setup program to install the Analysis ToolPak. After you install the Analysis ToolPak, you must enable it by using the **Add-Ins** command on the **Tools** menu.

Syntax

COUPDAYBS(settlement,maturity,frequency,basis)

Settlement   is the security's settlement date. The security settlement date is the date after the issue date when the security is traded to the buyer.

Maturity   is the security's maturity date. The maturity date is the date when the security expires.

Frequency   is the number of coupon payments per year. For annual payments, frequency = 1; for semiannual, frequency = 2; for quarterly, frequency = 4.

Basis   is the type of day count basis to use.

Basis	Day count basis
0 or omitted	US (NASD) 30/360
1	Actual/actual
2	Actual/360
3	Actual/365
4	European 30/360

Remarks

- The settlement date is the date a buyer purchases a coupon, such as a bond. The maturity date is the date when a coupon expires. For example, suppose a 30-year bond is issued on January 1, 1996, and is purchased by a buyer six months later. The issue date would be January 1, 1996, the settlement date would be July 1, 1996, and the maturity date would be January 1, 2026, 30 years after the January 1, 1996, issue date.

- All arguments are truncated to integers.

- If any argument is nonnumeric, COUPDAYBS returns the #VALUE! error value.

- If settlement or maturity is not a valid date, COUPDAYBS returns the #NUM! error value.

- If frequency is any number other than 1, 2, or 4, COUPDAYBS returns the #NUM! error value.

- If basis < 0 or if basis > 4, COUPDAYBS returns the #NUM! error value.

- If settlement ≥ maturity, COUPDAYBS returns the #NUM! error value.

Example

A bond has the following terms:

January 25, 1993, settlement date
November 15, 1994, maturity date
Semiannual coupon
Actual/actual basis

The number of days from the beginning of the coupon period to the settlement date (in the 1900 date system) is:

COUPDAYBS("1/25/93","11/15/94",2,1) equals 71

COUPDAYS

Returns the number of days in the coupon period that contains the settlement date.

If this function is not available, run the Setup program to install the Analysis ToolPak. After you install the Analysis ToolPak, you must enable it by using the **Add-Ins** command on the **Tools** menu.

Syntax

COUPDAYS(settlement,maturity,frequency,basis)

Settlement   is the security's settlement date. The security settlement date is the date after the issue date when the security is traded to the buyer.

Maturity   is the security's maturity date. The maturity date is the date when the security expires.

Frequency   is the number of coupon payments per year. For annual payments, frequency = 1; for semiannual, frequency = 2; for quarterly, frequency = 4.

Basis   is the type of day count basis to use.

Basis	Day count basis
0 or omitted	US (NASD) 30/360
1	Actual/actual
2	Actual/360
3	Actual/365
4	European 30/360

Remarks

- The settlement date is the date a buyer purchases a coupon, such as a bond. The maturity date is the date when a coupon expires. For example, suppose a 30-year bond is issued on January 1, 1996, and is purchased by a buyer six months later. The issue date would be January 1, 1996, the settlement date would be July 1, 1996, and the maturity date is January 1, 2026, 30 years after the January 1, 1996 issue date.

- All arguments are truncated to integers.

- If any argument is nonnumeric, COUPDAYS returns the #VALUE! error value.

- If settlement or maturity is not a valid date, COUPDAYS returns the #NUM! error value.

- If frequency is any number other than 1, 2, or 4, COUPDAYS returns the #NUM! error value.

- If basis < 0 or if basis > 4, COUPDAYS returns the #NUM! error value.

- If settlement ≥ maturity, COUPDAYS returns the #NUM! error value.

Example

A bond has the following terms:

January 25, 1993, settlement date
November 15, 1994, maturity date
Semiannual coupon
Actual/actual basis

The number of days in the coupon period that contains the settlement date (in the 1900 date system) is:

COUPDAYS("1/25/93","11/15/94",2,1) equals 181

COUPDAYSNC

Returns the number of days from the settlement date to the next coupon date.

If this function is not available, run the Setup program to install the Analysis ToolPak. After you install the Analysis ToolPak, you must enable it by using the **Add-Ins** command on the **Tools** menu.

Syntax

COUPDAYSNC(settlement,maturity,frequency,basis)

Settlement   is the security's settlement date. The security settlement date is the date after the issue date when the security is traded to the buyer.

Maturity   is the security's maturity date. The maturity date is the date when the security expires.

Frequency   is the number of coupon payments per year. For annual payments, frequency = 1; for semiannual, frequency = 2; for quarterly, frequency = 4.

Basis   is the type of day count basis to use.

Basis	Day count basis
0 or omitted	US (NASD) 30/360
1	Actual/actual
2	Actual/360
3	Actual/365
4	European 30/360

Remarks

- The settlement date is the date a buyer purchases a coupon, such as a bond. The maturity date is the date when a coupon expires. For example, suppose a 30-year bond is issued on January 1, 1996, and is purchased by a buyer six months later. The issue date would be January 1, 1996, the settlement date would be July 1, 1996, and the maturity date would be January 1, 2026, which is 30 years after the January 1, 1996, issue date.

- All arguments are truncated to integers.

- If any argument is nonnumeric, COUPDAYSNC returns the #VALUE! error value.

- If settlement or maturity is not a valid date, COUPDAYSNC returns the #NUM! error value.

- If frequency is any number other than 1, 2, or 4, COUPDAYSNC returns the #NUM! error value.

- If basis < 0 or if basis > 4, COUPDAYSNC returns the #NUM! error value.

- If settlement ≥ maturity, COUPDAYSNC returns the #NUM! error value.

Example

A bond has the following terms:

January 25, 1993, settlement date
November 15, 1994, maturity date
Semiannual coupon
Actual/actual basis

The number of days from the settlement date to the next coupon date (in the 1900 date system) is:

COUPDAYSNC("1/25/93","11/15/94",2,1) equals 110

COUPNCD

Returns a number that represents the next coupon date after the settlement date. To view the number as a date, click **Cells** on the **Format** menu, click **Date** in the **Category** box, and then click a date format in the **Type** box.

If this function is not available, run the Setup program to install the Analysis ToolPak. After you install the Analysis ToolPak, you must enable it by using the **Add-Ins** command on the **Tools** menu.

Syntax

COUPNCD(settlement,maturity,frequency,basis)

Settlement   is the security's settlement date. The security settlement date is the date after the issue date when the security is traded to the buyer.

Maturity   is the security's maturity date. The maturity date is the date when the security expires.

Frequency   is the number of coupon payments per year. For annual payments, frequency = 1; for semiannual, frequency = 2; for quarterly, frequency = 4.

Basis   is the type of day count basis to use.

Basis	Day count basis
0 or omitted	US (NASD) 30/360
1	Actual/actual
2	Actual/360
3	Actual/365
4	European 30/360

Remarks

- The settlement date is the date a buyer purchases a coupon, such as a bond. The maturity date is the date when a coupon expires. For example, suppose a 30-year bond is issued on January 1, 1996, and is purchased by a buyer six months later. The issue date would be January 1, 1996, the settlement date would be July 1, 1996, and the maturity date would be January 1, 2026, which is 30 years after the January 1, 1996, issue date.

- All arguments are truncated to integers.

- If any argument is nonnumeric, COUPNCD returns the #VALUE! error value.

- If settlement or maturity is not a valid date, COUPNCD returns the #NUM! error value.

- If frequency is any number other than 1, 2, or 4, COUPNCD returns the #NUM! error value.

- If basis < 0 or if basis > 4, COUPNCD returns the #NUM! error value.

- If settlement ≥ maturity, COUPNCD returns the #NUM! error value.

Example

A bond has the following terms:

January 25, 1993, settlement date
November 15, 1994, maturity date
Semiannual coupon
Actual/actual basis

The next coupon date after the settlement date (in the 1900 date system) is:

COUPNCD("1/25/93","11/15/94",2,1) equals 34104 or May 15, 1993

COUPNUM

Returns the number of coupons payable between the settlement date and maturity date, rounded up to the nearest whole coupon.

If this function is not available, run the Setup program to install the Analysis ToolPak. After you install the Analysis ToolPak, you must enable it by using the **Add-Ins** command on the **Tools** menu.

Syntax

COUPNUM(settlement,maturity,frequency,basis)

Settlement   is the security's settlement date. The security settlement date is the date after the issue date when the security is traded to the buyer.

Maturity   is the security's maturity date. The maturity date is the date when the security expires.

Frequency   is the number of coupon payments per year. For annual payments, frequency = 1; for semiannual, frequency = 2; for quarterly, frequency = 4.

Basis   is the type of day count basis to use.

Basis	Day count basis
0 or omitted	US (NASD) 30/360
1	Actual/actual
2	Actual/360
3	Actual/365
4	European 30/360

Remarks

- The settlement date is the date a buyer purchases a coupon, such as a bond. The maturity date is the date when a coupon expires. For example, suppose a 30-year bond is issued on January 1, 1996, and is purchased by a buyer six months later. The issue date would be January 1, 1996, the settlement date would be July 1, 1996, and the maturity date would be January 1, 2026, which is 30 years after the January 1, 1996, issue date.

- All arguments are truncated to integers.

- If any argument is nonnumeric, COUPNUM returns the #VALUE! error value.

- If settlement or maturity is not a valid date, COUPNUM returns the #NUM! error value.

- If frequency is any number other than 1, 2, or 4, COUPNUM returns the #NUM! error value.

- If basis < 0 or if basis > 4, COUPNUM returns the #NUM! error value.

- If settlement ≥ maturity, COUPNUM returns the #NUM! error value.

Example

A bond has the following terms:

January 25, 1993, settlement date
November 15, 1994, maturity date
Semiannual coupon
Actual/actual basis

The number of coupon payments (in the 1900 date system) is:

COUPNUM("1/25/93","11/15/94",2,1) equals 4

COUPPCD

Returns a number that represents the previous coupon date before the settlement date. To view the number as a date, click **Cells** on the **Format** menu, click **Date** in the **Category** box, and then click a date format in the **Type** box.

If this function is not available, run the Setup program to install the Analysis ToolPak. After you install the Analysis ToolPak, you must enable it by using the **Add-Ins** command on the **Tools** menu.

Syntax

COUPPCD(settlement,maturity,frequency,basis)

Settlement is the security's settlement date. The security settlement date is the date after the issue date when the security is traded to the buyer.

Maturity is the security's maturity date. The maturity date is the date when the security expires.

Frequency is the number of coupon payments per year. For annual payments, frequency = 1; for semiannual, frequency = 2; for quarterly, frequency = 4.

Basis   is the type of day count basis to use.

Basis	Day count basis
0 or omitted	US (NASD) 30/360
1	Actual/actual
2	Actual/360
3	Actual/365
4	European 30/360

Remarks

- The settlement date is the date a buyer purchases a coupon, such as a bond. The maturity date is the date when a coupon expires. For example, suppose a 30-year bond is issued on January 1, 1996, and is purchased by a buyer six months later. The issue date would be January 1, 1996, the settlement date would be July 1, 1996, and the maturity date would be January 1, 2026, which is 30 years after the January 1, 1996, issue date.

- All arguments are truncated to integers.

- If any argument is nonnumeric, COUPPCD returns the #VALUE! error value.

- If settlement or maturity is not a valid date, COUPPCD returns the #NUM! error value.

- If frequency is any number other than 1, 2, or 4, COUPPCD returns the #NUM! error value.

- If basis < 0 or if basis > 4, COUPPCD returns the #NUM! error value.

- If settlement ≥ maturity, COUPPCD returns the #NUM! error value.

Example

A bond has the following terms:

January 25, 1993, settlement date
November 15, 1994, maturity date
Semiannual coupon
Actual/actual basis

The previous coupon date before the settlement date (in the 1900 date system) is:

COUPPCD("1/25/93","11/15/94",2,1) equals 33923 or November 15, 1992

COVAR

Returns covariance, the average of the products of deviations for each data point pair. Use covariance to determine the relationship between two data sets. For example, you can examine whether greater income accompanies greater levels of education.

Syntax

COVAR(array1,array2)

Array1   is the first cell range of integers.

Array2   is the second cell range of integers.

Remarks

- The arguments must be either numbers or names, arrays, or references that contain numbers.
- If an array or reference argument contains text, logical values, or empty cells, those values are ignored; however, cells with the value zero are included.
- If array1 and array2 have different numbers of data points, COVAR returns the #N/A error value.
- If either array1 or array2 is empty, COVAR returns the #DIV/0! error value.
- The covariance is:

$$Cov(X,Y) = \frac{1}{n} \sum_{j-1}^{n} (x_j - \mu_x)(y_j - \mu_y)$$

Example

COVAR({3,2,4,5,6}, {9,7,12,15,17}) equals 5.2

CRITBINOM

Returns the smallest value for which the cumulative binomial distribution is greater than or equal to a criterion value. Use this function for quality assurance applications. For example, use CRITBINOM to determine the greatest number of defective parts that are allowed to come off an assembly line run without rejecting the entire lot.

Syntax

CRITBINOM(trials,probability_s,alpha)

Trials   is the number of Bernoulli trials.

Probability_s   is the probability of a success on each trial.

Alpha   is the criterion value.

Remarks

- If any argument is nonnumeric, CRITBINOM returns the #VALUE! error value.
- If trials is not an integer, it is truncated.
- If trials < 0, CRITBINOM returns the #NUM! error value.
- If probability_s is < 0 or probability_s > 1, CRITBINOM returns the #NUM! error value.
- If alpha < 0 or alpha > 1, CRITBINOM returns the #NUM! error value.

Example

CRITBINOM(6,0.5,0.75) equals 4

CUMIPMT

Returns the cumulative interest paid on a loan between start_period and end_period.

If this function is not available, run the Setup program to install the Analysis ToolPak. After you install the Analysis ToolPak, you must enable it by using the **Add-Ins** command on the **Tools** menu.

Syntax

CUMIPMT(rate,nper,pv,start_period,end_period,type)

Rate   is the interest rate.

Nper   is the total number of payment periods.

Pv   is the present value.

Start_period   is the first period in the calculation. Payment periods are numbered beginning with 1.

End_period   is the last period in the calculation.

Type   is the timing of the payment.

Type	Timing
0 (zero)	Payment at the end of the period
1	Payment at the beginning of the period

Remarks

- Make sure that you are consistent about the units you use for specifying rate and nper. If you make monthly payments on a four-year loan at an annual interest rate of 12 percent, use 12%/12 for rate and 4*12 for nper. If you make annual payments on the same loan, use 12% for rate and 4 for nper.

- Nper, start_period, end_period, and type are truncated to integers.

- If any argument is nonnumeric, CUMIPMT returns the #VALUE! error value.

- If rate ≤ 0, nper ≤ 0, or pv ≤ 0, CUMIPMT returns the #NUM! error value.

- If start_period < 1, end_period < 1, or start_period > end_period, CUMIPMT returns the #NUM! error value.

- If type is any number other than 0 or 1, CUMIPMT returns the #NUM! error value.

Example

A home mortgage loan has the following terms:

Interest rate, 9.00 percent per annum (rate = 9.00% ÷ 12 = 0.0075)
Term, 30 years (nper = 30 × 12 = 360)
Present value, $125,000

The total interest paid in the second year of payments (periods 13 through 24) is:

CUMIPMT(0.0075,360,125000,13,24,0) equals -11135.23

The interest paid in a single payment in the first month is:

CUMIPMT(0.0075,360,125000,1,1,0) equals -937.50

CUMPRINC

Returns the cumulative principal paid on a loan between start_period and end_period.

If this function is not available, run the Setup program to install the Analysis ToolPak. After you install the Analysis ToolPak, you must enable it by using the **Add-Ins** command on the **Tools** menu.

Syntax

CUMPRINC(rate,nper,pv,start_period,end_period,type)

Rate   is the interest rate.

Nper   is the total number of payment periods.

Pv   is the present value.

Start_period   is the first period in the calculation. Payment periods are numbered beginning with 1.

End_period   is the last period in the calculation.

Type   is the timing of the payment.

Type	Timing
0 (zero)	Payment at the end of the period
1	Payment at the beginning of the period

Remarks

- Make sure that you are consistent about the units you use for specifying rate and nper. If you make monthly payments on a four-year loan at an annual interest rate of 12 percent, use 12%/12 for rate and 4*12 for nper. If you make annual payments on the same loan, use 12% for rate and 4 for nper.

- Nper, start_period, end_period, and type are truncated to integers.

- If any argument is nonnumeric, CUMPRINC returns the #VALUE! error value.

- If rate ≤ 0, nper ≤ 0, or pv ≤ 0, CUMPRINC returns the #NUM! error value.

- If start_period < 1, end_period < 1, or start_period > end_period, CUMPRINC returns the #NUM! error value.

- If type is any number other than 0 or 1, CUMPRINC returns the #NUM! error value.

Example

A home mortgage loan has the following terms:

Interest rate, 9.00 percent per annum (rate = 9.00% ÷ 12 = 0.0075)
Term, 30 years (nper = 30 × 12 = 360)
Present value, $125,000

The total principal paid in the second year of payments (periods 13 through 24) is:

CUMPRINC(0.0075,360,125000,13,24,0) equals -934.1071

The principal paid in a single payment in the first month is:

CUMPRINC(0.0075,360,125000,1,1,0) equals -68.27827

Database Functions

Microsoft Excel includes 12 worksheet functions that analyze data stored in lists or databases. Each of these functions, referred to collectively as the Dfunctions, uses three arguments: database, field, and criteria. These arguments refer to the worksheet ranges that are used by the function.

Syntax

Dfunction(database,field,criteria)

Database   is the range of cells that make up the list or database.

- In Microsoft Excel, a database is a list of related data in which rows of related information are records and columns of data are fields. The first row of the list contains labels for each column. The reference can be entered as a cell range or as a name that represents the range that contains the list.

- In all database functions, if the database reference is to a cell inside a PivotTable, the calculation is done on only the PivotTable data.

- If you want to calculate subtotal values in your list, use the **Subtotals** command on the **Data** menu to insert subtotal values.

Field   indicates which column is used in the function. Columns of data in the list must have an identifying label in the first row. Field can be given as text with the column label enclosed between double quotation marks, such as "Age" or "Yield" in the example list below, or as a number that represents the position of the column in the list: 1 for the first column (Tree in the example below), 2 for the second (Height), and so on.

Criteria   is a reference to a range of cells that specify conditions for the function. The function returns information from the list that matches the conditions specified in the criteria range. The criteria range includes a copy of the column label in the list for the column you want the function to summarize. The criteria reference can be entered as a cell range, such as A1:F2 in the example database below, or as a name that represents the range, such as "Criteria."

Tips

- You can use any range for the criteria argument, as long as it includes at least one column label and at least one cell below the column label for specifying the condition.

- For example, if the range G1:G2 contains the column label Income in G1 and the amount 10,000 in G2, you could define the range as MatchIncome and use that name as the criteria argument in the database functions.

- Although the criteria range can be located anywhere on the worksheet, do not place the criteria range below the list. If you add more information to the list by using the **Form** command on the **Data** menu, the new information is added to the first row below the list. If the row below the list is not blank, Microsoft Excel cannot add the new information.

- Make sure the criteria range does not overlap the list.

- To perform an operation on an entire column in a database, enter a blank line below the column labels in the criteria range.

Examples

The following illustration shows a database for a small orchard. Each record contains information about one tree. The range A5:E11 is named Database, and the range A1:F3 is named Criteria.

	A	B	C	D	E	F
1	Tree	Height	Age	Yield	Profit	Height
2	Apple	>10				<16
3	Pear					
4						
5	Tree	Height	Age	Yield	Profit	
6	Apple	18	20	14	$105.00	
7	Pear	12	12	10	$96.00	
8	Cherry	13	14	10	$105.00	
9	Apple	14	15	10	$75.00	
10	Pear	9	8	8	$76.80	
11	Apple	9	9	6	$45.00	

DCOUNT(Database,"Age",A1:F2) equals 1. This function looks at the records of apple trees between a height of 10 and 16 and counts how many of the Age fields in those records contain numbers.

DCOUNTA(Database,"Profit",A1:F2) equals 1. This function looks at the records of apple trees between a height of 10 and 16 and counts how many of the Profit fields in those records are not blank.

DMAX(Database,"Profit",A1:A3) equals $105.00, the maximum profit of apple and pear trees.

DMIN(Database,"Profit",A1:B2) equals $75.00, the minimum profit of apple trees over 10.

DSUM(Database,"Profit",A1:A2) equals $225.00, the total profit from apple trees.

DSUM(Database,"Profit",A1:F2) equals $75.00, the total profit from apple trees with a height between 10 and 16.

DPRODUCT(Database,"Yield",A1:F2) equals 140, the product of the yields from apple trees with a height between 10 and 16.

DAVERAGE(Database,"Yield",A1:B2) equals 12, the average yield of apple trees over 10 feet in height.

DAVERAGE(Database,3,Database) equals 13, the average age of all trees in the database.

DSTDEV(Database,"Yield",A1:A3) equals 2.97, the estimated standard deviation in the yield of apple and pear trees if the data in the database is only a sample of the total orchard population.

DSTDEVP(Database,"Yield",A1:A3) equals 2.65, the true standard deviation in the yield of apple and pear trees if the data in the database is the entire population.

DVAR(Database,"Yield",A1:A3) equals 8.8, the estimated variance in the yield of apple and pear trees if the data in the database is only a sample of the total orchard population.

DVARP(Database,"Yield",A1:A3) equals 7.04, the true variance in the yield of apple and pear trees if the data in the database is the entire orchard population.

DGET(Database,"Yield",Criteria) returns the #NUM! error value because more than one record meets the criteria.

DATE

Returns the serial number of a particular date. For more information about serial numbers, see NOW.

Syntax

DATE(year,month,day)

Year   is a number from 1900 to 9999 in Microsoft Excel for Windows or 1904 to 9999 in Microsoft Excel for the Macintosh.

Month   is a number representing the month of the year. If month is greater than 12, then month adds that number of months to the first month in the year specified. For example, DATE(90,14,2) returns the serial number representing February 2, 1991.

Day   is a number representing the day of the month. If day is greater than the number of days in the month specified, then day adds that number of days to the first day in the month. For example, DATE(91,1,35) returns the serial number representing February 4, 1991.

Remarks

- Microsoft Excel for Windows and Microsoft Excel for the Macintosh use different date systems as their default. For more information, see NOW.

- The DATE function is most useful in formulas where year, month, and day are formulas, not constants.

Examples

Using the 1900 date system (the default in Microsoft Excel for Windows), DATE(91, 1, 1) equals 33239, the serial number corresponding to January 1, 1991.

Using the 1904 date system (the default in Microsoft Excel for the Macintosh), DATE(91, 1, 1) equals 31777, the serial number corresponding to January 1, 1991.

DATEVALUE

Returns the serial number of the date represented by date_text. Use DATEVALUE to convert a date represented by text to a serial number.

Syntax

DATEVALUE(date_text)

Date_text   is text that returns a date in a Microsoft Excel date format. Using the default date system in Microsoft Excel for Windows, date_text must represent a date from January 1, 1900, to December 31, 9999. Using the default date system in Microsoft Excel for the Macintosh, date_text must represent a date from January 1, 1904, to December 31, 9999. DATEVALUE returns the #VALUE! error value if date_text is out of this range.

If the year portion of date_text is omitted, DATEVALUE uses the current year from your computer's built-in clock. Time information in date_text is ignored.

Remarks

- Microsoft Excel for Windows and Microsoft Excel for the Macintosh use different date systems as their default. For more information, see NOW.

- Most functions automatically convert date values to serial numbers.

Examples

The following examples use the 1900 date system:

DATEVALUE("8/22/55") equals 20323

DATEVALUE("22-AUG-55") equals 20323

Assuming your computer's built-in clock is set to 1993 and you are using the 1900 date system:

DATEVALUE("5-JUL") equals 34155

DAVERAGE

Averages the values in a column in a list or database that match conditions you specify.

Syntax

DAVERAGE(database,field,criteria)

Database   is the range of cells that make up the list or database. A database is a list of related data in which rows of related information are records and columns of data are fields. The first row of the list contains labels for each column.

Field   indicates which column is used in the function. Field can be given as text with the column label enclosed between double quotation marks, such as "Age" or "Yield," or as a number that represents the position of the column within the list: 1 for the first column, 2 for the second column, and so on.

Criteria   is the range of cells that contains the conditions you specify. You can use any range for the criteria argument, as long as it includes at least one column label and at least one cell below the column label for specifying a condition for the column.

DAY

Returns the day of the month corresponding to serial_number. The day is given as an integer ranging from 1 to 31.

Syntax

DAY(serial_number)

Serial_number   is the date-time code used by Microsoft Excel for date and time calculations. You can give serial_number as text, such as "4-15-93" or "15-Apr-1993", instead of as a number. The text is automatically converted to a serial number. For more information about serial_number, see NOW.

Remarks

Microsoft Excel for Windows and Microsoft Excel for the Macintosh use different date systems as their default. For more information, see NOW.

Examples

DAY("4-Jan") equals 4

DAY("15-Apr-1993") equals 15

DAY("8/11/93") equals 11

DAYS360

Returns the number of days between two dates based on a 360-day year (twelve 30-day months), which is used in some accounting calculations. Use this function to help compute payments if your accounting system is based on twelve 30-day months.

Syntax

DAYS360(start_date,end_date,method)

Start_date   and end_date   are the two dates between which you want to know the number of days. If start_date occurs after end_date, DAYS360 returns a negative number.

Method   is a logical value that specifies whether to use the U.S. or European method in the calculation

Method	Defined
FALSE or omitted	U.S. (NASD). If the starting date is the 31st of a month, it becomes equal to the 30th of the same month. If the ending date is the 31st of a month and the starting date is less than the 30th of a month, the ending date becomes equal to the 1st of the next month, otherwise the ending date becomes equal to the 30th of the same month.
TRUE	European method. Starting dates or ending dates that occur on the 31st of a month become equal to the 30th of the same month.

Tip   To determine the number of days between two dates in a normal year, you can use normal subtraction—for example, "12/31/93"-"1/1/93" equals 364.

Example

DAYS360("1/30/93", "2/1/93") equals 1

If cell D10 contains the date 1/30/93 and cell D11 contains the date 2/1/93, then:

DAYS360(D10, D11) equals 1

DB

Returns the depreciation of an asset for a specified period using the fixed-declining balance method.

Syntax

DB(cost,salvage,life,period,month**)**

Cost   is the initial cost of the asset.

Salvage   is the value at the end of the depreciation (sometimes called the salvage value of the asset).

Life   is the number of periods over which the asset is being depreciated (sometimes called the useful life of the asset).

Period   is the period for which you want to calculate the depreciation. Period must use the same units as life.

Month   is the number of months in the first year. If month is omitted, it is assumed to be 12.

Remarks

The fixed-declining balance method computes depreciation at a fixed rate. DB uses the following formulas to calculate depreciation for a period:

(cost - total depreciation from prior periods) * rate

where:

rate = 1 - ((salvage / cost) ^ (1 / life)), rounded to three decimal places

Depreciation for the first and last periods is a special case. For the first period, DB uses this formula:

cost * rate * month / 12

For the last period, DB uses this formula:

((cost - total depreciation from prior periods) * rate * (12 - month)) / 12

Examples

Suppose a factory purchases a new machine. The machine costs $1,000,000 and has a lifetime of six years. The salvage value of the machine is $100,000. The following examples show depreciation over the life of the machine. The results are rounded to whole numbers.

DB(1000000,100000,6,1,7) equals $186,083
DB(1000000,100000,6,2,7) equals $259,639
DB(1000000,100000,6,3,7) equals $176,814
DB(1000000,100000,6,4,7) equals $120,411
DB(1000000,100000,6,5,7) equals $82,000
DB(1000000,100000,6,6,7) equals $55,842
DB(1000000,100000,6,7,7) equals $15,845

DCOUNT

Counts the cells that contain numbers in a column in a list or database that match conditions you specify.

The field argument is optional. If field is omitted, DCOUNT counts all records in the database that match the criteria.

Syntax

DCOUNT(database,field,criteria)

Database   is the range of cells that make up the list or database. A database is a list of related data in which rows of related information are records and columns of data are fields. The first row of the list contains labels for each column.

Field   indicates which column is used in the function. Field can be given as text with the column label enclosed between double quotation marks, such as "Age" or "Yield," or as a number that represents the position of the column within the list: 1 for the first column, 2 for the second column, and so on.

Criteria   is the range of cells that contains the conditions you specify. You can use any range for the criteria argument, as long as it includes at least one column label and at least one cell below the column label for specifying a condition for the column.

DCOUNTA

Counts all of the nonblank cells in a column in a list or database that match conditions you specify.

Syntax

DCOUNTA(database,field,**criteria)**

Database   is the range of cells that make up the list or database. A database is a list of related data in which rows of related information are records and columns of data are fields. The first row of the list contains labels for each column.

Field   indicates which column is used in the function. Field can be given as text with the column label enclosed between double quotation marks, such as "Age" or "Yield," or as a number that represents the position of the column within the list: 1 for the first column, 2 for the second column, and so on.

Criteria   is the range of cells that contains the conditions you specify. You can use any range for the criteria argument, as long as it includes at least one column label and at least one cell below the column label for specifying a condition for the column.

DDB

Returns the depreciation of an asset for a specified period using the double-declining balance method or some other method you specify.

Syntax

DDB(cost,salvage,life,period,factor)

Cost   is the initial cost of the asset.

Salvage   is the value at the end of the depreciation (sometimes called the salvage value of the asset).

Life   is the number of periods over which the asset is being depreciated (sometimes called the useful life of the asset).

Period   is the period for which you want to calculate the depreciation. Period must use the same units as life.

Factor   is the rate at which the balance declines. If factor is omitted, it is assumed to be 2 (the double-declining balance method).

All five arguments must be positive numbers.

Remarks

The double-declining balance method computes depreciation at an accelerated rate. Depreciation is highest in the first period and decreases in successive periods. DDB uses the following formula to calculate depreciation for a period:

cost - salvage(total depreciation from prior periods) * factor / life

Change factor if you do not want to use the double-declining balance method.

Examples

Suppose a factory purchases a new machine. The machine costs $2,400 and has a lifetime of 10 years. The salvage value of the machine is $300. The following examples show depreciation over several periods. The results are rounded to two decimal places.

DDB(2400,300,3650,1) equals $1.32, the first day's depreciation. Microsoft Excel automatically assumes that factor is 2.

DDB(2400,300,120,1,2) equals $40.00, the first month's depreciation.

DDB(2400,300,10,1,2) equals $480.00, the first year's depreciation.

DDB(2400,300,10,2,1.5) equals $306.00, the second year's depreciation using a factor of 1.5 instead of the double-declining balance method.

DDB(2400,300,10,10) equals $22.12, the 10th year's depreciation. Microsoft Excel automatically assumes that factor is 2.

DEC2BIN

Converts a decimal number to binary.

If this function is not available, run the Setup program to install the Analysis ToolPak. After you install the Analysis ToolPak, you must enable it by using the **Add-Ins** command on the **Tools** menu.

Syntax

DEC2BIN(number,places)

Number   is the decimal integer you want to convert. If number is negative, places is ignored and DEC2BIN returns a 10-character (10-bit) binary number in which the most significant bit is the sign bit. The remaining 9 bits are magnitude bits. Negative numbers are represented using two's-complement notation.

Places is the number of characters to use. If places is omitted, DEC2BIN uses the minimum number of characters necessary. Places is useful for padding the return value with leading 0s (zeros).

Remarks

- If number < -512 or if number > 511, DEC2BIN returns the #NUM! error value.
- If number is nonnumeric, DEC2BIN returns the #VALUE! error value.
- If DEC2BIN requires more than places characters, it returns the #NUM! error value.
- If places is not an integer, it is truncated.
- If places is nonnumeric, DEC2BIN returns the #VALUE! error value.
- If places is negative, DEC2BIN returns the #NUM! error value.

Examples

`DEC2BIN(9, 4)` equals 1001

`DEC2BIN(-100)` equals 1110011100

DEC2HEX

Converts a decimal number to hexadecimal.

If this function is not available, run the Setup program to install the Analysis ToolPak. After you install the Analysis ToolPak, you must enable it by using the **Add-Ins** command on the **Tools** menu.

Syntax

DEC2HEX(number,places)

Number is the decimal integer you want to convert. If number is negative, places is ignored and DEC2HEX returns a 10-character (40-bit) hexadecimal number in which the most significant bit is the sign bit. The remaining 39 bits are magnitude bits. Negative numbers are represented using two's-complement notation.

Places is the number of characters to use. If places is omitted, DEC2HEX uses the minimum number of characters necessary. Places is useful for padding the return value with leading 0s (zeros).

Remarks

- If number < -549,755,813,888 or if number > 549,755,813,887, DEC2HEX returns the #NUM! error value.
- If number is nonnumeric, DEC2HEX returns the #VALUE! error value.
- If DEC2HEX requires more than places characters, it returns the #NUM! error value.

- If places is not an integer, it is truncated.
- If places is nonnumeric, DEC2HEX returns the #VALUE! error value.
- If places is negative, DEC2HEX returns the #NUM! error value.

Examples

DEC2HEX(100, 4) equals 0064

DEC2HEX(-54) equals FFFFFFFFCA

DEC2OCT

Converts a decimal number to octal.

If this function is not available, run the Setup program to install the Analysis ToolPak. After you install the Analysis ToolPak, you must enable it by using the **Add-Ins** command on the **Tools** menu.

Syntax

DEC2OCT(number,places)

Number   is the decimal integer you want to convert. If number is negative, places is ignored and DEC2OCT returns a 10-character (30-bit) octal number in which the most significant bit is the sign bit. The remaining 29 bits are magnitude bits. Negative numbers are represented using two's-complement notation.

Places   is the number of characters to use. If places is omitted, DEC2OCT uses the minimum number of characters necessary. Places is useful for padding the return value with leading 0s (zeros).

Remarks

- If number < -536,870,912 or if number > 536,870,911, DEC2OCT returns the #NUM! error value.
- If number is nonnumeric, DEC2OCT returns the #VALUE! error value.
- If DEC2OCT requires more than places characters, it returns the #NUM! error value.
- If places is not an integer, it is truncated.
- If places is nonnumeric, DEC2OCT returns the #VALUE! error value.
- If places is negative, DEC2OCT returns the #NUM! error value.

Examples

DEC2OCT(58, 3) equals 072

DEC2OCT(-100) equals 7777777634

DEGREES

Converts radians into degrees.

Syntax

DEGREES(angle)

Angle   is the angle in radians that you want to convert.

Example

DEGREES(PI()) equals 180

DELTA

Tests whether two values are equal. Returns 1 if number1 = number2; returns 0 otherwise. Use this function to filter a set of values. For example, by summing several DELTA functions you calculate the count of equal pairs. This function is also known as the Kronecker Delta function.

If this function is not available, run the Setup program to install the Analysis ToolPak. After you install the Analysis ToolPak, you must enable it by using the **Add-Ins** command on the **Tools** menu.

Syntax

DELTA(number1,number2)

Number1   is the first number.

Number2   is the second number. If omitted, number2 is assumed to be zero.

Remarks

- If number1 is nonnumeric, DELTA returns the #VALUE! error value.
- If number2 is nonnumeric, DELTA returns the #VALUE! error value.

Examples

DELTA(5, 4) equals 0

DELTA(5, 5) equals 1

DELTA(0.5, 0) equals 0

DEVSQ

Returns the sum of squares of deviations of data points from their sample mean.

Syntax

DEVSQ(number1,number2, ...)

Number1,number2, ...   are 1 to 30 arguments for which you want to calculate the sum of squared deviations. You can also use a single array or a reference to an array instead of arguments separated by commas.

Remarks

- The arguments must be numbers, or names, arrays, or references that contain numbers.

- If an array or reference argument contains text, logical values, or empty cells, those values are ignored; however, cells with the value zero are included.

- The equation for the sum of squared deviations is:

$$DEVSQ = \sum (x - \bar{x})^2$$

Example

DEVSQ(4,5,8,7,11,4,3) equals 48

DGET

Extracts a single value from a column in a list or database that matches conditions you specify.

Syntax

DGET(database,field,criteria)

Database   is the range of cells that make up the list or database. A database is a list of related data in which rows of related information are records and columns of data are fields. The first row of the list contains labels for each column.

Field   indicates which column is used in the function. Field can be given as text with the column label enclosed between double quotation marks, such as "Age" or "Yield," or as a number that represents the position of the column within the list: 1 for the first column, 2 for the second column, and so on.

Criteria   is the range of cells that contains the conditions you specify. You can use any range for the criteria argument, as long as it includes at least one column label and at least one cell below the column label for specifying a condition for the column.

Remarks

- If no record matches the criteria, DGET returns the #VALUE! error value.
- If more than one record matches the criteria, DGET returns the #NUM! error value.

DISC

Returns the discount rate for a security.

If this function is not available, run the Setup program to install the Analysis ToolPak. After you install the Analysis ToolPak, you must enable it by using the **Add-Ins** command on the **Tools** menu.

Syntax

DISC(settlement,maturity,pr,redemption,basis)

Settlement   is the security's settlement date. The security settlement date is the date after the issue date when the security is traded to the buyer.

Maturity   is the security's maturity date. The maturity date is the date when the security expires.

Pr   is the security's price per $100 face value.

Redemption   is the security's redemption value per $100 face value.

Basis   is the type of day count basis to use.

Basis	Day count basis
0 or omitted	US (NASD) 30/360
1	Actual/actual
2	Actual/360
3	Actual/365
4	European 30/360

Remarks

- The settlement date is the date a buyer purchases a coupon, such as a bond. The maturity date is the date when a coupon expires. For example, suppose a 30-year bond is issued on January 1, 1996, and is purchased by a buyer six months later. The issue date would be January 1, 1996, the settlement date would be July 1, 1996, and the maturity date would be January 1, 2026, 30 years after the January 1, 1996, issue date.
- Settlement, maturity, and basis are truncated to integers.
- If any argument is nonnumeric, DISC returns the #VALUE! error value.
- If settlement or maturity is not a valid serial date number, DISC returns the #NUM! error value.
- If pr ≤ 0 or if redemption ≤ 0, DISC returns the #NUM! error value.

- If basis < 0 or if basis > 4, DISC returns the #NUM! error value.

- If settlement ≥ maturity, DISC returns the #NUM! error value.

- DISC is calculated as follows:

$$DISC = \frac{redemption - par}{par} \times \frac{B}{DSM}$$

Where:

B = number of days in a year, depending on the year basis.

DSM = number of days between settlement and maturity.

Example

A bond has the following terms:

February 15, 1993, settlement date
June 10, 1993, maturity date
$97.975 price
$100 redemption value
Actual/360 basis

The bond discount rate (in the 1900 date system) is:

DISC("2/15/93","6/10/93",97.975,100,2) equals 0.063391 or 6.3391 percent

DMAX

Returns the largest number in a column in a list or database that matches conditions you specify.

Syntax

DMAX(database,field,criteria)

Database   is the range of cells that make up the list or database. A database is a list of related data in which rows of related information are records and columns of data are fields. The first row of the list contains labels for each column.

Field   indicates which column is used in the function. Field can be given as text with the column label enclosed between double quotation marks, such as "Age" or "Yield," or as a number that represents the position of the column within the list: 1 for the first column, 2 for the second column, and so on.

Criteria   is the range of cells that contains the conditions you specify. You can use any range for the criteria argument, as long as it includes at least one column label and at least one cell below the column label for specifying a condition for the column.

DMIN

Returns the smallest number in a column in a list or database that matches conditions you specify.

Syntax

DMIN(database,field,criteria)

Database   is the range of cells that make up the list or database. A database is a list of related data in which rows of related information are records and columns of data are fields. The first row of the list contains labels for each column.

Field   indicates which column is used in the function. Field can be given as text with the column label enclosed between double quotation marks, such as "Age" or "Yield," or as a number that represents the position of the column within the list: 1 for the first column, 2 for the second column, and so on.

Criteria   is the range of cells that contains the conditions you specify. You can use any range for the criteria argument, as long as it includes at least one column label and at least one cell below the column label for specifying a condition for the column.

DOLLAR

Converts a number to text using currency format, with the decimals rounded to the specified place. The format used is $#,##0.00_);($#,##0.00).

Syntax

DOLLAR(number,decimals)

Number   is a number, a reference to a cell containing a number, or a formula that evaluates to a number.

Decimals   is the number of digits to the right of the decimal point. If decimals is negative, number is rounded to the left of the decimal point. If you omit decimals, it is assumed to be 2.

Remarks

The major difference between formatting a cell that contains a number with the **Cells** command (**Format** menu) and formatting a number directly with the DOLLAR function is that DOLLAR converts its result to text. A number formatted with the **Cells** command is still a number. You can continue to use numbers formatted with DOLLAR in formulas, because Microsoft Excel converts numbers entered as text values to numbers when it calculates.

Examples

DOLLAR(1234.567, 2) equals "$1,234.57"

DOLLAR(1234.567, -2) equals "$1,200"

DOLLAR(-1234.567, -2) equals "($1,200)"

DOLLAR(-0.123, 4) equals "($0.1230)"

DOLLAR(99.888) equals "$99.89"

DOLLARDE

Converts a dollar price expressed as a fraction into a dollar price expressed as a decimal number. Use DOLLARDE to convert fractional dollar numbers, such as securities prices, to decimal numbers.

If this function is not available, run the Setup program to install the Analysis ToolPak. After you install the Analysis ToolPak, you must enable it by using the **Add-Ins** command on the **Tools** menu.

Syntax

DOLLARDE(fractional_dollar,fraction)

Fractional_dollar   is a number expressed as a fraction.

Fraction   is the integer to use in the denominator of the fraction.

Remarks

- If either argument is nonnumeric, DOLLARDE returns the #VALUE! error value.
- If fraction is not an integer, it is truncated.
- If fraction ≤ 0, DOLLARDE returns the #NUM! error value.

Examples

DOLLARDE(1.02,16) equals 1.125

DOLLARDE(1.1,8) equals 1.125

DOLLARFR

Converts a dollar price expressed as a decimal number into a dollar price expressed as a fraction. Use DOLLARFR to convert decimal numbers to fractional dollar numbers, such as securities prices.

If this function is not available, run the Setup program to install the Analysis ToolPak. After you install the Analysis ToolPak, you must enable it by using the **Add-Ins** command on the **Tools** menu.

Syntax

DOLLARFR(decimal_dollar,fraction)

Decimal_dollar   is a decimal number.

Fraction   is the integer to use in the denominator of a fraction.

Remarks

- If either argument is nonnumeric, DOLLARFR returns the #VALUE! error value.
- If fraction is not an integer, it is truncated.
- If fraction ≤ 0, DOLLARFR returns the #NUM! error value.

Examples

DOLLARFR(1.125,16) equals 1.02

DOLLARFR(1.125,8) equals 1.1

DPRODUCT

Multiplies the values in a column in a list or database that match conditions you specify.

Syntax

DPRODUCT(database,field,criteria)

Database   is the range of cells that make up the list or database. A database is a list of related data in which rows of related information are records and columns of data are fields. The first row of the list contains labels for each column.

Field   indicates which column is used in the function. Field can be given as text with the column label enclosed between double quotation marks, such as "Age" or "Yield," or as a number that represents the position of the column within the list: 1 for the first column, 2 for the second column, and so on.

Criteria   is the range of cells that contains the conditions you specify. You can use any range for the criteria argument, as long as it includes at least one column label and at least one cell below the column label for specifying a condition for the column.

DSTDEV

Estimates the standard deviation of a population based on a sample, using the numbers in a column in a list or database that match conditions you specify.

Syntax

DSTDEV(database,field,criteria)

Database   is the range of cells that make up the list or database. A database is a list of related data in which rows of related information are records and columns of data are fields. The first row of the list contains labels for each column.

Field   indicates which column is used in the function. Field can be given as text with the column label enclosed between double quotation marks, such as "Age" or "Yield," or as a number that represents the position of the column within the list: 1 for the first column, 2 for the second column, and so on.

Criteria   is the range of cells that contains the conditions you specify. You can use any range for the criteria argument, as long as it includes at least one column label and at least one cell below the column label for specifying a condition for the column.

DSTDEVP

Calculates the standard deviation of a population based on the entire population, using the numbers in a column in a list or database that match conditions you specify.

Syntax

DSTDEVP(database,field,criteria)

Database   is the range of cells that make up the list or database. A database is a list of related data in which rows of related information are records and columns of data are fields. The first row of the list contains labels for each column.

Field   indicates which column is used in the function. Field can be given as text with the column label enclosed between double quotation marks, such as "Age" or "Yield," or as a number that represents the position of the column within the list: 1 for the first column, 2 for the second column, and so on.

Criteria   is the range of cells that contains the conditions you specify. You can use any range for the criteria argument, as long as it includes at least one column label and at least one cell below the column label for specifying a condition for the column.

DSUM

Adds the numbers in a column in a list or database that match conditions you specify.

Syntax

DSUM(database,field,criteria)

Database   is the range of cells that make up the list or database. A database is a list of related data in which rows of related information are records and columns of data are fields. The first row of the list contains labels for each column.

Field   indicates which column is used in the function. Field can be given as text with the column label enclosed between double quotation marks, such as "Age" or "Yield," or as a number that represents the position of the column within the list: 1 for the first column, 2 for the second column, and so on.

Criteria   is the range of cells that contains the conditions you specify. You can use any range for the criteria argument, as long as it includes at least one column label and at least one cell below the column label for specifying a condition for the column.

DURATION

Returns the Macauley duration for an assumed par value of $100. Duration is defined as the weighted average of the present value of the cash flows and is used as a measure of a bond price's response to changes in yield.

If this function is not available, run the Setup program to install the Analysis ToolPak. After you install the Analysis ToolPak, you must enable it by using the **Add-Ins** command on the **Tools** menu.

Syntax

DURATION(settlement,maturity,coupon yld,frequency,basis)

Settlement   is the security's settlement date. The security settlement date is the date after the issue date when the security is traded to the buyer.

Maturity   is the security's maturity date. The maturity date is the date when the security expires.

Coupon   is the security's annual coupon rate.

Yld   is the security's annual yield.

Frequency   is the number of coupon payments per year. For annual payments, frequency = 1; for semiannual, frequency = 2; for quarterly, frequency = 4.

Basis   is the type of day count basis to use.

Basis	Day count basis
0 or omitted	US (NASD) 30/360
1	Actual/actual
2	Actual/360
3	Actual/365
4	European 30/360

Remarks

- The settlement date is the date a buyer purchases a coupon, such as a bond. The maturity date is the date when a coupon expires. For example, suppose a 30-year bond is issued on January 1, 1996, and is purchased by a buyer six months later. The issue date would be January 1, 1996, the settlement date would be July 1, 1996, and the maturity date would be January 1, 2026, which is 30 years after the January 1, 1996, issue date.

- Settlement, maturity, frequency, and basis are truncated to integers.

- If any argument is nonnumeric, DURATION returns the #VALUE! error value.

- If settlement or maturity is not a valid date, DURATION returns the #NUM! error value.

- If coupon < 0 or if yld < 0, DURATION returns the #NUM! error value.

- If frequency is any number other than 1, 2, or 4, DURATION returns the #NUM! error value.

- If basis < 0 or if basis > 4, DURATION returns the #NUM! error value.

- If settlement ≥ maturity, DURATION returns the #NUM! error value.

Example

A bond has the following terms:

January 1, 1986, settlement date
January 1, 1994, maturity date
8 percent coupon
9.0 percent yield
Frequency is semiannual
Actual/actual basis

The duration (in the 1900 date system) is:

```
DURATION("1/1/86","1/1/94",0.08,0.09,2,1)
```
equals 5.993775

DVAR

Estimates the variance of a population based on a sample, using the numbers in a column in a list or database that match conditions you specify.

Syntax

DVAR(database,field,criteria)

Database   is the range of cells that make up the list or database. A database is a list of related data in which rows of related information are records and columns of data are fields. The first row of the list contains labels for each column.

Field   indicates which column is used in the function. Field can be given as text with the column label enclosed between double quotation marks, such as "Age" or "Yield," or as a number that represents the position of the column within the list: 1 for the first column, 2 for the second column, and so on.

Criteria   is the range of cells that contains the conditions you specify. You can use any range for the criteria argument, as long as it includes at least one column label and at least one cell below the column label for specifying a condition for the column.

DVARP

Calculates the variance of a population based on the entire population, using the numbers in a column in a list or database that match conditions you specify.

Syntax

DVARP(database,field,criteria)

Database   is the range of cells that make up the list or database. A database is a list of related data in which rows of related information are records and columns of data are fields. The first row of the list contains labels for each column.

Field   indicates which column is used in the function. Field can be given as text with the column label enclosed between double quotation marks, such as "Age" or "Yield," or as a number that represents the position of the column within the list: 1 for the first column, 2 for the second column, and so on.

Criteria   is the range of cells that contains the conditions you specify. You can use any range for the criteria argument, as long as it includes at least one column label and at least one cell below the column label for specifying a condition for the column.

EDATE

Returns the serial number that represents the date that is the indicated number of months before or after a specified date (the start_date). Use EDATE to calculate maturity dates or due dates that fall on the same day of the month as the date of issue.

If this function is not available, run the Setup program to install the Analysis ToolPak. After you install the Analysis ToolPak, you must enable it by using the **Add-Ins** command on the **Tools** menu.

Syntax

EDATE(start_date,months)

Start_date   is a date that represents the start date.

Months   is the number of months before or after start_date. A positive value for months yields a future date; a negative value yields a past date.

Remarks

- If either argument is nonnumeric, EDATE returns the #VALUE! error value.
- If start_date is not a valid date, EDATE returns the #NUM! error value.
- If months is not an integer, it is truncated.

Examples

EDATE(DATEVALUE("01/15/91"),1) equals 33284 or 02/15/91

EDATE(DATEVALUE("03/31/91"),-1) equals 33297 or 02/28/91

EFFECT

Returns the effective annual interest rate, given the nominal annual interest rate and the number of compounding periods per year.

If this function is not available, run the Setup program to install the Analysis ToolPak. After you install the Analysis ToolPak, you must enable it by using the **Add-Ins** command on the **Tools** menu.

Syntax

EFFECT(nominal_rate,npery)

Nominal_rate   is the nominal interest rate.

Npery   is the number of compounding periods per year.

Remarks

- Npery is truncated to an integer.
- If either argument is nonnumeric, EFFECT returns the #VALUE! error value.
- If nominal_rate ≤ 0 or if npery < 1, EFFECT returns the #NUM! error value.
- EFFECT is calculated as follows:

$$EFFECT = \left(1 + \frac{Nominal\_rate}{Npery}\right)^{Npery} - 1$$

Example

EFFECT(5.25%,4) equals 0.053543 or 5.3543 percent

EOMONTH

Returns the serial number date for the last day of the month that is the indicated number of months before or after start_date. Use EOMONTH to calculate maturity dates or due dates that fall on the last day of the month.

If this function is not available, run the Setup program to install the Analysis ToolPak. After you install the Analysis ToolPak, you must enable it by using the **Add-Ins** command on the **Tools** menu.

Syntax

EOMONTH(start_date,months)

Start_date   is a date that represents the start date.

Months   is the number of months before or after start_date. A positive value for months yields a future date; a negative value yields a past date.

Remarks

- If either argument is nonnumeric, EOMONTH returns the #VALUE! error value.
- If start_date is not a valid date, EOMONTH returns the #NUM! error value.
- If months is not an integer, it is truncated.
- If start_date plus months yields an invalid date, EOMONTH returns the #NUM! error value.

Examples

EOMONTH(DATEVALUE("01/01/93"), 1) equals 34028 or 2/28/93

EOMONTH(DATEVALUE("01/01/93"), -1) equals 33969 or 12/31/92

ERF

Returns the error function integrated between lower_limit and upper_limit.

If this function is not available, run the Setup program to install the Analysis ToolPak. After you install the Analysis ToolPak, you must enable it by using the **Add-Ins** command on the **Tools** menu.

Syntax

ERF(lower_limit,upper_limit)

Lower_limit   is the lower bound for integrating ERF.

Upper_limit   is the upper bound for integrating ERF. If omitted, ERF integrates between zero and lower_limit.

Remarks

- If lower_limit is nonnumeric, ERF returns the #VALUE! error value.
- If lower_limit is negative, ERF returns the #NUM! error value.
- If upper_limit is nonnumeric, ERF returns the #VALUE! error value.
- If upper_limit is negative, ERF returns the #NUM! error value.

$$\mathrm{ERF}(z) = \frac{2}{\sqrt{\pi}} \int_0^z e^{-t^2}\, dt$$

$$\mathrm{ERF}(a,b) = \frac{2}{\sqrt{\pi}} \int_a^b e^{-t^2}\, dt = \mathrm{ERF}(b) - \mathrm{ERF}(a)$$

Examples

ERF(0.74500) equals 0.70793

ERF(1) equals 0.84270

ERFC

Returns the complementary ERF function integrated between x and infinity.

If this function is not available, run the Setup program to install the Analysis ToolPak. After you install the Analysis ToolPak, you must enable it by using the **Add-Ins** command on the **Tools** menu.

Syntax

ERFC(x)

X   is the lower bound for integrating ERF.

Remarks

- If x is nonnumeric, ERFC returns the #VALUE! error value.

- If x is negative, ERFC returns the #NUM! error value.

$$ERFC(x) = \frac{2}{\sqrt{\pi}} \int_{x}^{\infty} e^{-t^2} dt = 1 - ERF(x)$$

Example

ERFC(1) equals 0.1573

ERROR.TYPE

Returns a number corresponding to one of the error values in Microsoft Excel. You can use ERROR.TYPE in an IF function to test for an error value and return a text string instead of the error value.

Syntax

ERROR.TYPE(error_val)

Error_val   is the error value whose identifying number you want to find. Although error_val can be the actual error value, it will usually be a reference to a cell containing a formula that you want to test.

If error_val is	ERROR.TYPE returns
#NULL!	1
#DIV/0!	2
#VALUE!	3
#REF!	4
#NAME?	5
#NUM!	6
#N/A	7
Anything else	#N/A

Example

The following formula checks cell E50 to see whether it contains a #N/A error value. If it does, the text "Value is not available" is displayed. Otherwise, the value in E50 is returned.

```
IF(ERROR.TYPE(E50)=7, "Value is not available", E50)
```

EVEN

Returns number rounded up to the nearest even integer. You can use this function for processing items that come in twos. For example, a packing crate accepts rows of one or two items. The crate is full when the number of items, rounded up to the nearest two, matches the crate's capacity.

Syntax

EVEN(number)

Number   is the value to round.

Remarks

- If number is nonnumeric, EVEN returns the #VALUE! error value.
- Regardless of the sign of number, a value is rounded up when adjusted away from zero. If number is an even integer, no rounding occurs.

Examples

EVEN(1.5) equals 2

EVEN(3) equals 4

EVEN(2) equals 2

EVEN(-1) equals -2

EXACT

Compares two text strings and returns TRUE if they are exactly the same, FALSE otherwise. EXACT is case-sensitive but ignores formatting differences. Use EXACT to test text being entered into a document.

Syntax

EXACT(text1,text2)

Text1   is the first text string.

Text2   is the second text string.

Examples

EXACT("word","word") equals TRUE

EXACT("Word","word") equals FALSE

EXACT("w ord","word") equals FALSE

To make sure that a user-entered value matches a value in a range, enter the following formula as an array in a cell. To enter an array formula, press CTRL+SHIFT+ENTER in Microsoft Excel 97 for Windows or COMMAND+ENTER in Microsoft Excel 97 for the Macintoch. The name TestValue refers to a cell containing a user-entered value; the name CompareRange refers to a list of text values to be checked.

```
{=OR(EXACT(TestValue, CompareRange))}
```

EXP

Returns e raised to the power of number. The constant e equals 2.71828182845904, the base of the natural logarithm.

Syntax

EXP(number)

Number   is the exponent applied to the base e.

Remarks

- To calculate powers of other bases, use the exponentiation operator (^).

- EXP is the inverse of LN, the natural logarithm of number.

Examples

EXP(1) equals 2.718282 (the approximate value of e)

EXP(2) equals e2, or 7.389056

EXP(LN(3)) equals 3

EXPONDIST

Returns the exponential distribution. Use EXPONDIST to model the time between events, such as how long an automated bank teller takes to deliver cash. For example, you can use EXPONDIST to determine the probability that the process takes at most 1 minute.

Syntax

EXPONDIST(x,lambda,cumulative)

X   is the value of the function.

Lambda   is the parameter value.

Cumulative   is a logical value that indicates which form of the exponential function to provide. If cumulative is TRUE, EXPONDIST returns the cumulative distribution function; if FALSE, it returns the probability density function.

Remarks

- If x or lambda is nonnumeric, EXPONDIST returns the #VALUE! error value.

- If x < 0, EXPONDIST returns the #NUM! error value.

- If lambda ≤ 0, EXPONDIST returns the #NUM! error value.

- The equation for the probability density function is:

$$f(x; \lambda) = \lambda e^{-\lambda x}$$

- The equation for the cumulative distribution function is:

$$F(x; \lambda) = 1 - e^{-\lambda x}$$

Examples

EXPONDIST(0.2,10,TRUE) equals 0.864665

EXPONDIST(0.2,10,FALSE) equals 1.353353

FACT

Returns the factorial of a number. The factorial of a number is equal to 1*2*3*...* number.

Syntax

FACT(number)

Number   is the nonnegative number you want the factorial of. If number is not an integer, it is truncated.

Examples

FACT(1) equals 1

FACT(1.9) equals FACT(1) equals 1

FACT(0) equals 1

FACT(-1) equals #NUM!

FACT(5) equals 1*2*3*4*5 equals 120

FACTDOUBLE

Returns the double factorial of a number.

If this function is not available, run the Setup program to install the Analysis ToolPak. After you install the Analysis ToolPak, you must enable it by using the **Add-Ins** command on the **Tools** menu.

Syntax

FACTDOUBLE(number)

Number   is the value for which to return the double factorial. If number is not an integer, it is truncated.

Remarks

- If number is nonnumeric, FACTDOUBLE returns the #VALUE! error value.
- If number is negative, FACTDOUBLE returns the #NUM! error value.
- If number is even:

$$n!! = n(n-2)(n-4)...(4)(2)$$

- If number is odd:

$$n!! = n(n-2)(n-4)...(3)(1)$$

Examples

FACTDOUBLE(6) equals 48

FACTDOUBLE(7) equals 105

FALSE

Returns the logical value FALSE.

Syntax

FALSE( )

Remarks

You can also type the word FALSE directly onto the worksheet or into the formula, and Microsoft Excel interprets it as the logical value FALSE.

FDIST

Returns the F probability distribution. You can use this function to determine whether two data sets have different degrees of diversity. For example, you can examine test scores given to men and women entering high school and determine if the variability in the females is different from that found in the males.

Syntax

FDIST(x,degrees_freedom1,degrees_freedom2)

X is the value at which to evaluate the function.

Degrees_freedom1 is the numerator degrees of freedom.

Degrees_freedom2 is the denominator degrees of freedom.

Remarks

- If any argument is nonnumeric, FDIST returns the #VALUE! error value.

- If x is negative, FDIST returns the #NUM! error value.

- If degrees_freedom1 or degrees_freedom2 is not an integer, it is truncated.

- If degrees_freedom1 < 1 or degrees_freedom1 $\geq 10\wedge10$, FDIST returns the #NUM! error value.

- If degrees_freedom2 < 1 or degrees_freedom2 $\geq 10\wedge10$, FDIST returns the #NUM! error value.

- FDIST is calculated as FDIST=P(F<x), where F is a random variable that has an F distribution.

Example

FDIST(15.20675,6,4) equals 0.01

FIND

Finds one text string (find_text) within another text string (within_text), and returns the number of the starting position of find_text, from the leftmost character of within_text. You can also use SEARCH to find one text string within another, but unlike SEARCH, FIND is case-sensitive and doesn't allow wildcard characters.

Syntax

FIND(find_text,within_text,start_num)

Find_text is the text you want to find.

- If find_text is "" (empty text), FIND matches the first character in the search string (that is, the character numbered start_num or 1).

- Find_text cannot contain any wildcard characters.

Within_text is the text containing the text you want to find.

Start_num specifies the character at which to start the search. The first character in within_text is character number 1. If you omit start_num, it is assumed to be 1.

Remarks

- If find_text does not appear in within_text, FIND returns the #VALUE! error value.

- If start_num is not greater than zero, FIND returns the #VALUE! error value.

- If start_num is greater than the length of within_text, FIND returns the #VALUE! error value.

Examples

FIND("M","Miriam McGovern") equals 1

FIND("m","Miriam McGovern") equals 6

FIND("M","Miriam McGovern",3) equals 8

Suppose you have a list of parts and serial numbers on a worksheet, and you want to extract the names of the parts, but not the serial numbers, from each cell. You can use the FIND function to find the # symbol and the MID function to omit the serial number. A2:A4 contain the following parts with serial numbers, respectively: "Ceramic Insulators #124-TD45-87", "Copper Coils #12-671-6772", "Variable Resistors #116010".

MID(A2,1,FIND(" #",A2,1)-1) returns "Ceramic Insulators"

MID(A3,1,FIND(" #",A3,1)-1) returns "Copper Coils"

MID(A4,1,FIND(" #",A4,1)-1) returns "Variable Resistors"

FINV

Returns the inverse of the F probability distribution. If $p = FDIST(x, ...)$, then $FINV(p, ...) = x$.

The F distribution can be used in an F-test that compares the degree of variability in two data sets. For example, you can analyze income distributions in the United States and Canada to determine whether the two countries have a similar degree of diversity.

Syntax

FINV(probability,degrees_freedom1,degrees_freedom2)

Probability is a probability associated with the F cumulative distribution.

Degrees_freedom1 is the numerator degrees of freedom.

Degrees_freedom2 is the denominator degrees of freedom.

Remarks

- If any argument is nonnumeric, FINV returns the #VALUE! error value.
- If probability < 0 or probability > 1, FINV returns the #NUM! error value.
- If degrees_freedom1 or degrees_freedom2 is not an integer, it is truncated.
- If degrees_freedom1 < 1 or degrees_freedom1 ≥ 10^10, FINV returns the #NUM! error value.
- If degrees_freedom2 < 1 or degrees_freedom2 ≥ 10^10, FINV returns the #NUM! error value.

FINV can be used to return critical values from the F distribution. For example, the output of an ANOVA calculation often includes data for the F statistic, F probability, and F critical value at the 0.05 significance level. To return the critical value of F, use the significance level as the probability argument to FINV.

FINV uses an iterative technique for calculating the function. Given a probability value, FINV iterates until the result is accurate to within ± 3x10^-7. If FINV does not converge after 100 iterations, the function returns the #N/A error value.

Example

FINV(0.01,6,4) equals 15.20675

FISHER

Returns the Fisher transformation at x. This transformation produces a function that is approximately normally distributed rather than skewed. Use this function to perform hypothesis testing on the correlation coefficient.

Syntax

FISHER(x)

X is a numeric value for which you want the transformation.

Remarks

- If x is nonnumeric, FISHER returns the #VALUE! error value.
- If x ≤ -1 or if x ≥ 1, FISHER returns the #NUM! error value.

The equation for the Fisher transformation is:

$$z' = \frac{1}{2}\ln\left(\frac{1+x}{1-x}\right)$$

Example

FISHER(0.75) equals 0.972955

FISHERINV

Returns the inverse of the Fisher transformation. Use this transformation when analyzing correlations between ranges or arrays of data. If y = FISHER(x), then FISHERINV(y) = x.

Syntax

FISHERINV(y)

Y   is the value for which you want to perform the inverse of the transformation.

Remarks

- If y is nonnumeric, FISHERINV returns the #VALUE! error value.

The equation for the inverse of the Fisher transformation is:

$$x = \frac{e^{2y} - 1}{e^{2y} + 1}$$

Example

FISHERINV(0.972955) equals 0.75

FIXED

Rounds a number to the specified number of decimals, formats the number in decimal format using a period and commas, and returns the result as text.

Syntax

FIXED(number,decimals,no_commas**)**

Number   is the number you want to round and convert to text.

Decimals   is the number of digits to the right of the decimal point.

No_commas   is a logical value that, if TRUE, prevents FIXED from including commas in the returned text. If no_commas is FALSE or omitted, then the returned text includes commas as usual.

- Numbers in Microsoft Excel can never have more than 15 significant digits, but decimals can be as large as 127.
- If decimals is negative, number is rounded to the left of the decimal point.
- If you omit decimals, it is assumed to be 2.

Remarks

The major difference between formatting a cell containing a number with the **Cells** command (**Format** menu) and formatting a number directly with the FIXED function is that FIXED converts its result to text. A number formatted with the **Cells** command is still a number.

Examples

FIXED(1234.567, 1) equals "1234.6"

FIXED(1234.567, -1) equals "1230"

FIXED(-1234.567, -1) equals "-1230"

FIXED(44.332) equals "44.33"

FLOOR

Rounds number down, toward zero, to the nearest multiple of significance.

Syntax

FLOOR(number,significance)

Number   is the numeric value you want to round.

Significance   is the multiple to which you want to round.

Remarks

- If either argument is nonnumeric, FLOOR returns the #VALUE! error value.
- If number and significance have different signs, FLOOR returns the #NUM! error value.
- Regardless of the sign of number, a value is rounded down when adjusted away from zero. If number is an exact multiple of significance, no rounding occurs.

Examples

FLOOR(2.5, 1) equals 2

FLOOR(-2.5, -2) equals -2

FLOOR(-2.5, 2) equals #NUM!

FLOOR(1.5, 0.1) equals 1.5

FLOOR(0.234, 0.01) equals 0.23

FORECAST

Calculates, or predicts, a future value by using existing values. The predicted value is a y-value for a given x-value. The known values are existing x-values and y-values, and the new value is predicted by using linear regression. You can use this function to predict future sales, inventory requirements, or consumer trends.

Syntax

FORECAST(x,known_y's,known_x's)

X   is the data point for which you want to predict a value.

Known_y's   is the dependent array or range of data.

Known_x's   is the independent array or range of data.

Remarks

- If x is nonnumeric, FORECAST returns the #VALUE! error value.
- If known_y's and known_x's are empty or contain a different number of data points, FORECAST returns the #N/A error value.
- If the variance of known_x's equals zero, then FORECAST returns the #DIV/0! error value.
- The equation for FORECAST is a+bx, where:

$$a = \overline{Y} - b\overline{X}$$

and:

$$b = \frac{n\Sigma xy - (\Sigma x)(\Sigma y)}{n\Sigma x^2 - (\Sigma x)^2}$$

Example

FORECAST(30,{6,7,9,15,21},{20,28,31,38,40}) equals 10.60725

FREQUENCY

Calculates how often values occur within a range of values, and then returns a vertical array of numbers. For example, use FREQUENCY to count the number of test scores that fall within ranges of scores. Because FREQUENCY returns an array, it must be entered as an array formula.

Syntax

FREQUENCY(data_array,bins_array)

Data_array   is an array of or reference to a set of values for which you want to count frequencies. If data_array contains no values, FREQUENCY returns an array of zeros.

Bins_array   is an array of or reference to intervals into which you want to group the values in data_array. If bins_array contains no values, FREQUENCY returns the number of elements in data_array.

Remarks

- FREQUENCY is entered as an array formula after you select a range of adjacent cells into which you want the returned distribution to appear.

- The number of elements in the returned array is one more than the number of elements in bins_array.

- FREQUENCY ignores blank cells and text.

- Formulas that return arrays must be entered as array formulas.

Example

Suppose a worksheet lists scores for a test. The scores are 79, 85, 78, 85, 83, 81, 95, 88, and 97 and are entered into A1:A9, respectively. The data_array would contain a column of these test scores. The bins_array would be another column of intervals by which the test scores are grouped. In this example, bins_array would be C4:C6 and would contain the values 70, 79, 89. When FREQUENCY is entered as an array, the number of scores corresponding to the letter grade ranges 0-70, 71-79, 80-89, and 90-100, are counted. This example assumes all test scores are integers. The following formula is entered as an array formula after you select four vertical cells adjacent to your data.

`FREQUENCY(A1:A9,C4:C6)` equals {0;2;5;2}

FTEST

Returns the result of an F-test. An F-test returns the one-tailed probability that the variances in array1 and array2 are not significantly different. Use this function to determine whether two samples have different variances. For example, given test scores from public and private schools, you can test whether these schools have different levels of diversity.

Syntax

FTEST(array1,array2)

Array1   is the first array or range of data.

Array2   is the second array or range of data.

Remarks

- The arguments must be either numbers or names, arrays, or references that contain numbers.

- If an array or reference argument contains text, logical values, or empty cells, those values are ignored; however, cells with the value zero are included.

- If the number of data points in array1 or array2 is less than 2, or if the variance of array1 or array2 is zero, FTEST returns the #DIV/0! error value.

Example

FTEST({6,7,9,15,21},{20,28,31,38,40}) equals 0.648318

FV

Returns the future value of an investment based on periodic, constant payments and a constant interest rate.

Syntax

FV(rate,nper,pmt,pv,type)

For a more complete description of the arguments in FV and for more information on annuity functions, see PV.

Rate   is the interest rate per period.

Nper   is the total number of payment periods in an annuity.

Pmt   is the payment made each period; it cannot change over the life of the annuity. Typically, pmt contains principal and interest but no other fees or taxes.

Pv   is the present value, or the lump-sum amount that a series of future payments is worth right now. If pv is omitted, it is assumed to be 0 (zero).

Type   is the number 0 or 1 and indicates when payments are due. If type is omitted, it is assumed to be 0.

Set type equal to	If payments are due
0	At the end of the period
1	At the beginning of the period

Remarks

- Make sure that you are consistent about the units you use for specifying rate and nper. If you make monthly payments on a four-year loan at 12 percent annual interest, use 12%/12 for rate and 4*12 for nper. If you make annual payments on the same loan, use 12% for rate and 4 for nper.

- For all the arguments, cash you pay out, such as deposits to savings, is represented by negative numbers; cash you receive, such as dividend checks, is represented by positive numbers.

Examples

    FV(0.5%, 10, -200, -500, 1) equals $2581.40

    FV(1%, 12, -1000) equals $12,682.50

    FV(11%/12, 35, -2000, , 1) equals $82,846.25

Suppose you want to save money for a special project occurring a year from now. You deposit $1,000 into a savings account that earns 6 percent annual interest compounded monthly (monthly interest of 6%/12, or 0.5%). You plan to deposit $100 at the beginning of every month for the next 12 months. How much money will be in the account at the end of 12 months?

    FV(0.5%, 12, -100, -1000, 1) equals $2301.40

FVSCHEDULE

Returns the future value of an initial principal after applying a series of compound interest rates. Use FVSCHEDULE to calculate future value of an investment with a variable or adjustable rate.

If this function is not available, run the Setup program to install the Analysis ToolPak. After you install the Analysis ToolPak, you must enable it by using the **Add-Ins** command on the **Tools** menu.

Syntax

FVSCHEDULE(principal,schedule)

Principal   is the present value.

Schedule   is an array of interest rates to apply.

Remarks

- If principal is nonnumeric, FVSCHEDULE returns the #VALUE! error value.

- The values in schedule can be numbers or blank cells; any other value produces the #VALUE! error value for FVSCHEDULE. Blank cells are taken as zeros (no interest).

Example

    FVSCHEDULE(1,{0.09,0.11,0.1}) equals 1.33089

GAMMADIST

Returns the gamma distribution. You can use this function to study variables that may have a skewed distribution. The gamma distribution is commonly used in queuing analysis.

Syntax

GAMMADIST(x,alpha,beta,cumulative)

X is the value at which you want to evaluate the distribution.

Alpha is a parameter to the distribution.

Beta is a parameter to the distribution. If beta = 1, GAMMADIST returns the standard gamma distribution.

Cumulative is a logical value that determines the form of the function. If cumulative is TRUE, GAMMADIST returns the cumulative distribution function; if FALSE, it returns the probability mass function.

Remarks

- If x, alpha, or beta is nonnumeric, GAMMADIST returns the #VALUE! error value.

- If x < 0, GAMMADIST returns the #NUM! error value.

- If alpha ≤ 0 or if beta ≤ 0, GAMMADIST returns the #NUM! error value.

- The equation for the gamma distribution is:

$$f(x;\alpha,\beta) = \frac{1}{\beta^{\alpha}\Gamma(\alpha)} x^{\alpha-1} e^{-\frac{x}{\beta}}$$

The standard gamma distribution is:

$$f(x;\alpha) = \frac{x^{\alpha-1}e^{-x}}{\Gamma(\alpha)}$$

- When alpha = 1, GAMMADIST returns the exponential distribution with:

$$\lambda = \frac{1}{\beta}$$

- For a positive integer n, when alpha = n/2, beta = 2, and cumulative = TRUE, GAMMADIST returns (1 - CHIDIST(x)) with n degrees of freedom.

- When alpha is a positive integer, GAMMADIST is also known as the Erlang distribution.

Examples

    GAMMADIST(10,9,2,FALSE) equals 0.032639

    GAMMADIST(10,9,2,TRUE) equals 0.068094

GAMMAINV

Returns the inverse of the gamma cumulative distribution. If p = GAMMADIST(x, ...), then GAMMAINV(p, ...) = x.

You can use this function to study a variable whose distribution may be skewed.

Syntax

GAMMAINV(probability,alpha,beta)

Probability   is the probability associated with the gamma distribution.

Alpha   is a parameter to the distribution.

Beta   is a parameter to the distribution. If beta = 1, GAMMAINV returns the standard gamma distribution.

Remarks

- If any argument is nonnumeric, GAMMAINV returns the #VALUE! error value.
- If probability < 0 or probability > 1, GAMMAINV returns the #NUM! error value.
- If alpha ≤ 0 or if beta ≤ 0, GAMMAINV returns the #NUM! error value.
- If beta ≤ 0, GAMMAINV returns the #NUM! error value.
- GAMMAINV uses an iterative technique for calculating the function. Given a probability value, GAMMAINV iterates until the result is accurate to within $\pm 3 \times 10^{-7}$. If GAMMAINV does not converge after 100 iterations, the function returns the #N/A error value.

Example

    GAMMAINV(0.068094,9,2) equals 10

GAMMALN

Returns the natural logarithm of the gamma function, $\Gamma(x)$.

Syntax

GAMMALN(x)

X   is the value for which you want to calculate GAMMALN.

Remarks

- If x is nonnumeric, GAMMALN returns the #VALUE! error value.

- If x ≤ 0, GAMMALN returns the #NUM! error value.

- The number e raised to the GAMMALN(i) power, where i is an integer, returns the same result as (i - 1)!.

- GAMMALN is calculated as follows:

$$GAMMALN = LN(\Gamma(x))$$

where:

$$\Gamma(x) = \int_0^\infty e^{-u} u^{x-1} du$$

Examples

GAMMALN(4) equals 1.791759

EXP(GAMMALN(4)) equals 6 or (4 - 1)!

GCD

Returns the greatest common divisor of two or more integers. The greatest common divisor is the largest integer that divides both number1 and number2 without a remainder.

If this function is not available, run the Setup program to install the Analysis ToolPak. After you install the Analysis ToolPak, you must enable it by using the **Add-Ins** command on the **Tools** menu.

Syntax

GCD(number1,number2, ...)

Number1,number2, ...   are 1 to 29 values. If any value is not an integer, it is truncated.

Remarks

- If any argument is nonnumeric, GCD returns the #VALUE! error value.

- If any argument is less than zero, GCD returns the #NUM! error value.

- One divides any value evenly.

- A prime number has only itself and one as even divisors.

Examples

GCD(5, 2) equals 1

GCD(24, 36) equals 12

GCD(7, 1) equals 1

GCD(5, 0) equals 5

GEOMEAN

Returns the geometric mean of an array or range of positive data. For example, you can use GEOMEAN to calculate average growth rate given compound interest with variable rates.

Syntax

GEOMEAN(number1,number2, ...)

Number1,number2, ...   are 1 to 30 arguments for which you want to calculate the mean. You can also use a single array or a reference to an array instead of arguments separated by commas.

Remarks

- The arguments must be either numbers or names, arrays, or references that contain numbers.

- If an array or reference argument contains text, logical values, or empty cells, those values are ignored; however, cells with the value zero are included.

- If any data point ≤ 0, GEOMEAN returns the #NUM! error value.

- The equation for the geometric mean is:

$$GM_{\bar{y}} = \sqrt[n]{y_1 y_2 y_3 \cdots y_n}$$

Example

GEOMEAN(4,5,8,7,11,4,3) equals 5.476987

GESTEP

Returns 1 if number $\geq$ step; returns 0 (zero) otherwise. Use this function to filter a set of values. For example, by summing several GESTEP functions you calculate the count of values that exceed a threshold.

If this function is not available, run the Setup program to install the Analysis ToolPak. After you install the Analysis ToolPak, you must enable it by using the **Add-Ins** command on the **Tools** menu.

Syntax

GESTEP(number,step)

Number   is the value to test against step.

Step   is the threshold value. If you omit a value for step, GESTEP uses zero.

Remarks

If any argument is nonnumeric, GESTEP returns the #VALUE! error value.

Examples

GESTEP(5, 4) equals 1

GESTEP(5, 5) equals 1

GESTEP(-4, -5) equals 1

GESTEP(-1, 0) equals 0

GETPIVOTDATA

Returns data stored in a PivotTable. You can use GETPIVOTDATA to retrieve summary data from a PivotTable, provided the summary data is visible in the PivotTable.

Syntax

GETPIVOTDATA(pivot_table,name)

Pivot_table   is the name of the PivotTable that contains the data you want to retrieve. Pivot_table can be a cell or range of cells in the PivotTable, a name for the range that contains the PivotTable, or a label stored in a cell above the PivotTable.

Name   is a text string enclosed in double quotation marks that describes the cell in the PivotTable that contains the value you want to retrieve. For example, if the PivotTable contains one row field labeled Salesperson and you want to retrieve the grand total value for a salesperson named Suyama, name would be "Suyama." If the column field in the PivotTable contains products and you want the total grand total value of beverage sales for a salesperson named Suyama, then name would be "Suyama Beverages."

Remarks

- Calculated fields or items and custom calculations are included in GETPIVOTDATA calculations.

- If pivot_table is a range that includes two or more PivotTables, data will be retrieved from whichever PivotTable was created most recently in the range.

- If name describes a single cell, the value of that cell is returned regardless of whether it is a string, number, error, and so on.

- If pivot_table is not a range in which a PivotTable is found, GETPIVOTDATA returns #VALUE!.

- If the syntax of name does not describe a visible field, if name is omitted, or if name includes a page field that is not displayed, GETPIVOTDATA returns #REF!.

Examples

Assuming the following PivotTable is stored on a worksheet, and the name PT1 refers to A2:E12, the range that contains the PivotTable is:

	A	B	C	D	E
2	Region	North			
3					
4	Sum of Sales		Product		
5	Month	Salesperson	Beverages	Produce	Grand Total
6	March	Buchanan	$3,522	$10,201	$13,723
7		Davolio	$8,725	$7,889	$16,614
8	March Total		$12,247	$18,090	$30,337
9	April	Buchanan	$5,594	$7,265	$12,859
10		Davolio	$5,461	$668	$6,129
11	April Total		$11,055	$7,933	$18,988
12	Grand Total		$23,302	$26,023	$49,325

GETPIVOTDATA(PT1,"Sum of Sales") returns the grand total of the Sales field, $49,325.

GETPIVOTDATA(PT1,"March") returns the grand total for March, $30,337.

The following examples refer to the same PivotTable above but use a cell within the PivotTable for the pivot_table argument:

GETPIVOTDATA(A4,"March Buchanan Produce") returns $10,201.

GETPIVOTDATA(A4,"March South") returns #REF! because the South region data is not visible.

GETPIVOTDATA(A4,"Davolio Beverages") returns #REF!; there is no total value of beverage sales for Davolio.

GROWTH

Calculates predicted exponential growth by using existing data. GROWTH returns the y-values for a series of new x-values that you specify by using existing x-values and y-values. You can also use the GROWTH worksheet function to fit an exponential curve to existing x-values and y-values.

Syntax

GROWTH(known_y's,known_x's,new_x's,const)

Known_y's is the set of y-values you already know in the relationship $y = b*m^x$.

- If the array known_y's is in a single column, then each column of known_x's is interpreted as a separate variable.

- If the array known_y's is in a single row, then each row of known_x's is interpreted as a separate variable.

- If any of the numbers in known_y's is 0 or negative, GROWTH returns the #NUM! error value.

Known_x's is an optional set of x-values that you may already know in the relationship $y = b*m^x$.

- The array known_x's can include one or more sets of variables. If only one variable is used, known_y's and known_x's can be ranges of any shape, as long as they have equal dimensions. If more than one variable is used, known_y's must be a vector (that is, a range with a height of one row or a width of one column).

- If known_x's is omitted, it is assumed to be the array {1,2,3, ...} that is the same size as known_y's.

New_x's are new x-values for which you want GROWTH to return corresponding y-values.

- New_x's must include a column (or row) for each independent variable, just as known_x's does. So, if known_y's is in a single column, known_x's and new_x's must have the same number of columns. If known_y's is in a single row, known_x's and new_x's must have the same number of rows.

- If new_x's is omitted, it is assumed to be the same as known_x's.

- If both known_x's and new_x's are omitted, they are assumed to be the array {1,2,3, ...} that is the same size as known_y's.

Const is a logical value specifying whether to force the constant b to equal 1.

- If const is TRUE or omitted, b is calculated normally.

- If const is FALSE, b is set equal to 1 and the m-values are adjusted so that $y = m^x$.

Remarks

- Formulas that return arrays must be entered as array formulas after selecting the correct number of cells.

- When entering an array constant for an argument such as known_x's, use commas to separate values in the same row and semicolons to separate rows.

Examples

This example uses the same data as the LOGEST example. The sales for the 11th through the 16th months are 33,100, 47,300, 69,000, 102,000, 150,000, and 220,000 units, respectively. Assume that these values are entered into six cells named UnitsSold.

When entered as an array formula, the following formula predicts sales for months 17 and 18 based on sales for the previous six months:

GROWTH(UnitsSold,{11;12;13;14;15;16},{17;18}) equals {320,197;468,536}

If the exponential trend continues, sales for months 17 and 18 will be 320,197 and 468,536 units, respectively.

You could use other sequential numbers for the x-value arguments, and the predicted sales would be the same. For example, you could use the default value for known_x's, {1;2;3;4;5;6}:

GROWTH(UnitsSold,,{7;8},) equals {320197;468536}

HARMEAN

Returns the harmonic mean of a data set. The harmonic mean is the reciprocal of the arithmetic mean of reciprocals.

Syntax

HARMEAN(number1,number2, ...)

Number1,number2, ...   are 1 to 30 arguments for which you want to calculate the mean. You can also use a single array or a reference to an array instead of arguments separated by commas.

Remarks

- The arguments must be either numbers or names, arrays, or references that contain numbers.

- If an array or reference argument contains text, logical values, or empty cells, those values are ignored; however, cells with the value zero are included.

- If any data point ≤ 0, HARMEAN returns the #NUM! error value.

- The harmonic mean is always less than the geometric mean, which is always less than the arithmetic mean.

- The equation for the harmonic mean is:

$$\frac{1}{H_\mu} = \frac{1}{n}\sum \frac{1}{Y_j}$$

Example

    HARMEAN(4,5,8,7,11,4,3) equals 5.028376

HEX2BIN

Converts a hexadecimal number to binary.

If this function is not available, run the Setup program to install the Analysis ToolPak. After you install the Analysis ToolPak, you must enable it by using the **Add-Ins** command on the **Tools** menu.

Syntax

HEX2BIN(number,places)

Number   is the hexadecimal number you want to convert. Number cannot contain more than 10 characters. The most significant bit of number is the sign bit (40th bit from the right). The remaining 9 bits are magnitude bits. Negative numbers are represented using two's-complement notation.

Places   is the number of characters to use. If places is omitted, HEX2BIN uses the minimum number of characters necessary. Places is useful for padding the return value with leading 0s (zeros).

Remarks

- If number is negative, HEX2BIN ignores places and returns a 10-character binary number.

- If number is negative, it cannot be less than FFFFFFFE00, and if number is positive, it cannot be greater than 1FF.

- If number is not a valid hexadecimal number, HEX2BIN returns the #NUM! error value.

- If HEX2BIN requires more than places characters, it returns the #NUM! error value.

- If places is not an integer, it is truncated.

- If places is nonnumeric, HEX2BIN returns the #VALUE! error value.

- If places is negative, HEX2BIN returns the #NUM! error value.

Examples

    HEX2BIN("F", 8) equals 00001111

    HEX2BIN("B7") equals 10110111

    HEX2BIN("FFFFFFFFFF") equals 1111111111

HEX2DEC

Converts a hexadecimal number to decimal.

If this function is not available, run the Setup program to install the Analysis ToolPak. After you install the Analysis ToolPak, you must enable it by using the **Add-Ins** command on the **Tools** menu.

Syntax

HEX2DEC(number)

Number   is the hexadecimal number you want to convert. Number cannot contain more than 10 characters (40 bits). The most significant bit of number is the sign bit. The remaining 39 bits are magnitude bits. Negative numbers are represented using two's-complement notation.

Remarks

If number is not a valid hexadecimal number, HEX2DEC returns the #NUM! error value.

Examples

HEX2DEC("A5") equals 165

HEX2DEC("FFFFFFFF5B") equals -165

HEX2DEC("3DA408B9") equals 1034160313

HEX2OCT

Converts a hexadecimal number to octal.

If this function is not available, run the Setup program to install the Analysis ToolPak. After you install the Analysis ToolPak, you must enable it by using the **Add-Ins** command on the **Tools** menu.

Syntax

HEX2OCT(number,places**)**

Number   is the hexadecimal number you want to convert. Number cannot contain more than 10 characters. The most significant bit of number is the sign bit. The remaining 39 bits are magnitude bits. Negative numbers are represented using two's-complement notation.

Places   is the number of characters to use. If places is omitted, HEX2OCT uses the minimum number of characters necessary. Places is useful for padding the return value with leading 0s (zeros).

Remarks

- If number is negative, HEX2OCT ignores places and returns a 10-character octal number.

- If number is negative, it cannot be less than FFE0000000, and if number is positive, it cannot be greater than 1FFFFFFF.

- If number is not a valid hexadecimal number, HEX2OCT returns the #NUM! error value.

- If HEX2OCT requires more than places characters, it returns the #NUM! error value.

- If places is not an integer, it is truncated.

- If places is nonnumeric, HEX2OCT returns the #VALUE! error value.

- If places is negative, HEX2OCT returns the #NUM! error value.

Examples

HEX2OCT("F", 3) equals 017

HEX2OCT("3B4E") equals 35516

HEX2OCT("FFFFFFFF00") equals 7777777400

HLOOKUP

Searches for a value in the top row of a table or an array of values, and then returns a value in the same column from a row you specify in the table or array. Use HLOOKUP when your comparison values are located in a row across the top of a table of data, and you want to look down a specified number of rows. Use VLOOKUP when your comparison values are located in a column to the left of the data you want to find.

Syntax

HLOOKUP(lookup_value,table_array,row_index_num,range_lookup)

Lookup_value   is the value to be found in the first row of the table. Lookup_value can be a value, a reference, or a text string.

Table_array   is a table of information in which data is looked up. Use a reference to a range or a range name.

- The values in the first row of table_array can be text, numbers, or logical values.

- If range_lookup is TRUE, the values in the first row of table_array must be placed in ascending order: ...-2, -1, 0), 1, 2, ... , A-Z, FALSE, TRUE; otherwise, HLOOKUP may not give the correct value. If range_lookup is FALSE, table_array does not need to be sorted.

- Uppercase and lowercase text are equivalent.

- You can put values in ascending order, left to right, by selecting the values and then clicking **Sort** on the **Data** menu. Click **Options,** click **Sort left to right,** and then click **OK.** Under **Sort by,** click the row in the list, and then click **Ascending.**

Row_index_num   is the row number in table_array from which the matching value will be returned. A row_index_num of 1 returns the first row value in table_array, a row_index_num of 2 returns the second row value in table_array, and so on. If row_index_num is less than 1, HLOOKUP returns the #VALUE! error value; if row_index_num is greater than the number of rows on table_array, HLOOKUP returns the #REF! error value.

Range_lookup   is a logical value that specifies whether you want HLOOKUP to find an exact match or an approximate match. If TRUE or omitted, an approximate match is returned. In other words, if an exact match is not found, the next largest value that is less than lookup_value is returned. If FALSE, HLOOKUP will find an exact match. If one is not found, the error value #N/A is returned.

Remarks

- If HLOOKUP can't find lookup_value, and range_lookup is TRUE, it uses the largest value that is less than lookup_value.

- If lookup_value is smaller than the smallest value in the first row of table_array, HLOOKUP returns the #N/A error value.

Examples

Suppose you have an inventory worksheet of auto parts. A1:A4 contain "Axles", 4, 5, 6. B1:B4 contain "Bearings", 4, 7, 8. C1:C4 contain "Bolts", 9, 10, 11.

HLOOKUP("Axles", A1:C4,2,TRUE) equals 4

HLOOKUP("Bearings",A1:C4,3,FALSE) equals 7

HLOOKUP("Bearings",A1:C4,3,TRUE) equals 7

HLOOKUP("Bolts",A1:C4,4,) equals 11

Table_array can also be an array constant:

HLOOKUP(3,{1,2,3;"a","b","c";"d","e","f"},2,TRUE) equals "c"

HOUR

Returns the hour corresponding to serial_number. The hour is given as an integer, ranging from 0 (12:00 A.M.) to 23 (11:00 P.M.).

Syntax

HOUR(serial_number)

Serial_number is the date-time code used by Microsoft Excel for date and time calculations. You can give serial_number as text, such as "16:48:00" or "4:48:00 PM", instead of as a number. The text is automatically converted to a serial number. For more information about serial numbers, see NOW.

Note Microsoft Excel for Windows and Microsoft Excel for the Macintosh use different date systems as their default. For more information, see NOW.

Examples

HOUR(0.7) equals 16

HOUR(29747.7) equals 16

HOUR("3:30:30 PM") equals 15

HYPERLINK

Creates a shortcut or jump that opens a document stored on a network server, an intranet, or the Internet. When you click the cell that contains the HYPERLINK function, Microsoft Excel 97 opens the file stored at link_location.

Syntax

HYPERLINK(link_location,cell_contents)

Link_location is the path and file name to the document to be opened as text. Link_location can refer to a place in a document—such as a specific cell or named range in a Microsoft Excel worksheet or workbook, or to a bookmark in a Microsoft Word document. The path can be to a file stored on a hard disk drive, or the path can be a universal naming convention (UNC) path on a server (in Microsoft Excel 97 for Windows) or a Uniform Resource Locator (URL) path on the Internet or an intranet.

Cell_contents is the jump text or numeric value that is displayed in the cell. The cell contents is displayed in blue and is underlined. If cell_contents is omitted, the cell displays the link_location as the jump text.

Remarks

- Link_location can be a text string enclosed in quotation marks or a cell that contains the link as a text string.

- Cell_contents can be a value, a text string, a name, or a cell that contains the jump text or value.

- If cell_contents returns an error value (for example, #VALUE!), the cell displays the error instead of the jump text.

- If the jump specified in link_location does not exist or cannot be navigated, an error appears when you click the cell.

- To select a cell that contains HYPERLINK, click a cell next to the cell, and then use an arrow key to move to the cell.

Examples

The following example opens a worksheet named Budget Report.xls that is stored on the Internet at the location named `www.business.com/report` and displays the text "Click for report":

`HYPERLINK("http://www.business.com/report/budget report.xls", "Click for report")`

The following example creates a hyperlink to cell F10 on the worksheet named Annual in the workbook Budget Report.xls, which is stored on the Internet at the location named `www.business.com/report`. The cell on the worksheet that contains the hyperlink displays the contents of cell D1 as the jump text:

`HYPERLINK("'[http://www.business.com/report/budget report.xls]Annual'!F10", D1)`

The following example creates a hyperlink to the range named DeptTotal on the worksheet named First Quarter in the workbook Budget Report.xls, which is stored on the Internet at the location named `www.business.com/report`. The cell on the worksheet that contains the hyperlink displays the text "Click to see First Quarter Department Total":

`HYPERLINK("'[http://www.business.com/report/budget report.xls]First Quarter'!DeptTotal", "Click to see First Quarter Department Total")`

To create a hyperlink to a specific location in a Microsoft Word document, you must use a bookmark to define the location you want to jump to in the document. The following example creates a hyperlink to the bookmark named QrtlyProfits in the document named Annual Report.doc located at `www.business.com`:

`HYPERLINK("'[http://www.business.com/Annual Report.doc]#QrtlyProfits", "Quarterly Profit Report")`

In Microsoft Excel 97 for Windows, the following example displays the contents of cell D5 as the jump text in the cell and opens the file named 1stqtr.xls, which is stored on the server named FINANCE in the Statements share. This example uses a UNC path:

`HYPERLINK("\\FINANCE\Statements\1stqtr.xls", D5)`

The following example opens the file 1stqtr.xls in Microsoft Excel 97 for Windows that is stored in a directory named Finance on drive D, and displays the numeric value stored in cell H10:

```
HYPERLINK("D:\FINANCE\1stqtr.xls", H10)
```

HYPGEOMDIST

Returns the hypergeometric distribution. HYPGEOMDIST returns the probability of a given number of sample successes, given the sample size, population successes, and population size. Use HYPGEOMDIST for problems with a finite population, where each observation is either a success or a failure, and where each subset of a given size is chosen with equal likelihood.

Syntax

HYPGEOMDIST(sample_s,number_sample,population_s,number_population)

Sample_s   is the number of successes in the sample.

Number_sample   is the size of the sample.

Population_s   is the number of successes in the population.

Number_population   is the population size.

Remarks

- All arguments are truncated to integers.
- If any argument is nonnumeric, HYPGEOMDIST returns the #VALUE! error value.
- If sample_s < 0 or sample_s is greater than the lesser of number_sample or population_s, HYPGEOMDIST returns the #NUM! error value.
- If sample_s is less than the larger of 0 or (number_sample - number_population + population_s), HYPGEOMDIST returns the #NUM! error value.
- If number_sample < 0 or number_sample > number_population, HYPGEOMDIST returns the #NUM! error value.
- If population_s < 0 or population_s > number_population, HYPGEOMDIST returns the #NUM! error value.
- If number_population < 0, HYPGEOMDIST returns the #NUM! error value.

- The equation for the hypergeometric distribution is:

$$P(X = x) = h(x;n,M,N) = \frac{\binom{M}{x}\binom{N-M}{n-x}}{\binom{N}{n}}$$

where:

x = sample_s

n = number_sample

M = population_s

N = number_population

HYPGEOMDIST is used in sampling without replacement from a finite population.

Example

A sampler of chocolates contains 20 pieces. Eight pieces are caramels, and the remaining 12 are nuts. If a person selects 4 pieces at random, the following function returns the probability that exactly 1 piece is a caramel:

`HYPGEOMDIST(1,4,8,20)` equals 0.363261

IF

Returns one value if a condition you specify evaluates to TRUE and another value if it evaluates to FALSE.

Use IF to conduct conditional tests on values and formulas.

Syntax 1

IF(logical_test,value_if_true,value_if_false)

Logical_test   is any value or expression that can be evaluated to TRUE or FALSE.

Value_if_true   is the value that is returned if logical_test is TRUE. If logical_test is TRUE and value_if_true is omitted, TRUE is returned. Value_if_true can be another formula.

Value_if_false   is the value that is returned if logical_test is FALSE. If logical_test is FALSE and value_if_false is omitted, FALSE is returned. Value_if_false can be another formula.

Remarks

- Up to seven IF functions can be nested as value_if_true and value_if_false arguments to construct more elaborate tests. See the following last example.

- When the value_if_true and value_if_false arguments are evaluated, IF returns the value returned by those statements.

- If any of the arguments to IF are arrays, every element of the array is evaluated when the IF statement is carried out. If some of the value_if_true and value_if_false arguments are action-taking functions, all of the actions are taken.

Examples

In the following example, if the value in cell A10 is 100, then logical_test is TRUE, and the total value for the range B5:B15 is calculated. Otherwise, logical_test is FALSE, and empty text ("") is returned that blanks the cell that contains the IF function.

```
IF(A10=100,SUM(B5:B15),"")
```

Suppose an expense worksheet contains in B2:B4 the following data for "Actual Expenses" for January, February, and March: 1500, 500, 500. C2:C4 contains the following data for "Predicted Expenses" for the same periods: 900, 900, 925.

You can write a formula to check whether you are over budget for a particular month, generating text for a message with the following formulas:

```
IF(B2>C2,"Over Budget","OK")
```
equals "Over Budget"

```
IF(B3>C3,"Over Budget","OK")
```
equals "OK"

Suppose you want to assign letter grades to numbers referenced by the name AverageScore. See the following table.

If AverageScore is	Then return
Greater than 89	A
From 80 to 89	B
From 70 to 79	C
From 60 to 69	D
Less than 60	F

You can use the following nested IF function:

```
IF(AverageScore>89,"A",IF(AverageScore>79,"B",
IF(AverageScore>69,"C",IF(AverageScore>59,"D","F"))))
```

In the preceding example, the second IF statement is also the value_if_false argument to the first IF statement. Similarly, the third IF statement is the value_if_false argument to the second IF statement. For example, if the first logical_test (Average>89) is TRUE, "A" is returned. If the first logical_test is FALSE, the second IF statement is evaluated, and so on.

IMABS

Returns the absolute value (modulus) of a complex number in x + yi or x + yj text format.

If this function is not available, run the Setup program to install the Analysis ToolPak. After you install the Analysis ToolPak, you must enable it by using the **Add-Ins** command on the **Tools** menu.

Syntax

IMABS(inumber)

Inumber   is a complex number for which you want the absolute value.

Remarks

- Use COMPLEX to convert real and imaginary coefficients into a complex number.
- If inumber is not in the form x + yi or x + yj, IMABS returns the #NUM! error value.
- The absolute value of a complex number is:

$$IMABS(z) = |z| = \sqrt{x^2 + y^2}$$

where:

z = x + yi

Example

IMABS("5+12i") equals 13

IMAGINARY

Returns the imaginary coefficient of a complex number in x + yi or x + yj text format.

If this function is not available, run the Setup program to install the Analysis ToolPak. After you install the Analysis ToolPak, you must enable it by using the **Add-Ins** command on the **Tools** menu.

Syntax

IMAGINARY(inumber)

Inumber   is a complex number for which you want the imaginary coefficient.

Remarks

- Use COMPLEX to convert real and imaginary coefficients into a complex number.
- If inumber is not in the form x + yi or x + yj, IMAGINARY returns the #NUM! error value.

Examples

IMAGINARY("3+4i") equals 4

IMAGINARY("0-j") equals -1

IMAGINARY(4) equals 0

IMARGUMENT

Returns the argument θ (theta), an angle expressed in radians, such that:

$$x + yi = |x + yi| \times e^{\theta} = |x + yi|(\cos\theta + i\sin\theta)$$

If this function is not available, run the Setup program to install the Analysis ToolPak. After you install the Analysis ToolPak, you must enable it by using the **Add-Ins** command on the **Tools** menu.

Syntax

IMARGUMENT(inumber)

Inumber   is a complex number for which you want the argument θ.

Remarks

- Use COMPLEX to convert real and imaginary coefficients into a complex number.
- If inumber is not in the form x + yi or x + yj, IMARGUMENT returns the #NUM! error value.
- IMARGUMENT is calculated as follows:

$$IMARGUMENT(z) = \tan^{-1}\left(\frac{y}{x}\right) = \theta$$

where:

$$\theta \in \left]-\pi; \pi\right]$$

and

z = x + yi

Example

IMARGUMENT("3+4i") equals 0.927295

IMCONJUGATE

Returns the complex conjugate of a complex number in x + yi or x + yj text format.

If this function is not available, run the Setup program to install the Analysis ToolPak. After you install the Analysis ToolPak, you must enable it by using the **Add-Ins** command on the **Tools** menu.

Syntax

IMCONJUGATE(inumber)

Inumber   is a complex number for which you want the conjugate.

Remarks

- Use COMPLEX to convert real and imaginary coefficients into a complex number.

- If inumber is not in the form x + yi or x + yj, IMCONJUGATE returns the #NUM! error value.

- The conjugate of a complex number is:

$$\text{IMCONJUGATE}(x + yi) = \bar{z} = (x - yi)$$

Example

IMCONJUGATE("3+4i") equals 3 - 4i

IMCOS

Returns the cosine of a complex number in x + yi or x + yj text format.

If this function is not available, run the Setup program to install the Analysis ToolPak. After you install the Analysis ToolPak, you must enable it by using the **Add-Ins** command on the **Tools** menu.

Syntax

IMCOS(inumber)

Inumber   is a complex number for which you want the cosine.

Remarks

- Use COMPLEX to convert real and imaginary coefficients into a complex number.
- If inumber is not text, IMCOS returns the #VALUE! error value.
- If inumber is not in the form x + yi or x + yj, IMCOS returns the #NUM! error value.
- The cosine of a complex number is:

$$\cos\left(x + yi\right) = \cos\left(x\right)\cosh\left(y\right) - \sin\left(x\right)\sinh\left(y\right)i$$

Example

IMCOS("1+i") equals 0.83373 - 0.988898i

IMDIV

Returns the quotient of two complex numbers in x + yi or x + yj text format.

If this function is not available, run the Setup program to install the Analysis ToolPak. After you install the Analysis ToolPak, you must enable it by using the **Add-Ins** command on the **Tools** menu.

Syntax

IMDIV(inumber1,inumber2)

Inumber1   is the complex numerator or dividend.

Inumber2   is the complex denominator or divisor.

Remarks

- Use COMPLEX to convert real and imaginary coefficients into a complex number.
- If inumber1 or inumber2 is not in the form x + yi or x + yj, IMDIV returns the #NUM! error value.
- The quotient of two complex numbers is:

$$\text{IMDIV}\left(z_1, z_2\right) = \frac{\left(a + bi\right)}{\left(c + di\right)} = \frac{\left(ac + bd\right) + \left(bc - ad\right)i}{c^2 + d^2}$$

Example

IMDIV("-238+240i","10+24i") equals 5 + 12i

IMEXP

Returns the exponential of a complex number in x + yi or x + yj text format.

If this function is not available, run the Setup program to install the Analysis ToolPak. After you install the Analysis ToolPak, you must enable it by using the **Add-Ins** command on the **Tools** menu.

Syntax

IMEXP(inumber)

Inumber is a complex number for which you want the exponential.

Remarks

- Use COMPLEX to convert real and imaginary coefficients into a complex number.

- If inumber is not in the form x + yi or x + yj, IMEXP returns the #NUM! error value.

- The exponential of a complex number is:

$$\text{IMEXP}(z) = e^{(x+yi)} = e^x e^{yi} = e^x(\cos y + i \sin y)$$

Example

IMEXP("1+i") equals 1.468694 + 2.287355i

IMLN

Returns the natural logarithm of a complex number in x + yi or x + yj text format.

If this function is not available, run the Setup program to install the Analysis ToolPak. After you install the Analysis ToolPak, you must enable it by using the **Add-Ins** command on the **Tools** menu.

Syntax

IMLN(inumber)

Inumber is a complex number for which you want the natural logarithm.

Remarks

- Use COMPLEX to convert real and imaginary coefficients into a complex number.
- If inumber is not in the form x + yi or x + yj, IMLN returns the #NUM! error value.
- The natural logarithm of a complex number is:

$$\ln(x + yi) = \ln\sqrt{x^2 + y^2} + i\tan^{-1}\left(\frac{y}{x}\right)$$

where:

$$\theta \in \left]-\pi; \pi\right]$$

Example

IMLN("3+4i") equals 1.609438 + 0.927295i

IMLOG10

Returns the common logarithm (base 10) of a complex number in x + yi or x + yj text format.

If this function is not available, run the Setup program to install the Analysis ToolPak. After you install the Analysis ToolPak, you must enable it by using the **Add-Ins** command on the **Tools** menu.

Syntax

IMLOG10(inumber)

Inumber   is a complex number for which you want the common logarithm.

Remarks

- Use COMPLEX to convert real and imaginary coefficients into a complex number.
- If inumber is not in the form x + yi or x + yj, IMLOG10 returns the #NUM! error value.
- The common logarithm of a complex number can be calculated from the natural logarithm as follows:

$$\log_{10}(x + yi) = (\log_{10} e)\ln(x + yi)$$

Example

IMLOG10("3+4i") equals 0.69897 + 0.402719i

IMLOG2

Returns the base-2 logarithm of a complex number in x + yi or x + yj text format.

If this function is not available, run the Setup program to install the Analysis ToolPak. After you install the Analysis ToolPak, you must enable it by using the **Add-Ins** command on the **Tools** menu.

Syntax

IMLOG2(inumber)

Inumber   is a complex number for which you want the base-2 logarithm.

Remarks

- Use COMPLEX to convert real and imaginary coefficients into a complex number.
- If inumber is not in the form x + yi or x + yj, IMLOG2 returns the #NUM! error value.
- The base-2 logarithm of a complex number can be calculated from the natural logarithm as follows:

$$\log_2(x + yi) = (\log_2 e)\ln(x + yi)$$

Example

IMLOG2("3+4i") equals 2.321928 + 1.337804i

IMPOWER

Returns a complex number in x + yi or x + yj text format raised to a power.

If this function is not available, run the Setup program to install the Analysis ToolPak. After you install the Analysis ToolPak, you must enable it by using the **Add-Ins** command on the **Tools** menu.

Syntax

IMPOWER(inumber,number)

Inumber   is a complex number you want to raise to a power.

Number   is the power to which you want to raise the complex number.

Remarks

- Use COMPLEX to convert real and imaginary coefficients into a complex number.

- If inumber is not in the form x + yi or x + yj, IMPOWER returns the #NUM! error value.

- If number is nonnumeric, IMPOWER returns the #VALUE! error value.

- Number can be an integer, fractional, or negative.

- A complex number raised to a power is calculated as follows:

$$(x + yi)^n = r^n e^{in\theta} = r^n \cos n\theta + i r^n \sin n\theta$$

where:

$$r = \sqrt{x^2 + y^2}$$

and:

$$\theta = \tan^{-1}\left(\frac{y}{x}\right)$$

and:

$$\theta \in \left]-\pi; \pi\right]$$

Example

IMPOWER("2+3i", 3) equals -46 + 9i

IMPRODUCT

Returns the product of 2 to 29 complex numbers in x + yi or x + yj text format.

If this function is not available, run the Setup program to install the Analysis ToolPak. After you install the Analysis ToolPak, you must enable it by using the **Add-Ins** command on the **Tools** menu.

Syntax

IMPRODUCT(inumber1,inumber2, ...)

Inumber1,inumber2, ...   are 1 to 29 complex numbers to multiply.

Remarks

- Use COMPLEX to convert real and imaginary coefficients into a complex number.

- If inumber1 or inumber2 is not in the form x + yi or x + yj, IMPRODUCT returns the #NUM! error value.

  The product of two complex numbers is:

$$(a + bi)(c + di) = (ac - bd) + (ad + bc)i$$

Examples

IMPRODUCT("3+4i","5-3i") equals 27 + 11i

IMPRODUCT("1+2i",30) equals 30 + 60i

IMREAL

Returns the real coefficient of a complex number in x + yi or x + yj text format.

If this function is not available, run the Setup program to install the Analysis ToolPak. After you install the Analysis ToolPak, you must enable it by using the **Add-Ins** command on the **Tools** menu.

Syntax

IMREAL(inumber)

Inumber   is a complex number for which you want the real coefficient.

Remarks

- Use COMPLEX to convert real and imaginary coefficients into a complex number.

- If inumber is not in the form x + yi or x + yj, IMREAL returns the #NUM! error value.

Example

IMREAL("6-9i") equals 6

IMSIN

Returns the sine of a complex number in x + yi or x + yj text format.

If this function is not available, run the Setup program to install the Analysis ToolPak. After you install the Analysis ToolPak, you must enable it by using the **Add-Ins** command on the **Tools** menu.

Syntax

IMSIN(inumber)

Inumber   is a complex number for which you want the sine.

Remarks

- Use COMPLEX to convert real and imaginary coefficients into a complex number.
- If inumber is not in the form x + yi or x + yj, IMSIN returns the #NUM! error value.
- The sine of a complex number is:

$$\sin\left(x + yi\right) = \sin\left(x\right)\cosh\left(y\right) - \cos\left(x\right)\sinh\left(y\right)i$$

Example

IMSIN("3+4i") equals 3.853738 - 27.016813i

IMSQRT

Returns the square root of a complex number in x + yi or x + yj text format.

If this function is not available, run the Setup program to install the Analysis ToolPak. After you install the Analysis ToolPak, you must enable it by using the **Add-Ins** command on the **Tools** menu.

Syntax

IMSQRT(inumber)

Inumber   is a complex number for which you want the square root.

Remarks

- Use COMPLEX to convert real and imaginary coefficients into a complex number.
- If inumber is not in the form x + yi or x + yj, IMSQRT returns the #NUM! error value.

- The square root of a complex number is:

$$\sqrt{x + yi} = \sqrt{r}\cos\left(\frac{\theta}{2}\right) + i\sqrt{r}\sin\left(\frac{\theta}{2}\right)$$

where:

$$r = \sqrt{x^2 + y^2}$$

and:

$$\theta = \tan^{-1}\left(\frac{y}{x}\right)$$

and:

$$\theta \in \left]-\pi; \pi\right]$$

Example

```
IMSQRT("1+i") equals 1.098684 + 0.45509i
```

IMSUB

Returns the difference of two complex numbers in x + yi or x + yj text format.

If this function is not available, run the Setup program to install the Analysis ToolPak. After you install the Analysis ToolPak, you must enable it by using the **Add-Ins** command on the **Tools** menu.

Syntax

IMSUB(inumber1,inumber2)

Inumber1   is the complex number from which to subtract inumber2.

Inumber2   is the complex number to subtract from inumber1.

Remarks

- Use COMPLEX to convert real and imaginary coefficients into a complex number.

- If either number is not in the form x + yi or x + yj, IMSUB returns the #NUM! error value.

- The difference of two complex numbers is:

$$(a + bi) - (c + di) = (a - c) + (b - d)i$$

Example

```
IMSUB("13+4i","5+3i") equals 8 + i
```

IMSUM

Returns the sum of two or more complex numbers in x + yi or x + yj text format.

If this function is not available, run the Setup program to install the Analysis ToolPak. After you install the Analysis ToolPak, you must enable it by using the **Add-Ins** command on the **Tools** menu.

Syntax

IMSUM(inumber1,inumber2, ...)

Inumber1,inumber2, ...   are 1 to 29 complex numbers to add.

Remarks

- Use COMPLEX to convert real and imaginary coefficients into a complex number.

- If any argument is not in the form x + yi or x + yj, IMSUM returns the #NUM! error value.

- The sum of two complex numbers is:

$$(a + bi) + (c + di) = (a + c) + (b + d)i$$

Example

IMSUM("3+4i","5-3i") equals 8 + i

INDEX (Array Form)

Returns the value of an element in a table or an array, selected by the row and column number indexes.

The INDEX function has two syntax forms: array and reference. The array form always returns a value or array of values; the reference form always returns a reference. Use the array form if the first argument to INDEX is an array constant.

Syntax 1

Array form

INDEX(array,row_num,column_num)

Array   is a range of cells or an array constant.

Row_num   selects the row in array from which to return a value. If row_num is omitted, column_num is required.

Column_num selects the column in array from which to return a value. If column_num is omitted, row_num is required.

- If both the row_num and column_num arguments are used, INDEX returns the value in the cell at the intersection of row_num and column_num.

- If array contains only one row or column, the corresponding row_num or column_num argument is optional.

- If array has more than one row and more than one column, and only row_num or column_num is used, INDEX returns an array of the entire row or column in array.

- If you set row_num or column_num to 0 (zero), INDEX returns the array of values for the entire column or row, respectively. To use values returned as an array, enter the INDEX function as an array formula in a horizontal range of cells. To enter an array formula, press CTRL+SHIFT+ENTER in Microsoft Excel 97 for Windows or COMMAND+ENTER in Microsoft Excel 97 for the Macintosh.

Remarks

Row_num and column_num must point to a cell within array; otherwise, INDEX returns the #REF! error value.

Examples

INDEX({1,2;3,4},2,2) equals 4

If entered as an array formula, then:

INDEX({1,2;3,4},0,2) equals {2;4}

If cells B5:B6 contain the text Apples and Bananas, and cells C5:C6 contain the text Lemons and Pears, respectively, then:

INDEX(B5:C6,2,2) equals Pears

INDEX(B5:C6,2,1) equals Bananas

INDEX (Reference Form)

Returns the reference of the cell at the intersection of a particular row and column. If the reference is made up of nonadjacent selections, you can pick the selection to look in.

The INDEX function has two syntax forms: array and reference. The array form always returns a value or an array of values; the reference form always returns a reference.

Syntax 2

Reference form

INDEX(**reference**,row_num,column_num,area_num)

Reference   is a reference to one or more cell ranges.

- If you are entering a nonadjacent selection for reference, enclose reference in parentheses. For an example of using INDEX with a nonadjacent selection, see the fifth example following.

- If each area in reference contains only one row or column, the row_num or column_num argument, respectively, is optional. For example, for a single row reference, use INDEX(reference,,column_num).

Row_num   is the number of the row in reference from which to return a reference.

Column_num   is the number of the column in reference from which to return a reference.

Area_num   selects a range in reference from which to return the intersection of row_num and column_num. The first area selected or entered is numbered 1, the second is 2, and so on. If area_num is omitted, INDEX uses area 1.

For example, if reference describes the cells (A1:B4,D1:E4,G1:H4), then area_num 1 is the range A1:B4, area_num 2 is the range D1:E4, and area_num 3 is the range G1:H4.

After reference and area_num have selected a particular range, row_num and column_num select a particular cell: row_num 1 is the first row in the range, column_num 1 is the first column, and so on. The reference returned by INDEX is the intersection of row_num and column_num.

If you set row_num or column_num to 0 (zero), INDEX returns the reference for the entire column or row, respectively.

Remarks

- Row_num, column_num, and area_num must point to a cell within reference; otherwise, INDEX returns the #REF! error value. If row_num and column_num are omitted, INDEX returns the area in reference specified by area_num.

- The result of the INDEX function is a reference and is interpreted as such by other formulas. Depending on the formula, the return value of INDEX may be used as a reference or as a value. For example, the formula CELL("width",INDEX(A1:B2,1,2)) is equivalent to CELL("width",B1). The CELL function uses the return value of INDEX as a cell reference. On the other hand, a formula such as 2*INDEX(A1:B2,1,2) translates the return value of INDEX into the number in cell B1.

Examples

On the following worksheet, the range A2:C6 is named Fruit, the range A8:C11 is named Nuts, and the range A1:C11 is named Stock.

	A	B	C
		Price	**Count (lbs.)**
1		**Price**	**Count (lbs.)**
2	Apples	$0.69	40
3	Bananas	$0.34	38
4	Lemons	$0.55	15
5	Oranges	$0.25	25
6	Pears	$0.59	40
7			
8	Almonds	$2.80	10
9	Cashews	$3.55	16
10	Peanuts	$1.25	20
11	Walnuts	$1.75	12

INDEX(Fruit,2,3) equals the reference C3, containing 38

INDEX((A1:C6,A8:C11),2,2,2) equals the reference B9, containing $3.55

SUM(INDEX(Stock,0,3,1)) equals SUM(C1:C11) equals 216

SUM(B2:INDEX(Fruit,5,2)) equals SUM(B2:B6) equals 2.42

INDIRECT

Returns the reference specified by a text string. References are immediately evaluated to display their contents. Use INDIRECT when you want to change the reference to a cell within a formula without changing the formula itself.

Syntax

INDIRECT(ref_text,a1)

Ref_text is a reference to a cell that contains an A1-style reference, an R1C1-style reference, a name defined as a reference, or a reference to a cell as a text string. If ref_text is not a valid cell reference, INDIRECT returns the #REF! error value.

A1 is a logical value that specifies what type of reference is contained in the cell ref_text.

- If a1 is TRUE or omitted, ref_text is interpreted as an A1-style reference.
- If a1 is FALSE, ref_text is interpreted as an R1C1-style reference.

Remarks

If ref_text refers to another workbook (an external reference), the other workbook must be open. If the source workbook is not open, INDIRECT returns the #REF! error value.

Examples

If cell A1 contains the text "B2", and cell B2 contains the value 1.333, then:

`INDIRECT($A$1)` equals 1.333

If you change the text in A1 to "C5", and cell C5 contains the value 45, then:

`INDIRECT($A$1)` equals 45

If the workspace is set to display R1C1-style references, cell R1C1 contains R2C2, and cell R2C2 contains the value 1.333, then:

`INT(INDIRECT(R1C1,FALSE))` equals 1

If B3 contains the text "George", and a cell defined as George contains the value 10, then:

`INDIRECT($B$3)` equals 10

When you create a formula that refers to a cell, the reference to the cell will be updated if the cell is moved by using the **Cut** command to delete the cell or if the cell is moved because rows or columns are inserted or deleted. If you always want the formula to refer to the same cell regardless of whether the row above the cell is deleted or the cell is moved, use the INDIRECT worksheet function. For example, if you always want to refer to cell A10, use the following syntax:

`INDIRECT("A10")`

INFO

Returns information about the current operating environment.

Syntax

INFO(type_text)

Type_text is text specifying what type of information you want returned.

Type_text	Returns
"directory"	Path of the current directory or folder.
"memavail"	Amount of memory available, in bytes.
"memused"	Amount of memory being used for data.
"numfile"	Number of active worksheets.
"origin"	Absolute A1-style reference, as text, prepended with "$A:" for Lotus 1-2-3 release 3.x compatibility. Returns the cell reference of the top and leftmost cell visible in the window, based on the current scrolling position.
"osversion"	Current operating system version, as text.
"recalc"	Current recalculation mode; returns "Automatic" or "Manual".
"release"	Version of Microsoft Excel, as text.
"system"	Name of the operating environment:
	Macintosh = "mac"
	Windows = "pcdos"
"totmem"	Total memory available, including memory already in use, in bytes.

Examples

The following formula returns 2 if two worksheets are currently open:

```
INFO("numfile")
```

INT

Rounds a number down to the nearest integer.

Syntax

INT(number)

Number is the real number you want to round down to an integer.

Examples

INT(8.9) equals 8

INT(-8.9) equals -9

The following formula returns the decimal part of a positive real number in cell A1:

A1-INT(A1)

INTERCEPT

Calculates the point at which a line will intersect the y-axis by using existing x-values and y-values. The intercept point is based on a best-fit regression line plotted through the known x-values and known y-values. Use the intercept when you want to determine the value of the dependent variable when the independent variable is 0 (zero). For example, you can use the INTERCEPT function to predict a metal's electrical resistance at 0°C when your data points were taken at room temperature and higher.

Syntax

INTERCEPT(known_y's,known_x's)

Known_y's is the dependent set of observations or data.

Known_x's is the independent set of observations or data.

Remarks

- The arguments should be either numbers or names, arrays, or references that contain numbers.

- If an array or reference argument contains text, logical values, or empty cells, those values are ignored; however, cells with the value zero are included.

- If known_y's and known_x's contain a different number of data points or contain no data points, INTERCEPT returns the #N/A error value.

- The equation for the intercept of the regression line is:

$$a = \overline{Y} - b\overline{X}$$

where the slope is calculated as:

$$b = \frac{n\Sigma xy - (\Sigma x)(\Sigma y)}{n\Sigma x^2 - (\Sigma x)^2}$$

Example

INTERCEPT({2, 3, 9, 1, 8}, {6, 5, 11, 7, 5}) equals 0.0483871

INTRATE

Returns the interest rate for a fully invested security.

If this function is not available, run the Setup program to install the Analysis ToolPak. After you install the Analysis ToolPak, you must enable it by using the **Add-Ins** command on the **Tools** menu.

Syntax

INTRATE(settlement,maturity,investment,redemption,basis)

Settlement   is the security's settlement date. The security settlement date is the date after the issue date when the security is traded to the buyer.

Maturity   is the security's maturity date. The maturity date is the date when the security expires.

Investment   is the amount invested in the security.

Redemption   is the amount to be received at maturity.

Basis   is the type of day count basis to use.

Basis	Day count basis
0 or omitted	US (NASD) 30/360
1	Actual/actual
2	Actual/360
3	Actual/365
4	European 30/360

Remarks

- The settlement date is the date a buyer purchases a coupon, such as a bond. The maturity date is the date when a coupon expires. For example, suppose a 30-year bond is issued on January 1, 1996, and is purchased by a buyer six months later. The issue date would be January 1, 1996, the settlement date would be July 1, 1996, and the maturity date would be January 1, 2026, which is 30 years after the January 1, 1996, issue date.

- Settlement, maturity, and basis are truncated to integers.

- If any argument is nonnumeric, INTRATE returns the #VALUE! error value.

- If settlement or maturity is not a valid date, INTRATE returns the #NUM! error value.

- If investment ≤ 0 or if redemption ≤ 0, INTRATE returns the #NUM! error value.

- If basis < 0 or if basis > 4, INTRATE returns the #NUM! error value.

- If settlement $\geq$ maturity, INTRATE returns the #NUM! error value.

- INTRATE is calculated as follows:

$$INTRATE = \frac{redemption - investment}{investment} \times \frac{B}{DIM}$$

Where:

B = number of days in a year, depending on the year basis.

DIM = number of days from settlement to maturity.

Example

A bond has the following terms:

February 15, 1993, settlement date
May 15, 1993, maturity date
1,000,000 investment
1,014,420 redemption value
Actual/360 basis

The bond discount rate (in the 1900 date system) is:

`INTRATE("2/15/93","5/15/93",1000000,1014420,2)` equals 0.058328 or 5.8328 percent

IPMT

Returns the interest payment for a given period for an investment based on periodic, constant payments and a constant interest rate. For a more complete description of the arguments in IPMT and for more information about annuity functions, see PV.

Syntax

IPMT(rate,per,nper,pv,fv,type)

Rate   is the interest rate per period.

Per   is the period for which you want to find the interest and must be in the range 1 to nper.

Nper   is the total number of payment periods in an annuity.

Pv   is the present value, or the lump-sum amount that a series of future payments is worth right now.

Fv   is the future value, or a cash balance you want to attain after the last payment is made. If fv is omitted, it is assumed to be 0 (the future value of a loan, for example, is 0).

Type   is the number 0 or 1 and indicates when payments are due. If type is omitted, it is assumed to be 0.

Set type equal to	If payments are due
0	At the end of the period
1	At the beginning of the period

Remarks

- Make sure that you are consistent about the units you use for specifying rate and nper. If you make monthly payments on a four-year loan at 12 percent annual interest, use 12%/12 for rate and 4*12 for nper. If you make annual payments on the same loan, use 12% for rate and 4 for nper.

- For all the arguments, cash you pay out, such as deposits to savings, is represented by negative numbers; cash you receive, such as dividend checks, is represented by positive numbers.

Examples

The following formula calculates the interest due in the first month of a three-year $8000 loan at 10 percent annual interest:

IPMT(0.1/12, 1, 36, 8000) equals -$66.67

The following formula calculates the interest due in the last year of a three-year $8000 loan at 10 percent annual interest, where payments are made yearly:

IPMT(0.1, 3, 3, 8000) equals -$292.45

IRR

Returns the internal rate of return for a series of cash flows represented by the numbers in values. These cash flows do not have to be even, as they would be for an annuity. However, the cash flows must occur at regular intervals, such as monthly or annually. The internal rate of return is the interest rate received for an investment consisting of payments (negative values) and income (positive values) that occur at regular periods.

Syntax

IRR(**values**,guess)

Values   is an array or a reference to cells that contain numbers for which you want to calculate the internal rate of return.

- Values must contain at least one positive value and one negative value to calculate the internal rate of return.

- IRR uses the order of values to interpret the order of cash flows. Be sure to enter your payment and income values in the sequence you want.

- If an array or reference argument contains text, logical values, or empty cells, those values are ignored.

Guess   is a number that you guess is close to the result of IRR.

- Microsoft Excel uses an iterative technique for calculating IRR. Starting with guess, IRR cycles through the calculation until the result is accurate within 0.00001 percent. If IRR can't find a result that works after 20 tries, the #NUM! error value is returned.

- In most cases you do not need to provide guess for the IRR calculation. If guess is omitted, it is assumed to be 0.1 (10 percent).

- If IRR gives the #NUM! error value, or if the result is not close to what you expected, try again with a different value for guess.

Remarks

IRR is closely related to NPV, the net present value function. The rate of return calculated by IRR is the interest rate corresponding to a 0 (zero) net present value. The following formula demonstrates how NPV and IRR are related:

NPV(IRR(B1:B6),B1:B6) equals 3.60E-08 [Within the accuracy of the IRR calculation, the value 3.60E-08 is effectively 0 (zero).]

Examples

Suppose you want to start a restaurant business. You estimate it will cost $70,000 to start the business and expect to net the following income in the first five years: $12,000, $15,000, $18,000, $21,000, and $26,000. B1:B6 contain the following values: $-70,000, $12,000, $15,000, $18,000, $21,000 and $26,000, respectively.

To calculate the investment's internal rate of return after four years:

IRR(B1:B5) equals -2.12 percent

To calculate the internal rate of return after five years:

IRR(B1:B6) equals 8.66 percent

To calculate the internal rate of return after two years, you need to include a guess:

IRR(B1:B3,-10%) equals -44.35 percent

IS Functions

This section describes the nine worksheet functions used for testing the type of a value or reference.

Each of these functions, referred to collectively as the IS functions, checks the type of value and returns TRUE or FALSE depending on the outcome. For example, the ISBLANK function returns the logical value TRUE if value is a reference to an empty cell; otherwise it returns FALSE.

Syntax

ISBLANK(value)
ISERR(value)
ISERROR(value)
ISLOGICAL(value)
ISNA(value)
ISNONTEXT(value)
ISNUMBER(value)
ISREF(value)
ISTEXT(value)

Value   is the value you want tested. Value can be a blank (empty cell), error, logical, text, number, or reference value, or a name referring to any of these, that you want to test.

Function	Returns TRUE if
ISBLANK	Value refers to an empty cell.
ISERR	Value refers to any error value except #N/A.
ISERROR	Value refers to any error value (#N/A, #VALUE!, #REF!, #DIV/0!, #NUM!, #NAME?, or #NULL!).
ISLOGICAL	Value refers to a logical value.
ISNA	Value refers to the #N/A (value not available) error value.
ISNONTEXT	Value refers to any item that is not text. (Note that this function returns TRUE if value refers to a blank cell.)
ISNUMBER	Value refers to a number.
ISREF	Value refers to a reference.
ISTEXT	Value refers to text.

Remarks

- The value arguments to the IS functions are not converted. For example, in most other functions where a number is required, the text value "19" is converted to the number 19. However, in the formula ISNUMBER("19"), "19" is not converted from a text value, and the ISNUMBER function returns FALSE.

- The IS functions are useful in formulas for testing the outcome of a calculation. When combined with the IF function, they provide a method for locating errors in formulas (see the following examples).

Examples

ISLOGICAL(TRUE) equals TRUE

ISLOGICAL("TRUE") equals FALSE

ISNUMBER(4) equals TRUE

Suppose C1:C5 on a worksheet of gold prices in different regions shows the following text values, number values, and error values: "Gold", "Region1", #REF!, $330.92, #N/A, respectively.

ISBLANK(C1) equals FALSE

ISERROR(C3) equals TRUE

ISNA(C3) equals FALSE

ISNA(C5) equals TRUE

ISERR(C5) equals FALSE

ISNUMBER(C4) equals TRUE (if the $330.92 was entered as a number and not as text)

ISREF(Region1) equals TRUE (if Region1 is defined as a range name)

ISTEXT(C2) equals TRUE (if Region1 is formatted as text)

On another worksheet, suppose you want to calculate the average of the range A1:A4, but you can't be sure that the cells contain numbers. The formula AVERAGE(A1:A4) returns the #DIV/0! error value if A1:A4 does not contain any numbers. To allow for this case, you can use the following formula to locate potential errors:

IF(ISERROR(AVERAGE(A1:A4)),"No Numbers",AVERAGE(A1:A4))

ISEVEN

Returns TRUE if number is even, or FALSE if number is odd.

If this function is not available, run the Setup program to install the Analysis ToolPak. After you install the Analysis ToolPak, you must enable it by using the **Add-Ins** command on the **Tools** menu.

Syntax

ISEVEN(number)

Number   is the value to test. If number is not an integer, it is truncated.

Remarks

If number is nonnumeric, ISEVEN returns the #VALUE! error value.

Examples

ISEVEN(-1) equals FALSE

ISEVEN(2.5) equals TRUE

ISEVEN(5) equals FALSE

ISODD

Returns TRUE if number is odd, or FALSE if number is even.

If this function is not available, run the Setup program to install the Analysis ToolPak. After you install the Analysis ToolPak, you must enable it by using the **Add-Ins** command on the **Tools** menu.

Syntax

ISODD(number)

Number   is the value to test. If number is not an integer, it is truncated.

Remarks

If number is nonnumeric, ISODD returns the #VALUE! error value.

Examples

ISODD(-1) equals TRUE

ISODD(2.5) equals FALSE

ISODD(5) equals TRUE

KURT

Returns the kurtosis of a data set. Kurtosis characterizes the relative peakedness or flatness of a distribution compared with the normal distribution. Positive kurtosis indicates a relatively peaked distribution. Negative kurtosis indicates a relatively flat distribution.

Syntax

KURT(number1,number2, ...)

Number1,number2, ...   are 1 to 30 arguments for which you want to calculate kurtosis. You can also use a single array or a reference to an array instead of arguments separated by commas.

Remarks

- The arguments must be either numbers or names, arrays, or references that contain numbers.

- If an array or reference argument contains text, logical values, or empty cells, those values are ignored; however, cells with the value zero are included.

- If there are fewer than four data points, or if the standard deviation of the sample equals zero, KURT returns the #DIV/0! error value.

- Kurtosis is defined as:

$$\left\{\frac{n(n+1)}{(n-1)(n-2)(n-3)}\sum\left(\frac{x_j-\bar{x}}{s}\right)^4\right\}$$
$$-\frac{3(n-1)^2}{(n-2)(n-3)}$$

where:

s is the sample standard deviation.

Example

KURT(3,4,5,2,3,4,5,6,4,7) returns -0.1518

LARGE

Returns the k-th largest value in a data set. You can use this function to select a value based on its relative standing. For example, you can use LARGE to return the highest, runner-up, or third-place score.

Syntax

LARGE(array,k)

Array   is the array or range of data for which you want to determine the k-th largest value.

K   is the position (from the largest) in the array or cell range of data to return.

Remarks

- If array is empty, LARGE returns the #NUM! error value.

- If k ≤ 0 or if k is greater than the number of data points, LARGE returns the #NUM! error value.

If n is the number of data points in a range, then LARGE(array,1) returns the largest value, and LARGE(array,n) returns the smallest value.

Examples

LARGE({3,4,5,2,3,4,5,6,4,7},3) equals 5

LARGE({3,4,5,2,3,4,5,6,4,7},7) equals 4

LCM

Returns the least common multiple of integers. The least common multiple is the smallest positive integer that is a multiple of all integer arguments number1, number2, and so on. Use LCM to add fractions with different denominators.

If this function is not available, run the Setup program to install the Analysis ToolPak. After you install the Analysis ToolPak, you must enable it by using the **Add-Ins** command on the **Tools** menu.

Syntax

LCM(number1,number2, ...)

Number1,number2, ...   are 1 to 29 values for which you want the least common multiple. If value is not an integer, it is truncated.

Remarks

- If any argument is nonnumeric, LCM returns the #VALUE! error value.

- If any argument is less than one, LCM returns the #NUM! error value.

Examples

LCM(5, 2) equals 10

LCM(24, 36) equals 72

LEFT

Returns the first (or leftmost) character or characters in a text string.

Syntax

LEFT(text,num_chars)

Text   is the text string that contains the characters you want to extract.

Num_chars   specifies how many characters you want LEFT to extract.

- Num_chars must be greater than or equal to zero.

- If num_chars is greater than the length of text, LEFT returns all of text.

- If num_chars is omitted, it is assumed to be 1.

Examples

LEFT("Sale Price", 4) equals "Sale"

If A1 contains "Sweden", then:

LEFT(A1) equals "S"

Some accounting programs display negative values with the negation sign (–) to the right of the value. If you import a file created in a program that stores negative values in this way, Microsoft Excel may import the values as text. To convert the text strings to values, you must return all of the characters of the text string except the rightmost character (the negation sign), and then multiply the result by –1. For the num_chars argument, use the LEN worksheet function to count the number of characters in the text string, and then subtract 1. For example, if the value in cell A2 is "156–" the following formula converts the text to the value –156.

LEFT(A2,LEN(A2)-1)*-1

LEN

Returns the number of characters in a text string.

Syntax

LEN(text)

Text   is the text whose length you want to find. Spaces count as characters.

Examples

LEN("Phoenix, AZ") equals 11

LEN("") equals 0

LINEST

Calculates the statistics for a line by using the "least squares" method to calculate a straight line that best fits your data, and returns an array that describes the line. Because this function returns an array of values, it must be entered as an array formula.

The equation for the line is:

$y = mx + b$ or $y = m1x1 + m2x2 + ... + b$ (if there are multiple ranges of x-values)

where the dependent y-value is a function of the independent x-values. The m-values are coefficients corresponding to each x-value, and b is a constant value. Note that y, x, and m can be vectors. The array that LINEST returns is {mn,mn-1, ...,m1,b}. LINEST can also return additional regression statistics.

Syntax

LINEST(known_y's,known_x's,const,stats)

Known_y's is the set of y-values you already know in the relationship y = mx + b.

- If the array known_y's is in a single column, then each column of known_x's is interpreted as a separate variable.

- If the array known_y's is in a single row, then each row of known_x's is interpreted as a separate variable.

Known_x's is an optional set of x-values that you may already know in the relationship y = mx + b.

- The array known_x's can include one or more sets of variables. If only one variable is used, known_y's and known_x's can be ranges of any shape, as long as they have equal dimensions. If more than one variable is used, known_y's must be a vector (that is, a range with a height of one row or a width of one column).

- If known_x's is omitted, it is assumed to be the array {1,2,3, ...} that is the same size as known_y's.

Const is a logical value specifying whether to force the constant b to equal 0.

- If const is TRUE or omitted, b is calculated normally.

- If const is FALSE, b is set equal to 0 and the m-values are adjusted to fit y = mx.

Stats is a logical value specifying whether to return additional regression statistics.

- If stats is TRUE, LINEST returns the additional regression statistics, so the returned array is {mn,mn-1, ...,m1,b;sen,sen-1, ...,se1,seb;r2,sey;F,df;ssreg,ssresid}.

- If stats is FALSE or omitted, LINEST returns only the m-coefficients and the constant b.

The additional regression statistics are as follows.

Statistic	Description
se1,se2, ...,sen	The standard error values for the coefficients m1,m2, ...,mn.
Seb	The standard error value for the constant b (seb = #N/A when const is FALSE).
r2	The coefficient of determination. Compares estimated and actual y-values, and ranges in value from 0 to 1. If it is 1, there is a perfect correlation in the sample—there is no difference between the estimated y-value and the actual y-value. At the other extreme, if the coefficient of determination is 0, the regression equation is not helpful in predicting a y-value. For information about how r2 is calculated, see "Remarks" later in this topic.
sey	The standard error for the y estimate.
F	The F statistic, or the F-observed value. Use the F statistic to determine whether the observed relationship between the dependent and independent variables occurs by chance.
df	The degrees of freedom. Use the degrees of freedom to help you find F-critical values in a statistical table. Compare the values you find in the table to the F statistic returned by LINEST to determine a confidence level for the model.
ssreg	The regression sum of squares.
ssresid	The residual sum of squares.

The following illustration shows the order in which the additional regression statistics are returned.

m_n	m_{n-1}	. . .	m_2	m_1	b
se_n	se_{n-1}	. . .	se_2	se_1	se_b
r^2	se_y				
F	df				
ss_{reg}	ss_{resid}				

Remarks

- You can describe any straight line with the slope and the y-intercept:

  Slope (m):
  To find the slope of a line, often written as m, take two points on the line, (x1,y1) and (x2,y2); the slope is equal to (y2 - y1)/(x2 - x1).

  Y-intercept (b):
  The y-intercept of a line, often written as b, is the value of y at the point where the line crosses the y-axis.

  The equation of a straight line is y = mx + b. Once you know the values of m and b, you can calculate any point on the line by plugging the y- or x-value into that equation. You can also use the TREND function. For more information, see TREND.

- When you have only one independent x-variable, you can obtain the slope and y-intercept values directly by using the following formulas:

  Slope:
  INDEX(LINEST(known_y's,known_x's),1)

  Y-intercept:
  INDEX(LINEST(known_y's,known_x's),2)

- The accuracy of the line calculated by LINEST depends on the degree of scatter in your data. The more linear the data, the more accurate the LINEST model. LINEST uses the method of least squares for determining the best fit for the data. When you have only one independent x-variable, the calculations for m and b are based on the following formulas:

$$m = \frac{n\left(\sum xy\right)\left(\sum x\right)\left(\sum y\right)}{n\left(\sum \left(x^2\right)\right) - \left(\sum x\right)^2}$$

$$b = \frac{\left(\sum y\right)\left(\sum \left(x^2\right)\right) - \left(\sum x\right)\left(\sum xy\right)}{n\left(\sum \left(x^2\right)\right) - \left(\sum x\right)^2}$$

- The line- and curve-fitting functions LINEST and LOGEST can calculate the best straight line or exponential curve that fits your data. However, you have to decide which of the two results best fits your data. You can calculate TREND(known_y's,known_x's) for a straight line, or GROWTH(known_y's, known_x's) for an exponential curve. These functions, without the new_x's argument, return an array of y-values predicted along that line or curve at your actual data points. You can then compare the predicted values with the actual values. You may want to chart them both for a visual comparison.

- In regression analysis, Microsoft Excel calculates for each point the squared difference between the y-value estimated for that point and its actual y-value. The sum of these squared differences is called the residual sum of squares. Microsoft Excel then calculates the sum of the squared differences between the actual y-values and the average of the y-values, which is called the total sum of squares (regression sum of squares + residual sum of squares). The smaller the residual sum of squares is, compared with the total sum of squares, the larger the value of the coefficient of determination, r2, which is an indicator of how well the equation resulting from the regression analysis explains the relationship among the variables.

- Formulas that return arrays must be entered as array formulas.

- When entering an array constant such as known_x's as an argument, use commas to separate values in the same row and semicolons to separate rows. Separator characters may be different depending on your country settings.

- Note that the y-values predicted by the regression equation may not be valid if they are outside the range of the y-values you used to determine the equation.

Example 1   Slope and Y-Intercept

LINEST({1,9,5,7},{0,4,2,3}) equals {2,1}, the slope = 2 and y-intercept = 1

Example 2   Simple Linear Regression

Suppose a small business has sales of $3,100, $4,500, $4,400, $5,400, $7,500, and $8,100 during the first six months of the fiscal year. Assuming that the values are entered in the range B2:B7, respectively, you can use the following simple linear regression model to estimate sales for the ninth month.

SUM(LINEST(B2:B7)*{9,1}) equals SUM({1000,2000}*{9,1}) equals $11,000

In general, SUM({m,b}*{x,1}) equals mx + b, the estimated y-value for a given x-value. You can also use the TREND function.

Example 3   Multiple Linear Regression

Suppose a commercial developer is considering purchasing a group of small office buildings in an established business district.

The developer can use multiple linear regression analysis to estimate the value of an office building in a given area based on the following variables.

Variable	Refers to the
y	Assessed value of the office building
x1	Floor space in square feet
x2	Number of offices
x3	Number of entrances
x4	Age of the office building in years

This example assumes that a straight-line relationship exists between each independent variable (x1, x2, x3, and x4) and the dependent variable (y), the value of office buildings in the area.

The developer randomly chooses a sample of 11 office buildings from a possible 1,500 office buildings and obtains the following data.

	A	B	C	D	E
1	x1 Floor Space	x2 Offices	x3 Entrances	x4 Age	y Value
2	2,310	2	2	20	$142,000
3	2,333	2	2	12	$144,000
4	2,356	3	1.5	33	$151,000
5	2,379	3	2	43	$150,000
6	2,402	2	3	53	$139,000
7	2,425	4	2	23	$169,000
8	2,448	2	1.5	99	$126,000
9	2,471	2	2	34	$142,900
10	2,494	3	3	23	$163,000
11	2,517	4	4	55	$169,000
12	2,540	2	3	22	$149,000

"Half an entrance" means an entrance for deliveries only. When entered as an array, the following formula:

```
LINEST(E2:E12,A2:D12,TRUE,TRUE)
```

returns the following output.

	A	B	C	D	E
14	-234.23716	2553.21066	12529.7682	27.6413874	52317.8305
15	13.2680115	530.669152	400.066838	5.42937404	12237.3616
16	0.99674799	970.578463	#N/A	#N/A	#N/A
17	459.753674	6	#N/A	#N/A	#N/A
18	1732393319	5652135.32	#N/A	#N/A	#N/A

The multiple regression equation, y = m1*x1 + m2*x2 + m3*x3 + m4*x4 + b, can now be obtained using the values from row 14:

y = 27.64*x1 + 12,530*x2 + 2,553*x3+ 234.24*x4 + 52,318

The developer can now estimate the assessed value of an office building in the same area that has 2,500 square feet, three offices, and two entrances and is 25 years old, by using the following equation:

y = 27.64*2500 + 12530*3 + 2553*2 - 234.24*25 + 52318 = $158,261

You can also use the TREND function to calculate this value. For more information, see TREND.

Example 4   Using The F And R2 Statistics

In the previous example, the coefficient of determination, or r2, is 0.99675 (see cell A16 in the output for LINEST), which would indicate a strong relationship between the independent variables and the sale price. You can use the F statistic to determine whether these results, with such a high r2 value, occurred by chance.

Assume for the moment that in fact there is no relationship among the variables, but that you have drawn a rare sample of 11 office buildings that causes the statistical analysis to demonstrate a strong relationship. The term "Alpha" is used for the probability of erroneously concluding that there is a relationship.

There is a relationship among the variables if the F-observed statistic is greater than the F-critical value. The F-critical value can be obtained by referring to a table of F-critical values in many statistics textbooks. To read the table, assume a single-tailed test, use an Alpha value of 0.05, and for the degrees of freedom (abbreviated in most tables as v1 and v2), use v1 = k = 4 and v2 = n - (k + 1) = 11 - (4 + 1) = 6, where k is the number of variables in the regression analysis and n is the number of data points. The F-critical value is 4.53.

The F-observed value is 459.753674 (cell A17), which is substantially greater than the F-critical value of 4.53. Therefore, the regression equation is useful in predicting the assessed value of office buildings in this area.

Example 5   Calculating The T-Statistics

Another hypothesis test will determine whether each slope coefficient is useful in estimating the assessed value of an office building in example 3. For example, to test the age coefficient for statistical significance, divide -234.24 (age slope coefficient) by 13.268 (the estimated standard error of age coefficients in cell A15). The following is the t-observed value:

$$t = m4 \div se4 = -234.24 \div 13.268 = -17.7$$

If you consult a table in a statistics manual, you will find that t-critical, single tail, with 6 degrees of freedom and Alpha = 0.05 is 1.94. Because the absolute value of t, 17.7, is greater than 1.94, age is an important variable when estimating the assessed value of an office building. Each of the other independent variables can be tested for statistical significance in a similar manner. The following are the t-observed values for each of the independent variables.

Variable	t-observed value
Floor space	5.1
Number of offices	31.3
Number of entrances	4.8
Age	17.7

These values all have an absolute value greater than 1.94; therefore, all the variables used in the regression equation are useful in predicting the assessed value of office buildings in this area.

LN

Returns the natural logarithm of a number. Natural logarithms are based on the constant e (2.71828182845904).

Syntax

LN(number)

Number   is the positive real number for which you want the natural logarithm.

Remarks

LN is the inverse of the EXP function.

Examples

LN(86) equals 4.454347

LN(2.7182818) equals 1

LN(EXP(3)) equals 3

EXP(LN(4)) equals 4

LOG

Returns the logarithm of a number to the base you specify.

Syntax

LOG(number,base)

Number   is the positive real number for which you want the logarithm.

Base   is the base of the logarithm. If base is omitted, it is assumed to be 10.

Examples

LOG(10) equals 1

LOG(8, 2) equals 3

LOG(86, 2.7182818) equals 4.454347

LOG10

Returns the base-10 logarithm of a number.

Syntax

LOG10(number)

Number   is the positive real number for which you want the base-10 logarithm.

Examples

LOG10(86) equals 1.934498451

LOG10(10) equals 1

LOG10(1E5) equals 5

LOG10(10^5) equals 5

LOGEST

In regression analysis, calculates an exponential curve that fits your data and returns an array of values that describes the curve. Because this function returns an array of values, it must be entered as an array formula.

The equation for the curve is:

$y = b*m^x$ or $y = (b*(m1^{x1})*(m2^{x2})*\_)$ (if there are multiple x-values)

where the dependent y-value is a function of the independent x-values. The m-values are bases corresponding to each exponent x-value, and b is a constant value. Note that y, x, and m can be vectors. The array that LOGEST returns is {mn,mn-1, ...,m1,b}.

Syntax

LOGEST(known_y's,known_x's,const,stats)

Known_y's   is the set of y-values you already know in the relationship $y = b*m^x$.

- If the array known_y's is in a single column, then each column of known_x's is interpreted as a separate variable.

- If the array known_y's is in a single row, then each row of known_x's is interpreted as a separate variable.

Known_x's   is an optional set of x-values that you may already know in the relationship $y = b*m^x$.

- The array known_x's can include one or more sets of variables. If only one variable is used, known_y's and known_x's can be ranges of any shape, as long as they have equal dimensions. If more than one variable is used, known_y's must be a range of cells with a height of one row or a width of one column (which is also known as a vector).

- If known_x's is omitted, it is assumed to be the array {1,2,3, ...} that is the same size as known_y's.

Const   is a logical value specifying whether to force the constant b to equal 1.

- If const is TRUE or omitted, b is calculated normally.

- If const is FALSE, b is set equal to 1, and the m-values are fitted to $y = m^x$.

Stats   is a logical value specifying whether to return additional regression statistics.

- If stats is TRUE, LOGEST returns the additional regression statistics, so the returned array is {mn,mn-1, ...,m1,b;sen,sen-1, ...,se1,seb;r 2,sey; F,df;ssreg,ssresid}.

- If stats is FALSE or omitted, LOGEST returns only the m-coefficients and the constant b.

For more information about additional regression statistics, see LINEST.

Remarks

- The more a plot of your data resembles an exponential curve, the better the calculated line will fit your data. Like LINEST, LOGEST returns an array of values that describes a relationship among the values, but LINEST fits a straight line to your data; LOGEST fits an exponential curve. For more information, see LINEST.

- When you have only one independent x-variable, you can obtain the slope (m) and y-intercept (b) values directly by using the following formulas:

  Slope (m):
  INDEX(LOGEST(known_y's,known_x's),1)

  Y-intercept (b):
  INDEX(LOGEST(known_y's,known_x's),2)

  You can use the $y = b*m^x$ equation to predict future values of y, but Microsoft Excel provides the GROWTH function to do this for you. For more information, see GROWTH.

- Formulas that return arrays must be entered as array formulas.

- When entering an array constant such as known_x's as an argument, use commas to separate values in the same row and semicolons to separate rows. Separator characters may be different depending on your country setting.

- You should note that the y-values predicted by the regression equation may not be valid if they are outside the range of y-values you used to determine the equation.

Example

After 10 months of sluggish sales, a company experiences exponential growth in sales after putting a new product on the market. In the subsequent 6 months, sales increased to 33,100, 47,300, 69,000, 102,000, 150,000, and 220,000 units per month. Assume that these values are entered into six cells named UnitsSold. When entered as a formula:

```
LOGEST(UnitsSold, {11;12;13;14;15;16}, TRUE, TRUE)
```

generates the following output in, for example, cells D1:E5:

{1.46327563, 495.30477; 0.0026334, 0.03583428; 0.99980862, 0.01101631; 20896.8011, 4; 2.53601883, 0.00048544}

$y = b*m1^{x1}$ or using the values from the array:

$y = 495.3 * 1.4633x$

You can estimate sales for future months by substituting the month number for x in this equation, or you can use the GROWTH function. For more information, see GROWTH.

You can use the additional regression statistics (cells D2:E5 in the above output array) to determine how useful the equation is for predicting future values.

Important The methods you use to test an equation using LOGEST are similar to the methods for LINEST. However, the additional statistics LOGEST returns are based on the following linear model:

ln y = x1 ln m1 + ... + xn ln mn + ln b

You should keep this in mind when you evaluate the additional statistics, especially the sei and seb values, which should be compared to ln mi and ln b, not to mi and b. For more information, consult an advanced statistics manual.

LOGINV

Returns the inverse of the lognormal cumulative distribution function of x, where ln(x) is normally distributed with parameters mean and standard_dev. If p = LOGNORMDIST(x, ...) then LOGINV(p, ...) = x.

Use the lognormal distribution to analyze logarithmically transformed data.

Syntax

LOGINV(probability,mean,standard_dev)

Probability is a probability associated with the lognormal distribution.

Mean is the mean of ln(x).

Standard_dev is the standard deviation of ln(x).

The inverse of the lognormal distribution function is:

$$LOGINV(p, \mu, \sigma) = e^{[\mu + \sigma \times (NORMSINV(p))]}$$

Remarks

- If any argument is nonnumeric, LOGINV returns the #VALUE! error value.
- If probability < 0 or probability > 1, LOGINV returns the #NUM! error value.
- If standard_dev <= 0, LOGINV returns the #NUM! error value.

Example

```
LOGINV(0.039084, 3.5, 1.2) equals 4.000014
```

LOGNORMDIST

Returns the cumulative lognormal distribution of x, where ln(x) is normally distributed with parameters mean and standard_dev. Use this function to analyze data that has been logarithmically transformed.

Syntax

LOGNORMDIST(x,**mean,standard_dev**)

X   is the value at which to evaluate the function.

Mean   is the mean of ln(x).

Standard_dev   is the standard deviation of ln(x).

Remarks

- If any argument is nonnumeric, LOGNORMDIST returns the #VALUE! error value.

- If x ≤ 0 or if standard_dev ≤ 0, LOGNORMDIST returns the #NUM! error value.

- The equation for the lognormal cumulative distribution function is:

$$\mathrm{LOGNORMDIST}(x,\mu,\sigma) = \mathrm{NORMSDIST}\left(\frac{\ln(x)-\mu}{\sigma}\right)$$

Example

LOGNORMDIST(4,3.5,1.2) equals 0.039084

LOOKUP (Vector Form)

The LOOKUP function has two syntax forms: vector and array.

A vector is a range of only one row or one column. The vector form of LOOKUP looks in a one-row or one-column range (known as a vector) for a value and returns a value from the same position in a second one-row or one-column range. Use this form of the LOOKUP function when you want to specify the range that contains the values you want to match. The other form of LOOKUP automatically looks in the first column or row.

Syntax 1

Vector form

LOOKUP(lookup_value,lookup_vector,result_vector)

Lookup_value   is a value that LOOKUP searches for in the first vector. Lookup_value can be a number, text, a logical value, or a name or reference that refers to a value.

Lookup_vector is a range that contains only one row or one column. The values in lookup_vector can be text, numbers, or logical values.

Important The values in lookup_vector must be placed in ascending order: ...,-2, -1, 0, 1, 2, ..., A-Z, FALSE, TRUE; otherwise, LOOKUP may not give the correct value. Uppercase and lowercase text are equivalent.

Result_vector is a range that contains only one row or column. It must be the same size as lookup_vector.

- If LOOKUP can't find the lookup_value, it matches the largest value in lookup_vector that is less than or equal to lookup_value.

- If lookup_value is smaller than the smallest value in lookup_vector, LOOKUP gives the #N/A error value.

Examples

	A	B	C
1	Frequency	Color	
2	4.14234	red	
3	4.19342	orange	
4	5.17234	yellow	
5	5.77343	green	
6	6.38987	blue	
7	7.31342	violet	

In the preceding worksheet:

LOOKUP(4.91,A2:A7,B2:B7) equals "orange"

LOOKUP(5.00,A2:A7,B2:B7) equals "orange"

LOOKUP(7.66,A2:A7,B2:B7) equals "violet"

LOOKUP(7.66E-14,A2:A7,B2:B7) equals #N/A, because 7.66E-14 is less than the smallest value in the lookup_vector A2:A7

LOOKUP (Array Form)

The LOOKUP function has two syntax forms: vector and array.

The array form of LOOKUP looks in the first row or column of an array for the specified value and returns a value from the same position in the last row or column of the array. Use this form of LOOKUP when the values you want to match are in the first row or column of the array. Use the other form of LOOKUP when you want to specify the location of the column or row.

Tip In general, it's best to use the HLOOKUP or VLOOKUP function instead of the array form of LOOKUP. This form of LOOKUP is provided for compatibility with other spreadsheet programs.

Syntax 2

Array form

LOOKUP(lookup_value,array)

Lookup_value   is a value that LOOKUP searches for in an array. Lookup_value can be a number, text, a logical value, or a name or reference that refers to a value.

- If LOOKUP can't find the lookup_value, it uses the largest value in the array that is less than or equal to lookup_value.

- If lookup_value is smaller than the smallest value in the first row or column (depending on the array dimensions), LOOKUP returns the #N/A error value.

Array   is a range of cells that contains text, numbers, or logical values that you want to compare with lookup_value.

The array form of LOOKUP is very similar to the HLOOKUP and VLOOKUP functions. The difference is that HLOOKUP searches for lookup_value in the first row, VLOOKUP searches in the first column, and LOOKUP searches according to the dimensions of array.

- If array covers an area that is wider than it is tall (more columns than rows), LOOKUP searches for lookup_value in the first row.

- If array is square or is taller than it is wide (more rows than columns), LOOKUP searches in the first column.

- With HLOOKUP and VLOOKUP, you can index down or across, but LOOKUP always selects the last value in the row or column.

Important The values must be placed in ascending order: ...,-2, -1, 0, 1, 2, ..., A-Z, FALSE, TRUE; otherwise, LOOKUP may not give the correct value. Uppercase and lowercase text are equivalent.

Examples

LOOKUP("C",{"a","b","c","d";1,2,3,4}) equals 3

LOOKUP("bump",{"a",1;"b",2;"c",3}) equals 2

LOWER

Converts all uppercase letters in a text string to lowercase.

Syntax

LOWER(text)

Text   is the text you want to convert to lowercase. LOWER does not change characters in text that are not letters.

Examples

LOWER("E. E. Cummings") equals "e. e. cummings"

LOWER("Apt. 2B") equals "apt. 2b"

LOWER is similar to PROPER and UPPER. Also see examples for PROPER.

MATCH

Returns the relative position of an item in an array that matches a specified value in a specified order. Use MATCH instead of one of the LOOKUP functions when you need the position of an item in a range instead of the item itself.

Syntax

MATCH(lookup_value,lookup_array,match_type)

Lookup_value   is the value you use to find the value you want in a table.

- Lookup_value is the value you want to match in lookup_array. For example, when you look up someone's number in a telephone book, you are using the person's name as the lookup value, but the telephone number is the value you want.

- Lookup_value can be a value (number, text, or logical value) or a cell reference to a number, text, or logical value.

Lookup_array   is a contiguous range of cells containing possible lookup values. Lookup_array can be an array or an array reference.

Lookup_array   is a contiguous range of cells containing possible lookup values. Lookup_array can be an array or an array reference.

Match_type   is the number -1, 0, or 1. Match_type specifies how Microsoft Excel matches lookup_value with values in lookup_array.

- If match_type is 1, MATCH finds the largest value that is less than or equal to lookup_value. Lookup_array must be placed in ascending order: ...-2, -1, 0, 1, 2, ..., A-Z, FALSE, TRUE.

- If match_type is 0, MATCH finds the first value that is exactly equal to lookup_value. Lookup_array can be in any order.

- If match_type is -1, MATCH finds the smallest value that is greater than or equal to lookup_value. Lookup_array must be placed in descending order: TRUE, FALSE, Z-A, ...,2, 1, 0, -1, -2, ..., and so on.

- If match_type is omitted, it is assumed to be 1.

Remarks

- MATCH returns the position of the matched value within lookup_array, not the value itself. For example, MATCH("b",{"a","b","c"},0) returns 2, the relative position of "b" within the array {"a","b","c"}.

- MATCH does not distinguish between uppercase and lowercase letters when matching text values.

- If MATCH is unsuccessful in finding a match, it returns the #N/A error value.

- If match_type is 0 and lookup_value is text, lookup_value can contain the wildcard characters, asterisk (*) and question mark (?). An asterisk matches any sequence of characters; a question mark matches any single character.

Examples

	A	B	C
1	Income (in Yen)	U.S. Dollars	U.S. Tax Rate
2	¥5,365,000.00	$37,000.00	21.50%
3	¥5,510,000.00	$38,000.00	21.67%
4	¥5,655,000.00	$39,000.00	21.84%
5	¥5,800,000.00	$40,000.00	21.99%
6	¥5,945,000.00	$41,000.00	22.14%
7	¥6,090,000.00	$42,000.00	22.28%
8	¥6,235,000.00	$43,000.00	22.41%

Note that C2:C8 contains text formatted as percent numbers.

In the preceding worksheet:

`MATCH(39000,B2:B8,1)` equals 3

`MATCH(38000,B2:B8,0)` equals 2

`MATCH(39000,B2:B8,-1)` equals the #N/A error value, because the range B2:B8 is ordered incorrectly for match_type -1 matching (the order must be descending to be correct).

Suppose Yen refers to A2:A8, YenDollar to A2:C8, and MyIncome to a cell containing the number ¥6,301,126.33. This formula:

`"Your tax rate is "&LOOKUP(MyIncome,YenDollar)&", which places you in tax bracket number "&MATCH(MyIncome,Yen)&"."`

produces this result:

"Your tax rate is 22.41%, which places you in tax bracket number 7."

MAX

Returns the largest value in a set of values.

Syntax

MAX(number1,number2, ...)

Number1,number2, ...   are 1 to 30 numbers for which you want to find the maximum value.

- You can specify arguments that are numbers, empty cells, logical values, or text representations of numbers. Arguments that are error values or text that cannot be translated into numbers cause errors.

- If an argument is an array or reference, only numbers in that array or reference are used. Empty cells, logical values, or text in the array or reference are ignored. If logical values and text must not be ignored, use MAXA instead.

- If the arguments contain no numbers, MAX returns 0 (zero).

Examples

If A1:A5 contains the numbers 10, 7, 9, 27, and 2, then:

`MAX(A1:A5)` equals 27

`MAX(A1:A5,30)` equals 30

MAXA

Returns the largest value in a list of arguments. Text and logical values such as TRUE and FALSE are compared as well as numbers.

MAXA is similar to MINA. For more information, see the examples for MINA.

Syntax

MAXA(value1,value2, ...)

Value1,value2, ...   are 1 to 30 values for which you want to find the largest value.

Remarks

- You can specify arguments that are numbers, empty cells, logical values, or text representations of numbers. Arguments that are error values cause errors. If the calculation must not include text or logical values, use the MAX worksheet function instead.

- If an argument is an array or reference, only values in that array or reference are used. Empty cells and text values in the array or reference are ignored.

- Arguments that contain TRUE evaluate as 1; arguments that contain text or FALSE evaluate as 0 (zero).

- If the arguments contain no values, MAXA returns 0 (zero).

Examples

If A1:A5 contains the numbers 10, 7, 9, 27, and 2, then:

MAXA(A1:A5) equals 27

MAXA(A1:A5,30) equals 30

If A1:A5 contains the values 0, 0.2, 0.5, 0.4, and TRUE, then:

MAXA(A1:A5) equals 1

MDETERM

Returns the matrix determinant of an array.

Syntax

MDETERM(array)

Array. is a numeric array with an equal number of rows and columns.

- Array can be given as a cell range, for example, A1:C3; as an array constant, such as {1,2,3;4,5,6;7,8,9}; or as a name to either of these.
- If any cells in array are empty or contain text, MDETERM returns the #VALUE! error value.
- MDETERM also returns #VALUE! if array does not have an equal number of rows and columns.

Remarks

- The matrix determinant is a number derived from the values in array. For a three-row, three-column array, A1:C3, the determinant is defined as:

  MDETERM(A1:C3) equals
  A1*(B2*C3-B3*C2) + A2*(B3*C1-B1*C3) + A3*(B1*C2-B2*C1)

- Matrix determinants are generally used for solving systems of mathematical equations that involve several variables.
- MDETERM is calculated with an accuracy of approximately 16 digits, which may lead to a small numeric error when the calculation is not complete. For example, the determinant of a singular matrix may differ from zero by 1E-16.

Examples

MDETERM({1,3,8,5;1,3,6,1;1,1,1,0;7,3,10,2}) equals 88

MDETERM({3,6,1;1,1,0;3,10,2}) equals 1

MDETERM({3,6;1,1}) equals -3

MDETERM({1,3,8,5;1,3,6,1}) equals #VALUE! because the array does not have an equal number of rows and columns.

MDURATION

Returns the modified duration for a security with an assumed par value of $100.

If this function is not available, run the Setup program to install the Analysis ToolPak. After you install the Analysis ToolPak, you must enable it by using the **Add-Ins** command on the **Tools** menu.

Syntax

MDURATION(settlement,maturity,coupon,yld,frequency,basis)

Settlement   is the security's settlement date. The security settlement date is the date after the issue date when the security is traded to the buyer.

Maturity   is the security's maturity date. The maturity date is the date when the security expires.

Coupon   is the security's annual coupon rate.

Yld   is the security's annual yield.

Frequency   is the number of coupon payments per year. For annual payments, frequency = 1; for semiannual, frequency = 2; for quarterly, frequency = 4.

Basis   is the type of day count basis to use.

Basis	Day count basis
0 or omitted	US (NASD) 30/360
1	Actual/actual
2	Actual/360
3	Actual/365
4	European 30/360

Remarks

- The settlement date is the date a buyer purchases a coupon, such as a bond. The maturity date is the date when a coupon expires. For example, suppose a 30-year bond is issued on January 1, 1996, and is purchased by a buyer six months later. The issue date would be January 1, 1996, the settlement date would be July 1, 1996, and the maturity date is January 1, 2026, which is 30 years after the January 1, 1996, issue date.

- Settlement, maturity, frequency, and basis are truncated to integers.

- If any argument is nonnumeric, MDURATION returns the #VALUE! error value.

- If settlement or maturity is not a valid date, MDURATION returns the #NUM! error value.

- If yld < 0 or if coupon < 0, MDURATION returns the #NUM! error value.

- If frequency is any number other than 1, 2, or 4, MDURATION returns the #NUM! error value.

- If basis < 0 or if basis > 4, MDURATION returns the #NUM! error value.

- If settlement ≥ maturity, MDURATION returns the #NUM! error value.

- Modified duration is defined as follows:

$$\text{MDURATION} = \frac{\text{DURATION}}{1 + \left(\dfrac{\text{Market yield}}{\text{Coupon payments per year}} \right)}$$

Example

A bond has the following terms:

January 1, 1986, settlement date
January 1, 1994, maturity date
8.0 percent coupon
9.0 percent yield
Frequency is semiannual
Actual/actual basis

The modified duration (in the 1900 date system) is:

`MDURATION("1/1/86","1/1/94",0.08,0.09,2,1)` equals 5.73567

MEDIAN

Returns the median of the given numbers. The median is the number in the middle of a set of numbers; that is, half the numbers have values that are greater than the median, and half have values that are less.

Syntax

MEDIAN(number1,number2, ...)

Number1,number2, ... are 1 to 30 numbers for which you want the median.

- The arguments should be either numbers or names, arrays, or references that contain numbers. Microsoft Excel examines all the numbers in each reference or array argument.

- If an array or reference argument contains text, logical values, or empty cells, those values are ignored; however, cells with the value zero are included.

Remarks

If there is an even number of numbers in the set, then MEDIAN calculates the average of the two numbers in the middle. See the second example following.

Examples

`MEDIAN(1, 2, 3, 4, 5)` equals 3

`MEDIAN(1, 2, 3, 4, 5, 6)` equals 3.5, the average of 3 and 4

MID

Returns a specific number of characters from a text string, starting at the position you specify.

Syntax

MID(text,start_num,num_chars)

Text   is the text string containing the characters you want to extract.

Start_num   is the position of the first character you want to extract in text. The first character in text has start_num 1, and so on.

- If start_num is greater than the length of text, MID returns "" (empty text).

- If start_num is less than the length of text, but start_num plus num_chars exceeds the length of text, MID returns the characters up to the end of text.

- If start_num is less than 1, MID returns the #VALUE! error value.

Num_chars   specifies how many characters to return from text. If num_chars is negative, MID returns the #VALUE! error value.

Examples

MID("Fluid Flow", 1, 5) equals "Fluid"

MID("Fluid Flow", 7, 20) equals "Flow"

MID("1234", 5, 5) equals "" (empty text)

Also see the examples for CODE and FIND.

MIN

Returns the smallest number in a set of values.

Syntax

MIN(number1,number2, ...)

Number1,number2, ...   are 1 to 30 numbers for which you want to find the minimum value.

- You can specify arguments that are numbers, empty cells, logical values, or text representations of numbers. Arguments that are error values or text that cannot be translated into numbers cause errors.

- If an argument is an array or reference, only numbers in that array or reference are used. Empty cells, logical values, or text in the array or reference are ignored. If logical values and text should not be ignored, use MINA instead.

- If the arguments contain no numbers, MIN returns 0.

Examples

If A1:A5 contains the numbers 10, 7, 9, 27, and 2, then:

`MIN(A1:A5)` equals 2

`MIN(A1:A5, 0)` equals 0

MIN is similar to MAX. Also see the examples for MAX.

MINA

Returns the smallest value in the list of arguments. Text and logical values such as TRUE and FALSE are compared as well as numbers.

Syntax

MINA(value1,value2, ...)

Value1,value2, ... are 1 to 30 values for which you want to find the smallest value.

- You can specify arguments that are numbers, empty cells, logical values, or text representations of numbers. Arguments that are error values cause errors. If the calculation must not include text or logical values, use the MIN worksheet function instead.

- If an argument is an array or reference, only values in that array or reference are used. Empty cells and text values in the array or reference are ignored.

- Arguments that contain TRUE evaluate as 1; arguments that contain text or FALSE evaluate as 0 (zero).

- If the arguments contain no values, MINA returns 0.

Examples

If A1:A5 contains the numbers 10, 7, 9, 27, and 2, then:

`MINA(A1:A5)` equals 2

`MINA(A1:A5, 0)` equals 0

If A1:A5 contains the values FALSE, 0.2, 0.5, 0.4, and 0.8, then:

`MINA(A1:A5)` equals 0

MINA is similar to MAXA. Also see the examples for MAXA.

MINUTE

Returns the minute corresponding to serial_number. The minute is given as an integer, ranging from 0 to 59.

Syntax

MINUTE(serial_number)

Serial_number is the date-time code used by Microsoft Excel for date and time calculations. You can give serial_number as text, such as "16:48:00" or "4:48:00 PM", instead of as a number. The text is automatically converted to a serial number. For more information about serial_number, see NOW.

Remarks

Microsoft Excel for Windows and Microsoft Excel for the Macintosh use different date systems as their default. For more information, see NOW.

Examples

MINUTE("4:48:00 PM") equals 48

MINUTE(0.01) equals 14

MINUTE(4.02) equals 28

MINVERSE

Returns the inverse matrix for the matrix stored in an array.

Syntax

MINVERSE(array)

Array is a numeric array with an equal number of rows and columns.

- Array can be given as a cell range, such as A1:C3; as an array constant, such as {1,2,3;4,5,6;7,8,9}; or as a name for either of these.

- If any cells in array are empty or contain text, MINVERSE returns the #VALUE! error value.

- MINVERSE also returns the #VALUE! error value if array does not have an equal number of rows and columns.

Remarks

- Formulas that return arrays must be entered as array formulas.

- Inverse matrices, like determinants, are generally used for solving systems of mathematical equations involving several variables. The product of a matrix and its inverse is the identity matrix—the square array in which the diagonal values equal 1, and all other values equal 0.

- As an example of how a two-row, two-column matrix is calculated, suppose that the range A1:B2 contains the letters a, b, c, and d that represent any four numbers. The following table shows the inverse of the matrix A1:B2.

	Column A	Column B
Row 1	d/(a*d-b*c)	b/(b*c-a*d)
Row 2	c/(b*c-a*d)	a/(a*d-b*c)

- MINVERSE is calculated with an accuracy of approximately 16 digits, which may lead to a small numeric error when the cancellation is not complete.

- Some square matrices cannot be inverted and will return the #NUM! error value with MINVERSE. The determinant for a noninvertible matrix is 0.

Examples

MINVERSE({4,-1;2,0}) equals {0,0.5;-1,2}

MINVERSE({1,2,1;3,4,-1;0,2,0}) equals {0.25,0.25,-0.75;0,0,0.5;0.75,-0.25, -0.25}

Tip   Use the INDEX function to access individual elements from the inverse matrix.

MIRR

Returns the modified internal rate of return for a series of periodic cash flows. MIRR considers both the cost of the investment and the interest received on reinvestment of cash.

Syntax

MIRR(values,finance_rate,reinvest_rate)

Values   is an array or a reference to cells that contain numbers. These numbers represent a series of payments (negative values) and income (positive values) occurring at regular periods.

- Values must contain at least one positive value and one negative value to calculate the modified internal rate of return. Otherwise, MIRR returns the #DIV/0! error value.

- If an array or reference argument contains text, logical values, or empty cells, those values are ignored; however, cells with the value zero are included.

Finance_rate   is the interest rate you pay on the money used in the cash flows.

Reinvest_rate   is the interest rate you receive on the cash flows as you reinvest them.

Remarks

- MIRR uses the order of values to interpret the order of cash flows. Be sure to enter your payment and income values in the sequence you want and with the correct signs (positive values for cash received, negative values for cash paid).

- If n is the number of cash flows in values, frate is the finance_rate, and rrate is the reinvest_rate, then the formula for MIRR is:

$$\left(\frac{-NPV(rrate, values[positive]) * (1 + rrate)^n}{NPV(frate, values[negative]) * (1 + frate)} \right)^{\frac{1}{n-1}} - 1$$

Examples

Suppose you're a commercial fisherman just completing your fifth year of operation. Five years ago, you borrowed $120,000 at 10 percent annual interest to purchase a boat. Your catches have yielded $39,000, $30,000, $21,000, $37,000, and $46,000. During these years you reinvested your profits, earning 12 percent annually. On a worksheet, your loan amount is entered as -$120,000 in B1, and your five annual profits are entered in B2:B6.

To calculate the investment's modified rate of return after five years:

MIRR(B1:B6, 10%, 12%) equals 12.61 percent

To calculate the modified rate of return after three years:

MIRR(B1:B4, 10%, 12%) equals -4.80 percent

To calculate the five-year modified rate of return based on a reinvest_rate of 14 percent

MIRR(B1:B6, 10%, 14%) equals 13.48 percent

MMULT

Returns the matrix product of two arrays. The result is an array with the same number of rows as array1 and the same number of columns as array2.

Syntax

MMULT(array1,array2)

Array1,array2   are the arrays you want to multiply.

- The number of columns in array1 must be the same as the number of rows in array2, and both arrays must contain only numbers.
- Array1 and array2 can be given as cell ranges, array constants, or references.
- If any cells are empty or contain text, or if the number of columns in array1 is different from the number of rows in array2, MMULT returns the #VALUE! error value.

Remarks

- The matrix product array a of two arrays b and c is:

$$a_{ij} = \sum_{k=1}^{n} b_{ik} c_{kj}$$

where i is the row number, and j is the column number.

- Formulas that return arrays must be entered as array formulas.

Examples

MMULT({1,3;7,2}, {2,0;0,2}) equals {2,6;14,4}

MMULT({3,0;2,0}, {2,0;0,2}) equals {6,0;4,0}

MMULT({1,3,0;7,2,0;1,0,0}, {2,0;0,2}) equals #VALUE!, because the first array has three columns, and the second array has only two rows.

MOD

Returns the remainder after number is divided by divisor. The result has the same sign as divisor.

Syntax

MOD(number,divisor)

Number   is the number for which you want to find the remainder.

Divisor   is the number by which you want to divide number. If divisor is 0, MOD returns the #DIV/0! error value.

Remarks

The MOD function can be expressed in terms of the INT function:

```
MOD(n, d) = n - d*INT(n/d)
```

Examples

MOD(3, 2) equals 1

MOD(-3, 2) equals 1

MOD(3, -2) equals -1

MOD(-3, -2) equals -1

MODE

Returns the most frequently occurring, or repetitive, value in an array or range of data. Like MEDIAN, MODE is a location measure.

Syntax

MODE(number1,number2, ...)

Number1,number2, ... are 1 to 30 arguments for which you want to calculate the mode. You can also use a single array or a reference to an array instead of arguments separated by commas.

Remarks

- The arguments should be numbers, names, arrays, or references that contain numbers.

- If an array or reference argument contains text, logical values, or empty cells, those values are ignored; however, cells with the value zero are included.

- If the data set contains no duplicate data points, MODE returns the #N/A error value.

In a set of values, the mode is the most frequently occurring value; the median is the middle value; and the mean is the average value. No single measure of central tendency provides a complete picture of the data. Suppose data is clustered in three areas, half around a single low value, and half around two large values. Both AVERAGE and MEDIAN may return a value in the relatively empty middle, and MODE may return the dominant low value.

Example

MODE({5.6, 4, 4, 3, 2, 4}) equals 4

MONTH

Returns the month corresponding to serial_number. The month is given as an integer, ranging from 1 (January) to 12 (December).

Syntax

MONTH(serial_number)

Serial_number is the date-time code used by Microsoft Excel for date and time calculations. You can give serial_number as text, such as "4-15-1993" or "15-Apr-1993", instead of as a number. The text is automatically converted to a serial number. For more information about serial_number, see NOW.

Remarks

Microsoft Excel for Windows and Microsoft Excel for the Macintosh use different date systems as their default. For more information, see NOW.

Examples

MONTH("6-May") equals 5

MONTH(366) equals 12

MONTH(367) equals 1

MROUND

Returns a number rounded to the desired multiple.

If this function is not available, run the Setup program to install the Analysis ToolPak. After you install the Analysis ToolPak, you must enable it by using the **Add-Ins** command on the **Tools** menu.

Syntax

MROUND(number,multiple)

Number is the value to round.

Multiple is the multiple to which you want to round number.

Remarks

MROUND rounds up, away from zero, if the remainder of dividing number by multiple is greater than or equal to half the value of multiple.

Examples

MROUND(10, 3) equals 9

MROUND(-10, -3) equals -9

MROUND(1.3, 0.2) equals 1.4

MROUND(5, -2) equals #NUM!

MULTINOMIAL

Returns the ratio of the factorial of a sum of values to the product of factorials.

If this function is not available, run the Setup program to install the Analysis ToolPak. After you install the Analysis ToolPak, you must enable it by using the **Add-Ins** command on the **Tools** menu.

Syntax

MULTINOMIAL(number1,number2, ...)

Number1,number2, ...   are 1 to 29 values for which you want the multinomial.

Remarks

- If any argument is nonnumeric, MULTINOMIAL returns the #VALUE! error value.

- If any argument is less than one, MULTINOMIAL returns the #NUM! error value.

- The multinomial is:

$$MULTINOMIAL(a,b,c) = \frac{(a+b+c)!}{a!b!c!}$$

Example

MULTINOMIAL(2, 3, 4) equals 1260

N

Returns a value converted to a number.

Syntax

N(value)

Value   is the value you want converted. N converts values listed in the following table.

If value is or refers to	N returns
A number	That number
A date, in one of the built-in date formats available in Microsoft Excel	The serial number of that date
TRUE	1
Anything else	0

Remarks

It is not generally necessary to use the N function in a formula, because Microsoft Excel automatically converts values as necessary. This function is provided for compatibility with other spreadsheet programs.

Examples

If A1 contains "7", A2 contains "Even", and A3 contains "TRUE", then:

N(A1) equals 7

N(A2) equals 0, because A2 contains text

N(A3) equals 1, because A3 contains TRUE

N("7") equals 0, because "7" is text

N("4/17/91") equals 0, because "4/17/91" is text

NA

Returns the error value #N/A. #N/A is the error value that means "no value is available." Use NA to mark empty cells. By entering #N/A in cells where you are missing information, you can avoid the problem of unintentionally including empty cells in your calculations. (When a formula refers to a cell containing #N/A, the formula returns the #N/A error value.)

Syntax

NA( )

Remarks

- You must include the empty parentheses with the function name. Otherwise, Microsoft Excel will not recognize it as a function.

- You can also type the value #N/A directly into a cell. The NA function is provided for compatibility with other spreadsheet programs.

NEGBINOMDIST

Returns the negative binomial distribution. NEGBINOMDIST returns the probability that there will be number_f failures before the number_s-th success, when the constant probability of a success is probability_s. This function is similar to the binomial distribution, except that the number of successes is fixed, and the number of trials is variable. Like the binomial, trials are assumed to be independent.

For example, you need to find 10 people with excellent reflexes, and you know the probability that a candidate has these qualifications is 0.3. NEGBINOMDIST calculates the probability that you will interview a certain number of unqualified candidates before finding all 10 qualified candidates.

Syntax

NEGBINOMDIST(number_f,number_s,probability_s)

Number_f   is the number of failures.

Number_s   is the threshold number of successes.

Probability_s   is the probability of a success.

Remarks

- Number_f and number_s are truncated to integers.

- If any argument is nonnumeric, NEGBINOMDIST returns the #VALUE! error value.

- If probability_s < 0 or if probability > 1, NEGBINOMDIST returns the #NUM! error value.

- If (number_f + number_s - 1) ≤ 0, NEGBINOMDIST returns the #NUM! error value.

- The equation for the negative binomial distribution is:

$$nb(x;r,p) = \binom{x+r-1}{r-1} p^r (1-p)^x$$

where:

x is number_f, r is number_s, and p is probability_s.

Example

`NEGBINOMDIST(10,5,0.25)` equals 0.055049

NETWORKDAYS

Returns the number of whole working days between start_date and end_date. Working days exclude weekends and any dates identified in holidays. Use NETWORKDAYS to calculate employee benefits that accrue based on the number of days worked during a specific term.

If this function is not available, run the Setup program to install the Analysis ToolPak. After you install the Analysis ToolPak, you must enable it by using the **Add-Ins** command on the **Tools** menu.

Syntax

NETWORKDAYS(start_date,end_date,holidays)

Start_date   is a date that represents the start date.

End_date   is a date that represents the end date.

Holidays   is an optional range of one or more dates to exclude from the working calendar, such as state and federal holidays and floating holidays.

Remarks

- If any argument is nonnumeric, NETWORKDAYS returns the #VALUE! error value.

- If any argument is not a valid date, NETWORKDAYS returns the #NUM! error value.

Example

```
NETWORKDAYS(DATEVALUE("10/01/91"), DATEVALUE("12/01/91"),
DATEVALUE("11/28/91")) equals 43
```

NOMINAL

Returns the nominal annual interest rate, given the effective rate and the number of compounding periods per year.

If this function is not available, run the Setup program to install the Analysis ToolPak. After you install the Analysis ToolPak, you must enable it by using the **Add-Ins** command on the **Tools** menu.

Syntax

NOMINAL(effect_rate,npery)

Effect_rate   is the effective interest rate.

Npery   is the number of compounding periods per year.

Remarks

- Npery is truncated to an integer.
- If either argument is nonnumeric, NOMINAL returns the #VALUE! error value.
- If effect_rate ≤ 0 or if npery < 1, NOMINAL returns the #NUM! error value.
- NOMINAL is related to EFFECT as shown in the following equation:

$$EFFECT = \left(1 + \frac{Nominal\_rate}{Npery}\right)^{Npery} - 1$$

Example

NOMINAL(5.3543%,4) equals 0.0525 or 5.25 percent

NORMDIST

Returns the normal cumulative distribution for the specified mean and standard deviation. This function has a very wide range of applications in statistics, including hypothesis testing.

Syntax

NORMDIST(x,mean,standard_dev,cumulative)

X   is the value for which you want the distribution.

Mean   is the arithmetic mean of the distribution.

Standard_dev   is the standard deviation of the distribution.

Cumulative   is a logical value that determines the form of the function. If cumulative is TRUE, NORMDIST returns the cumulative distribution function; if FALSE, it returns the probability mass function.

Remarks

- If mean or standard_dev is nonnumeric, NORMDIST returns the #VALUE! error value.
- If standard_dev ≤ 0, NORMDIST returns the #NUM! error value.
- If mean = 0 and standard_dev = 1, NORMDIST returns the standard normal distribution, NORMSDIST.
- The equation for the normal density function is:

$$f(x; \mu, \sigma) = \frac{1}{\sqrt{2\pi}\sigma} e^{-\left(\frac{(x-\mu)^2}{2\sigma^2}\right)}$$

Example

```
NORMDIST(42,40,1.5,TRUE) equals 0.908789
```

NORMINV

Returns the inverse of the normal cumulative distribution for the specified mean and standard deviation.

Syntax

NORMINV(probability,mean,standard_dev)

Probability   is a probability corresponding to the normal distribution.

Mean   is the arithmetic mean of the distribution.

Standard_dev   is the standard deviation of the distribution.

Remarks

- If any argument is nonnumeric, NORMINV returns the #VALUE! error value.
- If probability < 0 or if probability > 1, NORMINV returns the #NUM! error value.
- If standard_dev ≤ 0, NORMINV returns the #NUM! error value.

NORMINV uses the standard normal distribution if mean = 0 and standard_dev = 1 (see NORMSINV).

NORMINV uses an iterative technique for calculating the function. Given a probability value, NORMINV iterates until the result is accurate to within ± 3x10^-7. If NORMINV does not converge after 100 iterations, the function returns the #N/A error value.

Example

```
NORMINV(0.908789,40,1.5) equals 42
```

NORMSDIST

Returns the standard normal cumulative distribution function. The distribution has a mean of 0 (zero) and a standard deviation of one. Use this function in place of a table of standard normal curve areas.

Syntax

NORMSDIST(z)

Z   is the value for which you want the distribution.

Remarks

- If z is nonnumeric, NORMSDIST returns the #VALUE! error value.

- The equation for the standard normal density function is:

$$f(z;0,1) = \frac{1}{\sqrt{2\pi}}e^{-\frac{z^2}{2}}$$

Example

NORMSDIST(1.333333) equals 0.908789

NORMSINV

Returns the inverse of the standard normal cumulative distribution. The distribution has a mean of zero and a standard deviation of one.

Syntax

NORMSINV(probability)

Probability   is a probability corresponding to the normal distribution.

Remarks

- If probability is nonnumeric, NORMSINV returns the #VALUE! error value.

- If probability < 0 or if probability > 1, NORMSINV returns the #NUM! error value.

NORMSINV uses an iterative technique for calculating the function. Given a probability value, NORMSINV iterates until the result is accurate to within $\pm 3\times10^{-7}$. If NORMSINV does not converge after 100 iterations, the function returns the #N/A error value.

Example

NORMSINV(0.908789) equals 1.3333

NOT

Reverses the value of its argument. Use NOT when you want to make sure a value is not equal to one particular value.

Syntax

NOT(logical)

Logical   is a value or expression that can be evaluated to TRUE or FALSE. If logical is FALSE, NOT returns TRUE; if logical is TRUE, NOT returns FALSE.

Examples

NOT(FALSE) equals TRUE

NOT(1+1=2) equals FALSE

NOW

Returns the serial number of the current date and time.

Syntax

NOW( )

Remarks

- Microsoft Excel 97 for Windows and Microsoft Excel 97 for the Macintosh use different default date systems. Microsoft Excel for Windows uses the 1900 date system, in which serial numbers correspond to the dates January 1, 1900, through December 31, 9999. Microsoft Excel for the Macintosh uses the 1904 date system, in which serial numbers correspond to the dates January 1, 1904, through December 31, 9999.

- Numbers to the right of the decimal point in the serial number represent the time; numbers to the left represent the date. For example, in the 1900 date system, the serial number 367.5 represents the date-time combination 12:00 P.M., January 1, 1901.

- You can change the date system by selecting or clearing the **1904 date system** check box on the **Calculation** tab of the **Options** command (**Tools** menu).

- The date system is changed automatically when you open a document from another platform. For example, if you are working in Microsoft Excel for Windows and you open a document created in Microsoft Excel for the Macintosh, the **1904 date system** check box is selected automatically.

- The NOW function changes only when the worksheet is calculated or when a macro that contains the function is run. It is not updated continuously.

Examples

If you are using the 1900 date system and your computer's built-in clock is set to 12:30:00 P.M., 1-Jan-1987, then:

NOW( ) equals 31778.52083

Ten minutes later:

NOW( ) equals 31778.52778

NPER

Returns the number of periods for an investment based on periodic, constant payments and a constant interest rate.

Syntax

NPER(**rate**, pmt, **pv**, fv, type)

For a more complete description of the arguments in NPER and for more information about annuity functions, see PV.

Rate   is the interest rate per period.

Pmt   is the payment made each period; it cannot change over the life of the annuity. Typically, pmt contains principal and interest but no other fees or taxes.

Pv   is the present value, or the lump-sum amount that a series of future payments is worth right now.

Fv   is the future value, or a cash balance you want to attain after the last payment is made. If fv is omitted, it is assumed to be 0 (the future value of a loan, for example, is 0).

Type   is the number 0 or 1 and indicates when payments are due.

Set type equal to	If payments are due
0 or omitted	At the end of the period
1	At the beginning of the period

Examples

NPER(12%/12, -100, -1000, 10000, 1) equals 60

NPER(1%, -100, -1000, 10000) equals 60

NPER(1%, -100, 1000) equals 11

NPV

Calculates the net present value of an investment by using a discount rate and a series of future payments (negative values) and income (positive values).

Syntax

NPV(rate,value1,value2, ...)

Rate   is the rate of discount over the length of one period.

Value1,value2, ...   are 1 to 29 arguments representing the payments and income.

- Value1,value2, ... must be equally spaced in time and occur at the end of each period.
- NPV uses the order of value1,value2, ... to interpret the order of cash flows. Be sure to enter your payment and income values in the correct sequence.
- Arguments that are numbers, empty cells, logical values, or text representations of numbers are counted; arguments that are error values or text that cannot be translated into numbers are ignored.
- If an argument is an array or reference, only numbers in that array or reference are counted. Empty cells, logical values, text, or error values in the array or reference are ignored.

Remarks

- The NPV investment begins one period before the date of the value1 cash flow and ends with the last cash flow in the list. The NPV calculation is based on future cash flows. If your first cash flow occurs at the beginning of the first period, the first value must be added to the NPV result, not included in the values arguments. For more information, see the examples below.
- If n is the number of cash flows in the list of values, the formula for NPV is:

$$NPV = \sum_{i=1}^{n} \frac{values_i}{(1+rate)^i}$$

- NPV is similar to the PV function (present value). The primary difference between PV and NPV is that PV allows cash flows to begin either at the end or at the beginning of the period. Unlike the variable NPV cash flow values, PV cash flows must be constant throughout the investment. For information about annuities and financial functions, see PV.
- NPV is also related to the IRR function (internal rate of return). IRR is the rate for which NPV equals zero: NPV(IRR(...), ...) = 0.

Examples

Suppose you're considering an investment in which you pay $10,000 one year from today and receive an annual income of $3,000, $4,200, and $6,800 in the three years that follow. Assuming an annual discount rate of 10 percent, the net present value of this investment is:

`NPV(10%, -10000, 3000, 4200, 6800)` equals $1,188.44

In the preceding example, you include the initial $10,000 cost as one of the values, because the payment occurs at the end of the first period.

Consider an investment that starts at the beginning of the first period. Suppose you're interested in buying a shoe store. The cost of the business is $40,000, and you expect to receive the following income for the first five years of operation: $8,000, $9,200, $10,000, $12,000, and $14,500. The annual discount rate is 8 percent. This might represent the rate of inflation or the interest rate of a competing investment.

If the cost and income figures from the shoe store are entered in B1 through B6 respectively, then net present value of the shoe store investment is given by:

`NPV(8%, B2:B6)+B1` equals $1,922.06

In the preceding example, you don't include the initial $40,000 cost as one of the values, because the payment occurs at the beginning of the first period.

Suppose your shoe store's roof collapses during the sixth year and you assume a loss of $9000 for that year. The net present value of the shoe store investment after six years is given by:

`NPV(8%, B2:B6, -9000)+B1` equals -$3,749.47

OCT2BIN

Converts an octal number to binary.

If this function is not available, run the Setup program to install the Analysis ToolPak. After you install the Analysis ToolPak, you must enable it by using the **Add-Ins** command on the **Tools** menu.

Syntax

OCT2BIN(number,places)

Number   is the octal number you want to convert. Number may not contain more than 10 characters. The most significant bit of number is the sign bit. The remaining 29 bits are magnitude bits. Negative numbers are represented using two's-complement notation.

Places   is the number of characters to use. If places is omitted, OCT2BIN uses the minimum number of characters necessary. Places is useful for padding the return value with leading 0s (zeros).

Remarks

- If number is negative, OCT2BIN ignores places and returns a 10-character binary number.
- If number is negative, it cannot be less than or equal to 7777777000, and if number is positive, it cannot be greater than 777.
- If number is not a valid octal number, OCT2BIN returns the #NUM! error value.
- If OCT2BIN requires more than places characters, it returns the #NUM! error value.
- If places is not an integer, it is truncated.
- If places is nonnumeric, OCT2BIN returns the #VALUE! error value.
- If places is negative, OCT2BIN returns the #NUM! error value.

Examples

OCT2BIN(3, 3) equals 011

OCT2BIN(7777777000) equals 1000000000

OCT2DEC

Converts an octal number to decimal.

If this function is not available, run the Setup program to install the Analysis ToolPak. After you install the Analysis ToolPak, you must enable it by using the **Add-Ins** command on the **Tools** menu.

Syntax

OCT2DEC(number)

Number   is the octal number you want to convert. Number may not contain more than 10 octal characters (30 bits). The most significant bit of number is the sign bit. The remaining 29 bits are magnitude bits. Negative numbers are represented using two's-complement notation.

Remarks

If number is not a valid octal number, OCT2DEC returns the #NUM! error value.

Examples

OCT2DEC(54) equals 44

OCT2DEC(7777777533) equals -165

OCT2HEX

Converts an octal number to hexadecimal.

If this function is not available, run the Setup program to install the Analysis ToolPak. After you install the Analysis ToolPak, you must enable it by using the **Add-Ins** command on the **Tools** menu.

Syntax

OCT2HEX(number,places)

Number   is the octal number you want to convert. Number may not contain more than 10 octal characters (30 bits). The most significant bit of number is the sign bit. The remaining 29 bits are magnitude bits. Negative numbers are represented using two's-complement notation.

Places   is the number of characters to use. If places is omitted, OCT2HEX uses the minimum number of characters necessary. Places is useful for padding the return value with leading 0s (zeros).

Remarks

- If number is negative, OCT2HEX ignores places and returns a 10-character hexadecimal number.
- If number is not a valid octal number, OCT2HEX returns the #NUM! error value.
- If OCT2HEX requires more than places characters, it returns the #NUM! error value.
- If places is not an integer, it is truncated.
- If places is nonnumeric, OCT2HEX returns the #VALUE! error value.
- If places is negative, OCT2HEX returns the #NUM! error value.

Examples

OCT2HEX(100, 4) equals 0040

OCT2HEX(7777777533) equals FFFFFFFF5B

ODD

Returns number rounded up to the nearest odd integer.

Syntax

ODD(number)

Number   is the value to round.

Remarks

- If number is nonnumeric, ODD returns the #VALUE! error value.
- Regardless of the sign of number, a value is rounded up when adjusted away from zero. If number is an odd integer, no rounding occurs.

Examples

ODD(1.5) equals 3

ODD(3) equals 3

ODD(2) equals 3

ODD(-1) equals -1

ODD(-2) equals -3

ODDFPRICE

Returns the price per $100 face value of a security having an odd (short or long) first period.

If this function is not available, run the Setup program to install the Analysis ToolPak. After you install the Analysis ToolPak, you must enable it by using the **Add-Ins** command on the **Tools** menu.

Syntax

ODDFPRICE(settlement,maturity,issue,first_coupon,rate,yld,redemption,frequency,basis)

Settlement   is the security's settlement date. The security settlement date is the date after the issue date when the security is traded to the buyer.

Maturity   is the security's maturity date. The maturity date is the date when the security expires.

Issue   is the security's issue date.

First_coupon   is the security's first coupon date.

Rate   is the security's interest rate.

Yld   is the security's annual yield.

Redemption   is the security's redemption value per $100 face value.

Frequency   is the number of coupon payments per year. For annual payments, frequency = 1; for semiannual, frequency = 2; for quarterly, frequency = 4.

Basis   is the type of day count basis to use.

Basis	Day count basis
0 or omitted	US (NASD) 30/360
1	Actual/actual
2	Actual/360
3	Actual/365
4	European 30/360

Remarks

- The settlement date is the date a buyer purchases a coupon, such as a bond. The maturity date is the date when a coupon expires. For example, suppose a 30-year bond is issued on January 1, 1996, and is purchased by a buyer six months later. The issue date would be January 1, 1996, the settlement date would be July 1, 1996, and the maturity date would be January 1, 2026, which is 30 years after the January 1, 1996, issue date.

- Settlement, maturity, issue, first_coupon, and basis are truncated to integers.

- If any argument is nonnumeric, ODDFPRICE returns the #VALUE! error value.

- If settlement, maturity, issue, or first_coupon is not a valid date, ODDFPRICE returns the #NUM! error value.

- If rate < 0 or if yld < 0, ODDFPRICE returns the #NUM! error value.

- If basis < 0 or if basis > 4, ODDFPRICE returns the #NUM! error value.

- The following date condition must be satisfied; otherwise, ODDFPRICE returns the #NUM! error value:

  maturity > first_coupon > settlement > issue

- ODDFPRICE is calculated as follows:

Odd short first coupon:

$$ODDFPRICE = \left[\cfrac{redemption}{\left(1 + \cfrac{yld}{frequency}\right)^{\left(N-1+\frac{DSC}{E}\right)}} \right] + \left[\cfrac{100 \times \cfrac{rate}{frequency} \times \cfrac{DFC}{E}}{\left(1 + \cfrac{yld}{frequency}\right)^{\frac{DSC}{E}}} \right]$$

$$+ \sum_{k=2}^{N} \left[\cfrac{100 \times \cfrac{rate}{frequency}}{\left(1 + \cfrac{yld}{frequency}\right)^{\left(k-1+\frac{DSC}{E}\right)}} \right]$$

$$- \left[100 \times \cfrac{rate}{frequency} \times \cfrac{A}{E} \right]$$

Where:

A = number of days from the beginning of the coupon period to the settlement date (accrued days).

DSC = number of days from the settlement to the next coupon date.

DFC = number of days from the beginning of the odd first coupon to the first coupon date.

E = number of days in the coupon period.

N = number of coupons payable between the settlement date and the redemption date. (If this number contains a fraction, it is raised to the next whole number.)

Odd long first coupon:

$$ODDFPRICE = \left[\frac{redemption}{\left(1+\dfrac{yld}{frequency}\right)^{\left(N+N_q+\frac{DSC}{E}\right)}}\right]$$

$$+ \left[\frac{100 \times \dfrac{rate}{frequency} \times \left[\displaystyle\sum_{j=1}^{NC}\frac{DC_j}{NL_j}\right]}{\left(1+\dfrac{yld}{frequency}\right)^{\left(N_q+\frac{DSC}{E}\right)}}\right]$$

$$+ \left[\displaystyle\sum_{k=2}^{N}\frac{100 \times \dfrac{rate}{frequency}}{\left(1+\dfrac{yld}{frequency}\right)^{\left(k-N_q+\frac{DSC}{E}\right)}}\right]$$

$$- \left[100 \times \frac{rate}{frequency} \times \displaystyle\sum_{i=1}^{NC}\frac{A_i}{NL_i}\right]$$

Where:

A_i = number of days from the beginning of the ith, or last, quasi-coupon period within odd period.

DC_i = number of days from dated date (or issue date) to first quasi-coupon (i = 1) or number of days in quasi-coupon (i = 2, ..., i = NC).

DSC = number of days from settlement to next coupon date.

E = number of days in coupon period.

N = number of coupons payable between the first real coupon date and redemption date. (If this number contains a fraction, it is raised to the next whole number.)

NC = number of quasi-coupon periods that fit in odd period. (If this number contains a fraction, it is raised to the next whole number.)

NL_i = normal length in days of the full ith, or last, quasi-coupon period within odd period.

N_q = number of whole quasi-coupon periods between settlement date and first coupon.

Example

A treasury bond has the following terms:

November 11, 1986, settlement date
March 1, 1999, maturity date
October 15, 1986, issue date
March 1, 1987, first coupon date
7.85 percent coupon
6.25 percent yield
$100 redemptive value
Frequency is semiannual
Actual/actual basis

The price per $100 face value of a security having an odd (short or long) first period (in the 1900 date system) is:

```
ODDFPRICE("11/11/86","3/1/99","10/15/86","3/1/87",0.0785,0.0625,
100,2,1) equals 113.597717
```

ODDFYIELD

Returns the yield of a security that has an odd (short or long) first period.

If this function is not available, run the Setup program to install the Analysis ToolPak. After you install the Analysis ToolPak, you must enable it by using the **Add-Ins** command on the **Tools** menu.

Syntax

ODDFYIELD(settlement,maturity,issue,first_coupon,rate,pr,redemption,frequency,basis)

Settlement is the security's settlement date. The security settlement date is the date after the issue date when the security is traded to the buyer.

Maturity is the security's maturity date. The maturity date is the date when the security expires.

Issue is the security's issue date.

First_coupon is the security's first coupon date.

Rate is the security's interest rate.

Pr is the security's price.

Redemption is the security's redemption value per $100 face value.

Frequency is the number of coupon payments per year. For annual payments, frequency = 1; for semiannual, frequency = 2; for quarterly, frequency = 4.

Basis   is the type of day count basis to use.

Basis	Day count basis
0 or omitted	US (NASD) 30/360
1	Actual/actual
2	Actual/360
3	Actual/365
4	European 30/360

Remarks

- The settlement date is the date a buyer purchases a coupon, such as a bond. The maturity date is the date when a coupon expires. For example, suppose a 30-year bond is issued on January 1, 1996, and is purchased by a buyer six months later. The issue date would be January 1, 1996, the settlement date would be July 1, 1996, and the maturity date would be January 1, 2026, which is 30 years after the January 1, 1996, issue date.

- Settlement, maturity, issue, first_coupon, and basis are truncated to integers.

- If any argument is nonnumeric, ODDFYIELD returns the #VALUE! error value.

- If settlement, maturity, issue, or first_coupon is not a valid date, ODDFYIELD returns the #NUM! error value.

- If rate < 0 or if pr ≤ 0, ODDFYIELD returns the #NUM! error value.

- If basis < 0 or if basis > 4, ODDFYIELD returns the #NUM! error value.

- The following date condition must be satisfied; otherwise, ODDFYIELD returns the #NUM! error value:

maturity > first_coupon > settlement > issue

- Microsoft Excel uses an interative technique to calculate ODDFYIELD. This function uses the Newton method based on the formula used for the function ODDFPRICE. The yield is changed through 100 iterations until the estimated price with the given yield is close to the price.

Example

A bond has the following terms:

January 25, 1991, settlement date
January 1, 1996, maturity date
January 18, 1991, issue date
July 15, 1991, first coupon date
5.75 percent coupon
$84.50 price
$100 redemptive value
Frequency is semiannual
30/360 basis

The yield of a security that has an odd (short or long) first period is:

```
ODDFYIELD("1/25/91","1/1/96","1/18/91","7/15/91",0.0575,084.50,
100,2,0) equals .09758 or 9.76 percent
```

ODDLPRICE

Returns the price per $100 face value of a security having an odd (short or long) last coupon period.

If this function is not available, run the Setup program to install the Analysis ToolPak. After you install the Analysis ToolPak, you must enable it by using the **Add-Ins** command on the **Tools** menu.

Syntax

ODDLPRICE(settlement,maturity,last_interest,rate,yld,redemption,frequency,basis)

Settlement   is the security's settlement date. The security settlement date is the date after the issue date when the security is traded to the buyer.

Maturity   is the security's maturity date. The maturity date is the date when the security expires.

Last_interest   is the security's last coupon date.

Rate   is the security's interest rate.

Yld   is the security's annual yield.

Redemption   is the security's redemption value per $100 face value.

Frequency   is the number of coupon payments per year. For annual payments, frequency = 1; for semiannual, frequency = 2; for quarterly, frequency = 4.

Basis   is the type of day count basis to use.

Basis	Day count basis
0 or omitted	US (NASD) 30/360
1	Actual/actual
2	Actual/360
3	Actual/365
4	European 30/360

Remarks

- The settlement date is the date a buyer purchases a coupon, such as a bond. The maturity date is the date when a coupon expires. For example, suppose a 30-year bond is issued on January 1, 1996, and is purchased by a buyer six months later. The issue date would be January 1, 1996, the settlement date would be July 1, 1996, and the maturity date would be January 1, 2026, which is 30 years after the January 1, 1996, issue date.

- Settlement, maturity, last_interest, and basis are truncated to integers.

- If any argument is nonnumeric, ODDLPRICE returns the #VALUE! error value.

- If settlement, maturity, or last_interest is not a valid date, ODDLPRICE returns the #NUM! error value.

- If rate < 0 or if yld < 0, ODDLPRICE returns the #NUM! error value.

- If basis < 0 or if basis > 4, ODDLPRICE returns the #NUM! error value.

- The following date condition must be satisfied; otherwise, ODDLPRICE returns the #NUM! error value:

  maturity > settlement > last_interest

Example

A bond has the following terms:

February, 7, 1987, settlement date
June 15, 1987, maturity date
October 15, 1986, last interest date
3.75 percent coupon
4.05 percent yield
$100 redemptive value
Frequency is semiannual
30/360 basis

The price per $100 of a security having an odd (short or long) last coupon period is:

```
ODDLPRICE("2/7/87","6/15/87","10/15/86",0.0375,0.0405,100,2,0)
```
equals 99.87829

ODDLYIELD

Returns the yield of a security that has an odd (short or long) last period.

If this function is not available, run the Setup program to install the Analysis ToolPak. After you install the Analysis ToolPak, you must enable it by using the **Add-Ins** command on the **Tools** menu.

Syntax

ODDLYIELD(settlement,maturity,last_interest,rate,pr,redemption,frequency,basis)

Settlement is the security's settlement date. The security settlement date is the date after the issue date when the security is traded to the buyer.

Maturity is the security's maturity date. The maturity date is the date when the security expires.

Last_interest is the security's last coupon date.

Rate is the security's interest rate.

Pr is the security's price.

Redemption is the security's redemption value per $100 face value.

Frequency is the number of coupon payments per year. For annual payments, frequency = 1; for semiannual, frequency = 2; for quarterly, frequency = 4.

Basis is the type of day count basis to use.

Basis	Day count basis
0 or omitted	US (NASD) 30/360
1	Actual/actual
2	Actual/360
3	Actual/365
4	European 30/360

Remarks

- The settlement date is the date a buyer purchases a coupon, such as a bond. The maturity date is the date when a coupon expires. For example, suppose a 30-year bond is issued on January 1, 1996, and is purchased by a buyer six months later. The issue date would be January 1, 1996, the settlement date would be July 1, 1996, and the maturity date would be January 1, 2026, which is 30 years after the January 1, 1996, issue date.

- Settlement, maturity, last_interest, and basis are truncated to integers.

- If any argument is nonnumeric, ODDLYIELD returns the #VALUE! error value.

- If settlement, maturity, or last_interest is not a valid date, ODDLYIELD returns the #NUM! error value.

- If rate < 0 or if pr ≤ 0, ODDLYIELD returns the #NUM! error value.
- If basis < 0 or if basis > 4, ODDLYIELD returns the #NUM! error value.
- The following date condition must be satisfied; otherwise, ODDLYIELD returns the #NUM! error value:

maturity > settlement > last_interest

- ODDLYIELD is calculated as follows:

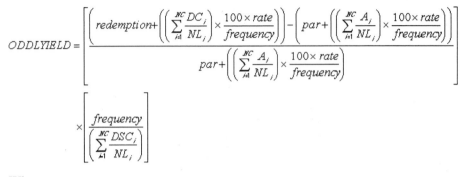

$$ODDLYIELD = \left[\frac{\left(redemption + \left(\left(\sum_{i=1}^{NC} \frac{DC_i}{NL_i} \right) \times \frac{100 \times rate}{frequency} \right) \right) - \left(par + \left(\left(\sum_{i=1}^{NC} \frac{A_i}{NL_i} \right) \times \frac{100 \times rate}{frequency} \right) \right)}{par + \left(\left(\sum_{i=1}^{NC} \frac{A_i}{NL_i} \right) \times \frac{100 \times rate}{frequency} \right)} \right]$$

$$\times \left[\frac{frequency}{\left(\sum_{i=1}^{NC} \frac{DSC_i}{NL_i} \right)} \right]$$

Where:

Ai = number of accrued days for the ith, or last, quasi-coupon period within odd period counting forward from last interest date before redemption.

DCi = number of days counted in the ith, or last, quasi-coupon period as delimited by the length of the actual coupon period.

NC = number of quasi-coupon periods that fit in odd period; if this number contains a fraction it will be raised to the next whole number.

NLi = normal length in days of the ith, or last, quasi-coupon period within odd coupon period.

Example

A bond has the following terms:

April 20, 1987, settlement date
June 15, 1987, maturity date
December 24, 1986, last interest date
3.75 percent coupon
$99.875 price
$100 redemptive value
Frequency is semiannual
30/360 basis

The yield of a security that has an odd (short or long) first period is:

```
ODDLYIELD("4/20/87","6/15/87","12/24/86",0.0375,99.875,100,2,0)
```
equals 0.045192

OFFSET

Returns a reference to a range that is a specified number of rows and columns from a cell or range of cells. The reference that is returned can be a single cell or a range of cells. You can specify the number of rows and the number of columns to be returned.

Syntax

OFFSET(reference,rows,cols,height,width)

Reference is the reference from which you want to base the offset. Reference must be a reference to a cell or range of adjacent cells; otherwise, OFFSET returns the #VALUE! error value.

Rows is the number of rows, up or down, that you want the upper-left cell to refer to. Using 5 as the rows argument specifies that the upper-left cell in the reference is five rows below reference. Rows can be positive (which means below the starting reference) or negative (which means above the starting reference).

Cols is the number of columns, to the left or right, that you want the upper-left cell of the result to refer to. Using 5 as the cols argument specifies that the upper-left cell in the reference is five columns to the right of reference. Cols can be positive (which means to the right of the starting reference) or negative (which means to the left of the starting reference).

If rows and cols offset reference over the edge of the worksheet, OFFSET returns the #REF! error value.

Height is the height, in number of rows, that you want the returned reference to be. Height must be a positive number.

Width is the width, in number of columns, that you want the returned reference to be. Width must be a positive number.

If height or width is omitted, it is assumed to be the same height or width as reference.

Remarks

OFFSET doesn't actually move any cells or change the selection; it just returns a reference. OFFSET can be used with any function expecting a reference argument. For example, the formula SUM(OFFSET(C2,1,2,3,1)) calculates the total value of a 3-row by 1-column range that is 1 row below and 2 columns to the right of cell C2.

Examples

OFFSET(C3,2,3,1,1) equals F5. If you enter this formula on a worksheet, Microsoft Excel displays the value contained in cell F5.

OFFSET(C3:E5,-1,0,3,3) equals C2:E4

OFFSET(C3:E5,0,-3,3,3) equals #REF!

OR

Returns TRUE if any argument is TRUE; returns FALSE if all arguments are FALSE.

Syntax

OR(logical1,logical2, ...)

Logical1,logical2, ...   are 1 to 30 conditions you want to test that can be either TRUE or FALSE.

- The arguments must evaluate to logical values such as TRUE or FALSE, or in arrays or references that contain logical values.

- If an array or reference argument contains text, numbers, or empty cells, those values are ignored.

- If the specified range contains no logical values, OR returns the #VALUE! error value.

- You can use an OR array formula to see if a value occurs in an array. To enter an array formula, press CTRL+SHIFT+ENTER in Microsoft Excel 97 for Windows or COMMAND+ENTER in Microsoft Excel 97 for the Macintosh.

Examples

OR(TRUE) equals TRUE

OR(1+1=1,2+2=5) equals FALSE

If A1:A3 contains the values TRUE, FALSE, and TRUE, then:

OR(A1:A3) equals TRUE

Also see the example for EXACT

PEARSON

Returns the Pearson product moment correlation coefficient, r, a dimensionless index that ranges from -1.0 to 1.0 inclusive and reflects the extent of a linear relationship between two data sets.

Syntax

PEARSON(array1,array2)

Array1   is a set of independent values.

Array2   is a set of dependent values.

Remarks

- The arguments must be either numbers or names, array constants, or references that contain numbers.

- If an array or reference argument contains text, logical values, or empty cells, those values are ignored; however, cells with the value zero are included.

- If array1 and array2 are empty or have a different number of data points, PEARSON returns the #N/A error value.

- The r value of the regression line is:

$$r = \frac{n(\Sigma XY) - (\Sigma X)(\Sigma Y)}{\sqrt{\left[n\Sigma X^2 - (\Sigma X)^2\right]\left[n\Sigma Y^2 - (\Sigma Y)^2\right]}}$$

Example

PEARSON({9,7,5,3,1},{10,6,1,5,3}) equals 0.699379

PERCENTILE

Returns the k-th percentile of values in a range. You can use this function to establish a threshold of acceptance. For example, you can decide to examine candidates who score above the 90th percentile.

Syntax

PERCENTILE(array,k)

Array   is the array or range of data that defines relative standing.

K   is the percentile value in the range 0..1, inclusive.

Remarks

- If array is empty or contains more than 8,191 data points, PERCENTILE returns the #NUM! error value.

- If k is nonnumeric, PERCENTILE returns the #VALUE! error value.

- If k is < 0 or if k > 1, PERCENTILE returns the #NUM! error value.

- If k is not a multiple of $1/(n - 1)$, PERCENTILE interpolates to determine the value at the kth percentile.

Example

PERCENTILE({1,2,3,4},0.3) equals 1.9

PERCENTRANK

Returns the rank of a value in a data set as a percentage of the data set. This function can be used to evaluate the relative standing of a value within a data set. For example, you can use PERCENTRANK to evaluate the standing of an aptitude test score among all scores for the test.

Syntax

PERCENTRANK(array,x,significance)

Array   is the array or range of data with numeric values that defines relative standing.

X   is the value for which you want to know the rank.

Significance   is an optional value that identifies the number of significant digits for the returned percentage value. If omitted, PERCENTRANK uses three digits (0.xxx%).

Remarks

- If array is empty, PERCENTRANK returns the #NUM! error value.

- If significance < 1, PERCENTRANK returns the #NUM! error value.

- If x does not match one of the values in array, PERCENTRANK interpolates to return the correct percentage rank.

Example

```
PERCENTRANK({1,2,3,4,5,6,7,8,9,10},4) equals 0.333
```

PERMUT

Returns the number of permutations for a given number of objects that can be selected from number objects. A permutation is any set or subset of objects or events where internal order is significant. Permutations are different from combinations, for which the internal order is not significant. Use this function for lottery-style probability calculations.

Syntax

PERMUT(number,number_chosen)

Number   is an integer that describes the number of objects.

Number_chosen   is an integer that describes the number of objects in each permutation.

Remarks

- Both arguments are truncated to integers.

- If number or number_chosen is nonnumeric, PERMUT returns the #VALUE! error value.

- If number ≤ 0 or if number_chosen < 0, PERMUT returns the #NUM! error value.

- If number < number_chosen, PERMUT returns the #NUM! error value.

- The equation for the number of permutations is:

$$P_{k,n} = \frac{n!}{(n-k)!}$$

Example

Suppose you want to calculate the odds of selecting a winning lottery number. Each lottery number contains three numbers, each of which can be between 0 (zero) and 99, inclusive. The following function calculates the number of possible permutations:

`PERMUT(100,3)` equals 970,200

PI

Returns the number 3.14159265358979, the mathematical constant π, accurate to 15 digits.

Syntax

PI( )

Examples

`PI()/2` equals 1.57079...

`SIN(PI()/2)` equals 1

If the radius of a circle is stored in a cell named Radius, the following formula calculates the area of the circle:

`PI()*(Radius^2)`

PMT

Calculates the payment for a loan based on constant payments and a constant interest rate.

Syntax

PMT(rate,nper,pv,fv,type)

For a more complete description of the arguments in PMT, see PV.

Rate   is the interest rate for the loan.

Nper   is the total number of payments for the loan.

Pv   is the present value, or the total amount that a series of future payments is worth now; also known as the principal.

Fv   is the future value, or a cash balance you want to attain after the last payment is made. If fv is omitted, it is assumed to be 0 (zero), that is, the future value of a loan is 0.

Type   is the number 0 (zero) or 1 and indicates when payments are due.

Set type equal to	If payments are due
0 or omitted	At the end of the period
1	At the beginning of the period

Remarks

- The payment returned by PMT includes principal and interest but no taxes, reserve payments, or fees sometimes associated with loans.

- Make sure that you are consistent about the units you use for specifying rate and nper. If you make monthly payments on a four-year loan at an annual interest rate of 12 percent, use 12%/12 for rate and 4*12 for nper. If you make annual payments on the same loan, use 12 percent for rate and 4 for nper.

  Tip   To find the total amount paid over the duration of the loan, multiply the returned PMT value by nper.

Examples

The following formula returns the monthly payment on a $10,000 loan at an annual rate of 8 percent that you must pay off in 10 months:

PMT(8%/12, 10, 10000) equals -$1,037.03

For the same loan, if payments are due at the beginning of the period, the payment is:

PMT(8%/12, 10, 10000, 0, 1) equals -$1,030.16

The following formula returns the amount someone must pay to you each month if you loan that person $5,000 at 12 percent and want to be paid back in five months:

PMT(12%/12, 5, -5000) equals $1,030.20

You can use PMT to determine payments to annuities other than loans. For example, if you want to save $50,000 in 18 years by saving a constant amount each month, you can use PMT to determine how much you must save. If you assume you'll be able to earn 6 percent interest on your savings, you can use PMT to determine how much to save each month.

PMT(6%/12, 18*12, 0, 50000) equals -$129.08

If you pay $129.08 into a 6 percent savings account every month for 18 years, you will have $50,000.

POISSON

Returns the Poisson distribution. A common application of the Poisson distribution is predicting the number of events over a specific time, such as the number of cars arriving at a toll plaza in 1 minute.

Syntax

POISSON(x,mean,cumulative)

X   is the number of events.

Mean   is the expected numeric value.

Cumulative   is a logical value that determines the form of the probability distribution returned. If cumulative is TRUE, POISSON returns the cumulative Poisson probability that the number of random events occurring will be between zero and x inclusive; if FALSE, it returns the Poisson probability mass function that the number of events occurring will be exactly x.

Remarks

- If x is not an integer, it is truncated.
- If x or mean is nonnumeric, POISSON returns the #VALUE! error value.
- If $x \leq 0$, POISSON returns the #NUM! error value.
- If mean ≤ 0, POISSON returns the #NUM! error value.

- POISSON is calculated as follows.

  For cumulative = FALSE:

  $$POISSON = \frac{e^{-\lambda} \lambda^x}{x!}$$

  For cumulative = TRUE:

  $$CUMPOISSON = \sum_{k=0}^{x} \frac{e^{-\lambda} \lambda^k}{k!}$$

Examples

POISSON(2,5,FALSE) equals 0.084224

POISSON(2,5,TRUE) equals 0.124652

POWER

Returns the result of a number raised to a power.

Syntax

POWER(number,power)

Number   is the base number. It can be any real number.

Power   is the exponent to which the base number is raised.

Remark

The "^" operator can be used instead of POWER to indicate to what power the base number is to be raised, such as in 5^2.

Examples

POWER(5,2) equals 25

POWER(98.6,3.2) equals 2401077

POWER(4,5/4) equals 5.656854

PPMT

Returns the payment on the principal for a given period for an investment based on periodic, constant payments and a constant interest rate.

Syntax

PPMT(rate,per,nper,pv,fv,type)

For a more complete description of the arguments in PPMT, see PV.

Rate   is the interest rate per period.

Per   specifies the period and must be in the range 1 to nper.

Nper   is the total number of payment periods in an annuity.

Pv   is the present value—the total amount that a series of future payments is worth now.

Fv   is the future value, or a cash balance you want to attain after the last payment is made. If fv is omitted, it is assumed to be 0 (zero), that is, the future value of a loan is 0.

Type   is the number 0 or 1 and indicates when payments are due.

Set type equal to	If payments are due
0 or omitted	At the end of the period
1	At the beginning of the period

Remarks

Make sure that you are consistent about the units you use for specifying rate and nper. If you make monthly payments on a four-year loan at 12 percent annual interest, use 12%/12 for rate and 4*12 for nper. If you make annual payments on the same loan, use 12% for rate and 4 for nper.

Examples

The following formula returns the principal payment for the first month of a two-year $2,000 loan at 10 percent annual interest:

PPMT(10%/12, 1, 24, 2000) equals -$75.62

The following function returns the principal payment for the last year of a 10-year $200,000 loan at 8 percent annual interest:

PPMT(8%, 10, 10, 200000) equals -$27,598.05

PRICE

Returns the price per $100 face value of a security that pays periodic interest.

If this function is not available, run the Setup program to install the Analysis ToolPak. After you install the Analysis ToolPak, you must enable it by using the **Add-Ins** command on the **Tools** menu.

Syntax

PRICE(settlement,maturity,rate,yld,redemption,frequency,basis)

Settlement   is the security's settlement date. The security settlement date is the date after the issue date when the security is traded to the buyer.

Maturity   is the security's maturity date. The maturity date is the date when the security expires.

Rate   is the security's annual coupon rate.

Yld   is the security's annual yield.

Redemption   is the security's redemption value per $100 face value.

Frequency   is the number of coupon payments per year. For annual payments, frequency = 1; for semiannual, frequency = 2; for quarterly, frequency = 4.

Basis   is the type of day count basis to use.

Basis	Day count basis
0 or omitted	US (NASD) 30/360
1	Actual/actual
2	Actual/360
3	Actual/365
4	European 30/360

Remarks

- The settlement date is the date a buyer purchases a coupon, such as a bond. The maturity date is the date when a coupon expires. For example, suppose a 30-year bond is issued on January 1, 1996, and is purchased by a buyer six months later. The issue date would be January 1, 1996, the settlement date would be July 1, 1996, and the maturity date would be January 1, 2026, which is 30 years after the January 1, 1996, issue date.

- Settlement, maturity, frequency, and basis are truncated to integers.

- If any argument is nonnumeric, PRICE returns the #VALUE! error value.

- If settlement or maturity is not a valid date, PRICE returns the #NUM! error value.

- If yld < 0 or if rate < 0, PRICE returns the #NUM! error value.

- If redemption ≤ 0, PRICE returns the #NUM! error value.

- If frequency is any number other than 1, 2, or 4, PRICE returns the #NUM! error value.
- If basis < 0 or if basis > 4, PRICE returns the #NUM! error value.
- If settlement ≥ maturity, PRICE returns the #NUM! error value.
- PRICE is calculated as follows:

$$PRICE = \left[\frac{redemption}{\left(1 + \frac{yld}{frequency} \right)^{\left(N-1+\frac{DSC}{E} \right)}} \right] + \left[\sum_{k=1}^{N} \frac{100 \times \frac{rate}{frequency}}{\left(1 + \frac{yld}{frequency} \right)^{\left(k-1+\frac{DSC}{E} \right)}} \right]$$

$$- \left(100 \times \frac{rate}{frequency} \times \frac{A}{E} \right)$$

Where:

DSC = number of days from settlement to next coupon date.

E = number of days in coupon period in which the settlement date falls.

N = number of coupons payable between settlement date and redemption date.

A = number of days from beginning of coupon period to settlement date.

Example

A bond has the following terms:

February 15, 1991, settlement date
November 15, 1999, maturity date
5.75 percent semiannual coupon
6.50 percent yield
$100 redemption value
Frequency is semiannual
30/360 basis

The bond price (in the 1900 date system) is:

`PRICE("2/15/91","11/15/99",0.0575,0.065,100,2,0)` equals 95.04287

PRICEDISC

Returns the price per $100 face value of a discounted security.

If this function is not available, run the Setup program to install the Analysis ToolPak. After you install the Analysis ToolPak, you must enable it by using the **Add-Ins** command on the **Tools** menu.

Syntax

PRICEDISC(settlement,maturity,discount,redemption,basis)

Settlement   is the security's settlement date. The security settlement date is the date after the issue date when the security is traded to the buyer.

Maturity   is the security's maturity date. The maturity date is the date when the security expires.

Discount   is the security's discount rate.

Redemption   is the security's redemption value per $100 face value.

Basis   is the type of day count basis to use.

Basis	Day count basis
0 or omitted	US (NASD) 30/360
1	Actual/actual
2	Actual/360
3	Actual/365
4	European 30/360

Remarks

- The settlement date is the date a buyer purchases a coupon, such as a bond. The maturity date is the date when a coupon expires. For example, suppose a 30-year bond is issued on January 1, 1996, and is purchased by a buyer six months later. The issue date would be January 1, 1996, the settlement date would be July 1, 1996, and the maturity date would be January 1, 2026, which is 30 years after the January 1, 1996, issue date.

- Settlement, maturity, and basis are truncated to integers.

- If any argument is nonnumeric, PRICEDISC returns the #VALUE! error value.

- If settlement or maturity is not a valid date, PRICEDISC returns the #NUM! error value.

- If discount ≤ 0 or if redemption ≤ 0, PRICEDISC returns the #NUM! error value.

- If basis < 0 or if basis > 4, PRICEDISC returns the #NUM! error value.

- If settlement ≥ maturity, PRICEDISC returns the #NUM! error value.

- PRICEDISC is calculated as follows:

$$PRICEDISC = redemption - discount \times redemption \times \frac{DSM}{B}$$

Where:

B = number of days in year, depending on year basis.

DSM = number of days from settlement to maturity.

Example

A bond has the following terms:

February 15, 1993, settlement date
March 1, 1993, maturity date
5.25 percent discount rate
$100 redemption value
Actual/360 basis

The bond price (in the 1900 date system) is:

`PRICEDISC("2/15/93","3/1/93",0.0525,100,2)` equals 99.79583

PRICEMAT

Returns the price per $100 face value of a security that pays interest at maturity.

If this function is not available, run the Setup program to install the Analysis ToolPak. After you install the Analysis ToolPak, you must enable it by using the **Add-Ins** command on the **Tools** menu.

Syntax

PRICEMAT(**settlement,maturity,issue,rate,yld**,basis)

Settlement   is the security's settlement date. The security settlement date is the date after the issue date when the security is traded to the buyer.

Maturity   is the security's maturity date. The maturity date is the date when the security expires.

Issue   is the security's issue date, expressed as a serial date number.

is the security's interest rate at date of issue.

Yld   is the security's annual yield.

Basis   is the type of day count basis to use.

Basis	Day count basis
0 (zero) or omitted	US (NASD) 30/360
1	Actual/actual
2	Actual/360
3	Actual/365
4	European 30/360

Remarks

- The settlement date is the date a buyer purchases a coupon, such as a bond. The maturity date is the date when a coupon expires. For example, suppose a 30-year bond is issued on January 1, 1996, and is purchased by a buyer six months later. The issue date would be January 1, 1996, the settlement date would be July 1, 1996, and the maturity date would be January 1, 2026, which is 30 years after the January 1, 1996, issue date.

- Settlement, maturity, issue, and basis are truncated to integers.

- If any argument is nonnumeric, PRICEMAT returns the #VALUE! error value.

- If settlement, maturity, or issue is not a valid date, PRICEMAT returns the #NUM! error value.

- If rate < 0 or if yld < 0, PRICEMAT returns the #NUM! error value.

- If basis < 0 or if basis > 4, PRICEMAT returns the #NUM! error value.

- If settlement ≥ maturity, PRICEMAT returns the #NUM! error value.

- PRICEMAT is calculated as follows:

$$PRICEMAT = \frac{100 + (\frac{DIM}{B} \times rate \times 100)}{1 + (\frac{DSM}{B} \times yld)} - \left(\frac{A}{B} \times rate \times 100\right)$$

Where:

B = number of days in year, depending on year basis.

DSM = number of days from settlement to maturity.

DIM = number of days from issue to maturity.

A = number of days from issue to settlement.

Example

A bond has the following terms:

February 15, 1993, settlement date
April 13, 1993, maturity date
November 11, 1992, issue date
6.1 percent semiannual coupon
6.1 percent yield
30/360 basis

The price (in the 1900 date system) is:

PRICEMAT("2/15/93","4/13/93","11/11/92",0.061,0.061,0) equals
99.98449888

PROB

Returns the probability that values in a range are between two limits. If upper_limit is not supplied, returns the probability that values in x_range are equal to lower_limit.

Syntax

PROB(x_range,prob_range,lower_limit,upper_limit)

X_range   is the range of numeric values of x with which there are associated probabilities.

Prob_range   is a set of probabilities associated with values in x_range.

Lower_limit   is the lower bound on the value for which you want a probability.

Upper_limit   is the optional upper bound on the value for which you want a probability.

Remarks

- If any value in prob_range ≤ 0 or if any value in prob_range > 1, PROB returns the #NUM! error value.

- If the sum of the values in prob_range ≠ 1, PROB returns the #NUM! error value.

- If upper_limit is omitted, PROB returns the probability of being equal to lower_limit.

- If x_range and prob_range contain a different number of data points, PROB returns the #N/A error value.

Examples

PROB({0,1,2,3},{0.2,0.3,0.1,0.4},2) equals 0.1

PROB({0,1,2,3},{0.2,0.3,0.1,0.4},1,3) equals 0.8

PRODUCT

Multiplies all the numbers given as arguments and returns the product.

Syntax

PRODUCT(number1,number2, ...)

Number1,number2, ...   are 1 to 30 numbers that you want to multiply.

Remarks

- Arguments that are numbers, logical values, or text representations of numbers are counted; arguments that are error values or text that cannot be translated into numbers cause errors.

- If an argument is an array or reference, only numbers in the array or reference are counted. Empty cells, logical values, text, or error values in the array or reference are ignored.

Examples

If cells A2:C2 contain 5, 15, and 30:

PRODUCT(A2:C2) equals 2,250

PRODUCT(A2:C2, 2) equals 4,500

PROPER

Capitalizes the first letter in a text string and any other letters in text that follow any character other than a letter. Converts all other letters to lowercase letters.

Syntax

PROPER(text)

Text   is text enclosed in quotation marks, a formula that returns text, or a reference to a cell containing the text you want to partially capitalize.

Examples

PROPER("this is a TITLE") equals "This Is A Title"

PROPER("2-cent's worth") equals "2-Cent'S Worth"

PROPER("76BudGet") equals "76Budget"

PV

Returns the present value of an investment. The present value is the total amount that a series of future payments is worth now. For example, when you borrow money, the loan amount is the present value to the lender.

Syntax

PV(**rate**,**nper**,pmt,fv,type)

Rate   is the interest rate per period. For example, if you obtain an automobile loan at a 10 percent annual interest rate and make monthly payments, your interest rate per month is 10%/12, or 0.83%. You would enter 10%/12, or 0.83%, or 0.0083, into the formula as the rate.

Nper   is the total number of payment periods in an annuity. For example, if you get a four-year car loan and make monthly payments, your loan has 4*12 (or 48) periods. You would enter 48 into the formula for nper.

Pmt   is the payment made each period and cannot change over the life of the annuity. Typically, pmt includes principal and interest but no other fees or taxes. For example, the monthly payments on a $10,000, four-year car loan at 12 percent are $263.33. You would enter -263.33 into the formula as the pmt.

Fv   is the future value, or a cash balance you want to attain after the last payment is made. If fv is omitted, it is assumed to be 0 (the future value of a loan, for example, is 0). For example, if you want to save $50,000 to pay for a special project in 18 years, then $50,000 is the future value. You could then make a conservative guess at an interest rate and determine how much you must save each month.

Type   is the number 0 or 1 and indicates when payments are due.

Set type equal to	If payments are due
0 or omitted	At the end of the period
1	At the beginning of the period

Remarks

- Make sure that you are consistent about the units you use for specifying rate and nper. If you make monthly payments on a four-year loan at 12 percent annual interest, use 12%/12 for rate and 4*12 for nper. If you make annual payments on the same loan, use 12% for rate and 4 for nper.

- The following functions apply to annuities:

CUMIPMT	PPMT
CUMPRINC	PV
FV	RATE
FVSCHEDULE	XIRR
IPMT	XNPV
PMT	

An annuity is a series of constant cash payments made over a continuous period. For example, a car loan or a mortgage is an annuity. For more information, see the description for each annuity function.

- In annuity functions, cash you pay out, such as a deposit to savings, is represented by a negative number; cash you receive, such as a dividend check, is represented by a positive number. For example, a $1,000 deposit to the bank would be represented by the argument -1000 if you are the depositor and by the argument 1000 if you are the bank.

- Microsoft Excel solves for one financial argument in terms of the others. If rate is not 0, then:

$$pv * (1 + rate)^{nper} + pmt(1 + rate * type) *$$
$$\left(\frac{(1 + rate)^{nper} - 1}{rate} \right) + fv = 0$$

If rate is 0, then:

(pmt * nper) + pv + fv = 0

Example

Suppose you're thinking of buying an insurance annuity that pays $500 at the end of every month for the next 20 years. The cost of the annuity is $60,000, and the money paid out will earn 8 percent. You want to determine whether this would be a good investment. Using the PV function, you find that the present value of the annuity is:

```
PV(0.08/12, 12*20, 500, , 0) equals -$59,777.15
```

The result is negative because it represents money that you would pay, an outgoing cash flow. The present value of the annuity ($59,777.15) is less than what you are asked to pay ($60,000). Therefore, you determine this would not be a good investment.

QUARTILE

Returns the quartile of a data set. Quartiles often are used in sales and survey data to divide populations into groups. For example, you can use QUARTILE to find the top 25 percent of incomes in a population.

Syntax

QUARTILE(array,quart)

Array   is the array or cell range of numeric values for which you want the quartile value.

Quart   indicates which value to return.

If quart equals	QUARTILE returns
0	Minimum value
1	First quartile (25th percentile)
2	Median value (50th percentile)
3	Third quartile (75th percentile)
4	Maximum value

Remarks

- If array is empty or contains more than 8,191 data points, QUARTILE returns the #NUM! error value.

- If quart is not an integer, it is truncated.

- If quart < 0 or if quart > 4, QUARTILE returns the #NUM! error value.

- MIN, MEDIAN, and MAX return the same value as QUARTILE when quart is equal to 0 (zero), 2, and 4, respectively.

Example

QUARTILE({1,2,4,7,8,9,10,12},1) equals 3.5

QUOTIENT

Returns the integer portion of a division. Use this function when you want to discard the remainder of a division.

If this function is not available, run the Setup program to install the Analysis ToolPak. After you install the Analysis ToolPak, you must enable it by using the **Add-Ins** command on the **Tools** menu.

Syntax

QUOTIENT(numerator,denominator)

Numerator   is the dividend.

Denominator   is the divisor.

Remarks

If either argument is nonnumeric, QUOTIENT returns the #VALUE! error value.

Examples

QUOTIENT(5, 2) equals 2

QUOTIENT(4.5, 3.1) equals 1

QUOTIENT(-10, 3) equals -3

RADIANS

Converts degrees to radians.

Syntax

RADIANS(angle)

Angle   is an angle in degrees that you want to convert.

Example

RADIANS(270) equals 4.712389 ($3\pi/2$ radians)

RAND

Returns an evenly distributed random number greater than or equal to 0 and less than 1. A new random number is returned every time the worksheet is calculated.

Syntax

RAND( )

Remarks

- To generate a random real number between a and b, use:

  RAND()*(b-a)+a

- If you want to use RAND to generate a random number but don't want the numbers to change every time the cell is calculated, you can enter =RAND() in the formula bar, and then press F9 to change the formula to a random number.

Examples

To generate a random number greater than or equal to 0 but less than 100:

RAND()*100

RANDBETWEEN

Returns a random number between the numbers you specify. A new random number is returned every time the worksheet is calculated.

If this function is not available, run the Setup program to install the Analysis ToolPak. After you install the Analysis ToolPak, you must enable it by using the **Add-Ins** command on the **Tools** menu.

Syntax

RANDBETWEEN(bottom,top)

Bottom   is the smallest integer RANDBETWEEN will return.

Top   is the largest integer RANDBETWEEN will return.

RANK

Returns the rank of a number in a list of numbers. The rank of a number is its size relative to other values in a list. (If you were to sort the list, the rank of the number would be its position.)

Syntax

RANK(number,ref,order)

Number   is the number whose rank you want to find.

Ref   is an array of, or a reference to, a list of numbers. Nonnumeric values in ref are ignored.

Order   is a number specifying how to rank number.

- If order is 0 (zero) or omitted, Microsoft Excel ranks number as if ref were a list sorted in descending order.

- If order is any nonzero value, Microsoft Excel ranks number as if ref were a list sorted in ascending order.

Remarks

RANK gives duplicate numbers the same rank. However, the presence of duplicate numbers affects the ranks of subsequent numbers. For example, in a list of integers, if the number 10 appears twice and has a rank of 5, then 11 would have a rank of 7 (no number would have a rank of 6).

Examples

If A1:A5 contain the numbers 7, 3.5, 3.5, 1, and 2, respectively, then:

RANK(A2,A1:A5,1) equals 3
RANK(A1,A1:A5,1) equals 5

RATE

Returns the interest rate per period of an annuity. RATE is calculated by iteration and can have zero or more solutions. If the successive results of RATE do not converge to within 0.0000001 after 20 iterations, RATE returns the #NUM! error value.

Syntax

RATE(nper,pmt,**pv**,fv,type,guess)

For a complete description of the arguments nper, pmt, pv, fv, and type, see PV.

Nper   is the total number of payment periods in an annuity.

Pmt   is the payment made each period and cannot change over the life of the annuity. Typically, pmt includes principal and interest but no other fees or taxes.

Pv   is the present value—the total amount that a series of future payments is worth now.

Fv   is the future value, or a cash balance you want to attain after the last payment is made. If fv is omitted, it is assumed to be 0 (the future value of a loan, for example, is 0).

Type   is the number 0 or 1 and indicates when payments are due.

Set type equal to	If payments are due
0 or omitted	At the end of the period
1	At the beginning of the period

Guess   is your guess for what the rate will be.

- If you omit guess, it is assumed to be 10 percent.
- If RATE does not converge, try different values for guess. RATE usually converges if guess is between 0 and 1.

Remarks

Make sure that you are consistent about the units you use for specifying guess and nper. If you make monthly payments on a four-year loan at 12 percent annual interest, use 12%/12 for guess and 4*12 for nper. If you make annual payments on the same loan, use 12% for guess and 4 for nper.

Example

To calculate the rate of a four-year $8,000 loan with monthly payments of $200:

`RATE(48, -200, 8000)` equals 0.77 percent

This is the monthly rate, because the period is monthly. The annual rate is 0.77%*12, which equals 9.24 percent.

RECEIVED

Returns the amount received at maturity for a fully invested security.

If this function is not available, run the Setup program to install the Analysis ToolPak. After you install the Analysis ToolPak, you must enable it by using the **Add-Ins** command on the **Tools** menu.

Syntax

RECEIVED(**settlement,maturity,investment,discount**,basis)

Settlement is the security's settlement date. The security settlement date is the date after the issue date when the security is traded to the buyer.

Maturity is the security's maturity date. The maturity date is the date when the security expires.

Investment is the amount invested in the security.

Discount is the security's discount rate.

Basis is the type of day count basis to use.

Basis	Day count basis
0 or omitted	US (NASD) 30/360
1	Actual/actual
2	Actual/360
3	Actual/365
4	European 30/360

Remarks

- The settlement date is the date a buyer purchases a coupon, such as a bond. The maturity date is the date when a coupon expires. For example, suppose a 30-year bond is issued on January 1, 1996, and is purchased by a buyer six months later. The issue date would be January 1, 1996, the settlement date would be July 1, 1996, and the maturity date would be January 1, 2026, which is 30 years after the January 1, 1996, issue date.

- Settlement, maturity, and basis are truncated to integers.

- If any argument is nonnumeric, RECEIVED returns the #VALUE! error value.

- If settlement or maturity is not a valid date, RECEIVED returns the #NUM! error value.

- If investment ≤ 0 or if discount ≤ 0, RECEIVED returns the #NUM! error value.

- If basis < 0 or if basis > 4, RECEIVED returns the #NUM! error value.

- If settlement ≥ maturity, RECEIVED returns the #NUM! error value.

- RECEIVED is calculated as follows:

$$RECEIVED = \frac{investment}{1 - (discount \times \frac{DIM}{B})}$$

Where:

B = number of days in a year, depending on the year basis.

DIM = number of days from issue to maturity.

Example

A bond has the following terms:

February 15, 1993, settlement (issue) date
May 15, 1993, maturity date
1,000,000 investment
5.75 percent discount rate
Actual/360 basis

The total amount to be received at maturity (in the 1900 date system) is:

RECEIVED("2/15/93","5/15/93",1000000,0.0575,2) equals 1,014,420.266

REGISTER.ID

Returns the register ID of the specified dynamic link library (DLL) or code resource that has been previously registered. If the DLL or code resource has not been registered, this function registers the DLL or code resource and then returns the register ID.

REGISTER.ID can be used on worksheets (unlike REGISTER), but you cannot specify a function name and argument names with REGISTER.ID.

Note Because Microsoft Excel for Windows and Microsoft Excel for the Macintosh use different types of code resources, REGISTER.ID has a slightly different syntax for each operating environment.

Syntax 1

For Microsoft Excel for Windows

REGISTER.ID(module_text,procedure,type_text)

Syntax 2

For Microsoft Excel for the Macintosh

REGISTER.ID(file_text,resource,type_text)

Module_text   is text specifying the name of the DLL that contains the function in Microsoft Excel for Windows.

Procedure   is text specifying the name of the function in the DLL in Microsoft Excel for Windows. You can also use the ordinal value of the function from the EXPORTS statement in the module-definition file (.DEF). The ordinal value or resource ID number must not be in text form.

Type_text   is text specifying the data type of the return value and the data types of all arguments to the DLL. The first letter of type_text specifies the return value. If the function or code resource is already registered, you can omit this argument.

File_text   is text specifying the name of the file that contains the code resource in Microsoft Excel for the Macintosh.

Resource   is text specifying the name of the function in the code resource in Microsoft Excel for the Macintosh. You can also use the resource ID number. The ordinal value or resource ID number must not be in text form.

Examples (32-Bit Microsoft Excel)

The following formula registers the GetTickCount function from 32-bit Microsoft Windows (Windows 95 or Windows NT) and returns the register ID:

```
REGISTER.ID("Kernel32", "GetTickCount", "J!")
```

Assuming that GetTickCount was already registered on another sheet using the preceding formula, the following formula returns the register ID for GetTickCount:

```
REGISTER.ID("Kernel32", "GetTickCount")
```

Examples (16-Bit Microsoft Excel)

The following formula registers the GetTickCount function from 16-bit Microsoft Windows and returns the register ID:

```
REGISTER.ID("User", "GetTickCount", "J!")
```

Assuming that GetTickCount was already registered on another sheet using the preceding formula, the following formula returns the register ID for GetTickCount:

```
REGISTER.ID("User", "GetTickCount")
```

REPLACE

Replaces part of a text string with a different text string.

Syntax

REPLACE(old_text,start_num,num_chars,new_text)

Old_text   is text in which you want to replace some characters.

Start_num   is the position of the character in old_text that you want to replace with new_text.

Num_chars   is the number of characters in old_text that you want to replace with new_text.

New_text   is the text that will replace characters in old_text.

Examples

The following formula replaces five characters with new_text, starting with the sixth character in old_text:

`REPLACE("abcdefghijk", 6, 5, "*")` equals "abcde*k"

The sixth through tenth characters are all replaced by "*".

The following formula replaces the last two digits of 1990 with 91:

`REPLACE("1990", 3, 2, "91")` equals "1991"

If cell A2 contains "123456", then:

`REPLACE(A2, 1, 3, "@")` equals "@456"

If the RIGHT function returns "ABCDEF", then:

`REPLACE(RIGHT(A3, 6), 1, 6, "*")` equals "*"

REPT

Repeats text a given number of times. Use REPT to fill a cell with a number of instances of a text string.

Syntax

REPT(text,number_times)

Text   is the text you want to repeat.

Number_times   is a positive number specifying the number of times to repeat text. If number_times is 0 (zero), REPT returns ""(empty text). If number_times is not an integer, it is truncated. The result of the REPT function cannot be longer than 255 characters.

Tip   You can use this function to create a simple histogram on your worksheet.

Examples

REPT("*-", 3) equals "*-*-*-"

If A3 contains "Sales", then:

REPT($A$3, 2.9) equals "SalesSales"

RIGHT

Returns the last (or rightmost) character or characters in a text string.

Syntax

RIGHT(text,num_chars)

Text   is the text string containing the characters you want to extract.

Num_chars   specifies how many characters you want to extract.

- Num_chars must be greater than or equal to zero.
- If num_chars is greater than the length of text, RIGHT returns all of text.
- If num_chars is omitted, it is assumed to be 1.

Examples

RIGHT("Sale Price", 5) equals "Price"

RIGHT("Stock Number") equals "r"

RIGHT is similar to LEFT; for more examples, see LEFT.

ROMAN

Converts an arabic numeral to roman, as text.

Syntax

ROMAN(number,form)

Number   is the arabic numeral you want converted.

Form   is a number specifying the type of roman numeral you want. The roman numeral style ranges from Classic to Simplified, becoming more concise as the value of form increases. See the example following ROMAN(499,0) below.

Form	Type
0 or omitted	Classic.
1	More concise. See example below.
2	More concise. See example below.
3	More concise. See example below.
4	Simplified.
TRUE	Classic.
FALSE	Simplified.

Remarks

- If number is negative, the #VALUE! error value is returned.

- If number is greater than 3999, the #VALUE! error value is returned.

Examples

ROMAN(499,0) equals "CDXCIX"

ROMAN(499,1) equals "LDVLIV"

ROMAN(499,2) equals "XDIX"

ROMAN(499,3) equals "VDIV"

ROMAN(499,4) equals "ID"

ROMAN(1993,0) equals "MCMXCIII"

ROUND

Rounds a number to a specified number of digits.

Syntax

ROUND(number,num_digits)

Number   is the number you want to round.

Num_digits   specifies the number of digits to which you want to round number.

- If num_digits is greater than 0 (zero), then number is rounded to the specified number of decimal places.

- If num_digits is 0, then number is rounded to the nearest integer.

- If num_digits is less than 0, then number is rounded to the left of the decimal point.

Examples

ROUND(2.15, 1) equals 2.2

ROUND(2.149, 1) equals 2.1

ROUND(-1.475, 2) equals -1.48

ROUND(21.5, -1) equals 20

ROUNDDOWN

Rounds a number down, toward zero.

Syntax

ROUNDDOWN(number,num_digits)

Number is any real number that you want rounded down.

Num_digits is the number of digits to which you want to round number.

Remark

- ROUNDDOWN behaves like ROUND, except that it always rounds a number down.
- If num_digits is greater than 0 (zero), then number is rounded down to the specified number of decimal places.
- If num_digits is 0 or omitted, then number is rounded down to the nearest integer.
- If num_digits is less than 0, then number is rounded down to the left of the decimal point.

Examples

ROUNDDOWN(3.2, 0) equals 3

ROUNDDOWN(76.9,0) equals 76

ROUNDDOWN(3.14159, 3) equals 3.141

ROUNDDOWN(-3.14159, 1) equals -3.1

ROUNDDOWN(31415.92654, -2) equals 31,400

ROUNDUP

Rounds a number up, away from 0 (zero).

Syntax

ROUNDUP(number,num_digits)

Number   is any real number that you want rounded up.

Num_digits   is the number of digits to which you want to round number.

Remarks

- ROUNDUP behaves like ROUND, except that it always rounds a number up.
- If num_digits is greater than 0 (zero), then number is rounded up to the specified number of decimal places.
- If num_digits is 0 or omitted, then number is rounded up to the nearest integer.
- If num_digits is less than 0, then number is rounded up to the left of the decimal point.

Examples

ROUNDUP(3.2,0) equals 4

ROUNDUP(76.9,0) equals 77

ROUNDUP(3.14159, 3) equals 3.142

ROUNDUP(-3.14159, 1) equals -3.2

ROUNDUP(31415.92654, -2) equals 31,500

ROW

Returns the row number of a reference.

Syntax

ROW(reference)

Reference   is the cell or range of cells for which you want the row number.

- If reference is omitted, it is assumed to be the reference of the cell in which the ROW function appears.
- If reference is a range of cells, and if ROW is entered as a vertical array, ROW returns the row numbers of reference as a vertical array.
- Reference cannot refer to multiple areas.

Examples

ROW(A3) equals 3

When entered as an array formula in three vertical cells:

ROW(A3:B5) equals {3;4;5}

If ROW is entered in C5, then:

ROW() equals ROW(C5) equals 5

ROWS

Returns the number of rows in a reference or array.

Syntax

ROWS(array)

Array   is an array, an array formula, or a reference to a range of cells for which you want the number of rows.

Examples

ROWS(A1:C4) equals 4

ROWS({1,2,3;4,5,6}) equals 2

RSQ

Returns the square of the Pearson product moment correlation coefficient through data points in known_y's and known_x's. For more information, see PEARSON. The r-squared value can be interpreted as the proportion of the variance in y attributable to the variance in x.

Syntax

RSQ(known_y's,known_x's)

Known_y's   is an array or range of data points.

Known_x's   is an array or range of data points.

Remarks

- The arguments must be either numbers or names, arrays, or references that contain numbers.

- If an array or reference argument contains text, logical values, or empty cells, those values are ignored; however, cells with the value zero are included.

- If known_y's and known_x's are empty or have a different number of data points, RSQ returns the #N/A error value.

- The equation for the r value of the regression line is:

$$r = \frac{n(\Sigma XY) - (\Sigma X)(\Sigma Y)}{\sqrt{\left[n\Sigma X^2 - (\Sigma X)^2\right]\left[n\Sigma Y^2 - (\Sigma Y)^2\right]}}$$

Example

RSQ({2,3,9,1,8,7,5},{6,5,11,7,5,4,4}) equals 0.05795

SEARCH

Returns the number of the character at which a specific character or text string is first found, reading from left to right. Use SEARCH to discover the location of a character or text string within another text string, so that you can use the MID or REPLACE functions to change the text.

Syntax

SEARCH(find_text,within_text,start_num**)**

Find_text   is the text you want to find. You can use the wildcard characters, question mark (?) and asterisk (*), in find_text. A question mark matches any single character; an asterisk matches any sequence of characters. If you want to find an actual question mark or asterisk, type a tilde (~) before the character. If find_text is not found, the #VALUE! error value is returned.

Within_text   is the text in which you want to search for find_text.

Start_num   is the character number in within_text, counting from the left, at which you want to start searching.

- If start_num is omitted, it is assumed to be 1.
- If start_num is not greater than 0 (zero) or is greater than the length of within_text, the #VALUE! error value is returned.

Tip   Use start_num to skip a specified number of characters from the left of the text. For example, suppose you are working with a text string such as "AYF0093.YoungMensApparel". To find the number of the first "Y" in the descriptive part of the text string, set start_num equal to 8 so that the serial-number portion of the text is not searched. SEARCH begins with character 8, finds find_text at the next character, and returns the number 9. SEARCH always returns the number of characters from the left of the text string, not from start_num.

Remarks

- SEARCH does not distinguish between uppercase and lowercase letters when searching text.
- SEARCH is similar to FIND, except that FIND is case-sensitive.

Examples

SEARCH("e","Statements",6) equals 7

If cell B17 contains the word "margin", and cell A14 contains "Profit Margin", then:

SEARCH($B$17,$A$14) equals 8

Use SEARCH with the REPLACE function to provide REPLACE with the correct start_num at which to begin inserting new text. Using the same cell references as the previous example:

REPLACE($A$14,SEARCH($B$17,$A$14),6,"Amount") returns the text "Profit Amount"

SECOND

Returns the second corresponding to serial_number. The second is given as an integer in the range 0 (zero) to 59. Use SECOND to get the time in seconds indicated by a serial number.

Syntax

SECOND(serial_number)

Serial_number is the date-time code used by Microsoft Excel for date and time calculations. You can give serial_number as text, such as "16:48:23" or "4:48:47 PM", instead of as a number. The text is automatically converted to a serial number. For more information about serial_number, see NOW.

Remarks

Microsoft Excel for Windows and Microsoft Excel for the Macintosh use different date systems as their default. For more information, see NOW.

Examples

SECOND("4:48:18 PM") equals 18

SECOND(0.01) equals 24

SECOND(4.02) equals 48

SERIESSUM

Returns the sum of a power series based on the formula:

$$SERIES(x,n,m,a) = a_1x^n + a_2x^{(n+m)} + a_3x^{(n+2m)}$$
$$+ ... + a_ix^{(n+(i-1)m)}$$

Many functions can be approximated by a power series expansion.

If this function is not available, run the Setup program to install the Analysis ToolPak. After you install the Analysis ToolPak, you must enable it by using the **Add-Ins** command on the **Tools** menu.

Syntax

SERIESSUM(x,n,m,coefficients)

X   is the input value to the power series.

N   is the initial power to which you want to raise x.

M   is the step by which to increase n for each term in the series.

Coefficients   is a set of coefficients by which each successive power of x is multiplied. The number of values in coefficients determines the number of terms in the power series. For example, if there are three values in coefficients, then there will be three terms in the power series.

Remarks

If any argument is nonnumeric, SERIESSUM returns the #VALUE! error value.

Example

Given that cell A1 contains the formula =PI()/4, and cells E1:E4 contain the following set of values for coefficients (calculated using the FACT function):

$$\left[1, -\frac{1}{2!}, \frac{1}{4!}, -\frac{1}{6!}\right]$$

SIGN

Determines the sign of a number. Returns 1 if the number is positive, zero (0) if the number is 0, and -1 if the number is negative.

Syntax

SIGN(number)

Number   is any real number.

Examples

SIGN(10) equals 1

SIGN(4-4) equals 0

SIGN(-0.00001) equals -1

SIN

Returns the sine of the given angle.

Syntax

SIN(number)

Number   is the angle in radians for which you want the sine. If your argument is in degrees, multiply it by PI()/180 to convert it to radians.

Examples

SIN(PI()) equals 1.22E-16, which is approximately 0 (zero). The sine of π is zero.

SIN(PI()/2) equals 1

SIN(30*PI()/180) equals 0.5, the sine of 30 degrees

SINH

Returns the hyperbolic sine of a number.

Syntax

SINH(number)

Number   is any real number.

The formula for the hyperbolic sine is:

$$SINH(z) = \frac{e^z - e^{-z}}{2}$$

Examples

SINH(1) equals 1.175201194

SINH(-1) equals -1.175201194

You can use the hyperbolic sine function to approximate a cumulative probability distribution. Suppose a laboratory test value varies between 0 and 10 seconds. An empirical analysis of the collected history of experiments shows that the probability of obtaining a result, x, of less than t seconds is approximated by the following equation:

P(x<t) = 2.868 * SINH(0.0342 * t), where 0<t<10

To calculate the probability of obtaining a result of less than 1.03 seconds, substitute 1.03 for t:

2.868*SINH(0.0342*1.03) equals 0.101049063

You can expect this result to occur about 101 times for every 1000 experiments.

SKEW

Returns the skewness of a distribution. Skewness characterizes the degree of asymmetry of a distribution around its mean. Positive skewness indicates a distribution with an asymmetric tail extending toward more positive values. Negative skewness indicates a distribution with an asymmetric tail extending toward more negative values.

Syntax

SKEW(number1,number2, ...)

Number1,number2, ...   are 1 to 30 arguments for which you want to calculate skewness. You can also use a single array or a reference to an array instead of arguments separated by commas.

Remarks

- The arguments must be either numbers or names, arrays, or references that contain numbers.

- If an array or reference argument contains text, logical values, or empty cells, those values are ignored; however, cells with the value zero are included.

- If there are fewer than three data points, or the sample standard deviation is zero, SKEW returns the #DIV/0! error value.

- The equation for skewness is defined as:

$$\frac{n}{(n-1)(n-2)} \sum \left(\frac{x_j - \bar{x}}{s} \right)^3$$

Example

SKEW(3,4,5,2,3,4,5,6,4,7) equals 0.359543

SLN

Returns the straight-line depreciation of an asset for one period.

Syntax

SLN(cost,salvage,life)

Cost   is the initial cost of the asset.

Salvage   is the value at the end of the depreciation (sometimes called the salvage value of the asset).

Life   is the number of periods over which the asset is being depreciated (sometimes called the useful life of the asset).

Example

Suppose you've bought a truck for $30,000 that has a useful life of 10 years and a salvage value of $7,500. The depreciation allowance for each year is:

SLN(30000, 7500, 10) equals $2,250

SLOPE

Returns the slope of the linear regression line through data points in known_y's and known_x's. The slope is the vertical distance divided by the horizontal distance between any two points on the line, which is the rate of change along the regression line.

Syntax

SLOPE(known_y's,known_x's)

Known_y's is an array or cell range of numeric dependent data points.

Known_x's is the set of independent data points.

Remarks

- The arguments must be either numbers or names, arrays, or references that contain numbers.

- If an array or reference argument contains text, logical values, or empty cells, those values are ignored; however, cells with the value zero are included.

- If known_y's and known_x's are empty or have a different number of data points, SLOPE returns the #N/A error value.

- The equation for the slope of the regression line is:

$$b = \frac{n\sum xy - \left(\sum x\right)\left(\sum y\right)}{n\sum x^2 - \left(\sum x\right)^2}$$

Example

SLOPE({2,3,9,1,8,7,5},{6,5,11,7,5,4,4}) equals 0.305556

SMALL

Returns the k-th smallest value in a data set. Use this function to return values with a particular relative standing in a data set.

Syntax

SMALL(array,k)

Array is an array or range of numerical data for which you want to determine the k-th smallest value.

K is the position (from the smallest) in the array or range of data to return.

Remarks

- If array is empty, SMALL returns the #NUM! error value.
- If k ≤ 0 or if k exceeds the number of data points, SMALL returns the #NUM! error value.
- If n is the number of data points in array, SMALL(array,1) equals the smallest value, and SMALL(array,n) equals the largest value.

Example

SMALL({3,4,5,2,3,4,5,6,4,7},4) equals 4

SMALL({1,4,8,3,7,12,54,8,23},2) equals 3

SQL.REQUEST

Connects with an external data source, and runs a query from a worksheet. SQL.REQUEST then returns the result as an array without the need for macro programming. If this function is not available, you must install the Microsoft Excel ODBC add-in (XLODBC.XLA).

Syntax

SQL.REQUEST(connection_string,output_ref,driver_prompt,query_text,col_names_logical)

Connection_string supplies information, such as the data source name, user ID, and passwords, required by the driver being used to connect to a data source and must follow the driver's format. The following table provides three example connection strings for three drivers.

Driver	Connection_string
dBASE	DSN=NWind;PWD=test
SQL Server	DSN=MyServer;UID=dbayer; PWD=123;Database=Pubs
ORACLE	DNS=My Oracle Data Source;DBQ=MYSER VER;UID=JohnS; PWD=Sesame

- You must define the data source name (DSN) used in connection_string before you try to connect to it.

- You can enter connection_string as an array or a string. If connection_string exceeds 250 characters, you must enter it as an array.

- If SQL.REQUEST is unable to gain access to the data source using connection_string, it returns the #N/A error value.

Output_ref   is a cell reference where you want the completed connection string placed. If you enter SQL.REQUEST on a worksheet, then output_ref is ignored.

- Use output_ref when you want SQL.REQUEST to return the completed connection string (you must enter SQL.REQUEST on a macro sheet in this case).

- If you omit output_ref, SQL.REQUEST does not return a completed connection string.

Driver_prompt   specifies when the driver dialog box is displayed and which options are available. Use one of the numbers described in the following table. If driver_prompt is omitted, SQL.REQUEST uses 2 as the default.

Driver_prompt	Description
1	Driver dialog box is always displayed.
2	Driver dialog box is displayed only if information provided by the connection string and the data source specification is not sufficient to complete the connection. All dialog box options are available.
3	Driver dialog box is displayed only if information provided by the connection string and the data source specification is not sufficient to complete the connection. Dialog box options appear dimmed and unavailable if they are not required.
4	Driver dialog box is not displayed. If the connection is not successful, it returns an error.

Query_text   is the SQL statement that you want to execute on the data source.

- If SQL.REQUEST is unable to execute query_text on the specified data source, it returns the #N/A error value.

- You can update a query by concatenating references into query_text. In the following example, every time $A$3 changes, SQL.REQUEST uses the new value to update the query.

"SELECT Name FROM Customers WHERE Balance > "&$A$3&"".

Microsoft Excel limits strings to a length of 255 characters. If query_text exceeds that length, enter the query in a vertical range of cells, and use the entire range as the query_text. The values of the cells are concatenated to form the complete SQL statement.

Column_names_logical   indicates whether column names are returned as the first row of the results. Set this argument to TRUE if you want the column names to be returned as the first row of the results. Use FALSE if you do not want the column names returned. If column_names_logical is omitted, SQL.REQUEST does not return column names.

Return Value

- If this function completes all of its actions, it returns an array of query results or the number of rows affected by the query.

- If SQL.REQUEST is unable to access the data source using connection_string, it returns the #N/A error value.

Remarks

- SQL.REQUEST can be entered as an array. When you enter SQL.REQUEST as an array, it returns an array to fit that range.

- If the range of cells is larger than the result set, SQL.REQUEST adds empty cells to the returned array to increase it to the necessary size.

- If the result set is larger than the range entered as an array, SQL.REQUEST returns the whole array.

- The arguments to SQL.REQUEST are in a different order than the arguments to the SQLRequest function in Visual Basic® for Applications.

Example

Suppose you want to make a query of a dBASE database named DBASE4. When you enter the following formula in a cell, an array of query results is returned, with the first row being the column names:

```
SQL.REQUEST("DSN=NWind;DBQ=c:\msquery;FIL=dBASE4", c15, 2,
"Select Custmr_ID, Due_Date from Orders WHERE order_Amt>100", TRUE)
```

SQRT

Returns a positive square root.

Syntax

SQRT(number)

Number   is the number for which you want the square root. If number is negative, SQRT returns the #NUM! error value.

Examples

SQRT(16) equals 4

SQRT(-16) equals #NUM!

SQRT(ABS(-16)) equals 4

SQRTPI

Returns the square root of (number * π).

If this function is not available, run the Setup program to install the Analysis ToolPak. After you install the Analysis ToolPak, you must enable it by using the **Add-Ins** command on the **Tools** menu.

Syntax

SQRTPI(number)

Number   is the number by which pi is multiplied.

Remark

If number < 0, SQRTPI returns the #NUM! error value.

Examples

SQRTPI(1) equals 1.772454

SQRTPI(2) equals 2.506628

STANDARDIZE

Returns a normalized value from a distribution characterized by mean and standard_dev.

Syntax

STANDARDIZE(x,mean,standard_dev)

X   is the value you want to normalize.

Mean   is the arithmetic mean of the distribution.

Standard_dev   is the standard deviation of the distribution.

Remarks

- If standard_dev ≤ 0, STANDARDIZE returns the #NUM! error value.

- The equation for the normalized value is:

$$Z = \frac{X - \mu}{\sigma}$$

Example

STANDARDIZE(42,40,1.5) equals 1.333333

STDEV

Estimates standard deviation based on a sample. The standard deviation is a measure of how widely values are dispersed from the average value (the mean).

Syntax

STDEV(number1,number2, ...)

Number1,number2, ... are 1 to 30 number arguments corresponding to a sample of a population. You can also use a single array or a reference to an array instead of arguments separated by commas.

Logical values such as TRUE and FALSE and text are ignored. If logical values and text must not be ignored, use the STDEVA worksheet function.

Remarks

- STDEV assumes that its arguments are a sample of the population. If your data represents the entire population, then compute the standard deviation using STDEVP.

- The standard deviation is calculated using the "nonbiased" or "n-1" method.

- STDEV uses the following formula:

$$\sqrt{\frac{n \sum x^2 - \left(\sum x\right)^2}{n(n-1)}}$$

Example

Suppose 10 tools stamped from the same machine during a production run are collected as a random sample and measured for breaking strength. The sample values (1345, 1301, 1368, 1322, 1310, 1370, 1318, 1350, 1303, 1299) are stored in A2:E3, respectively. STDEV estimates the standard deviation of breaking strengths for all the tools.

STDEV(A2:E3) equals 27.46

STDEVA

Estimates standard deviation based on a sample. The standard deviation is a measure of how widely values are dispersed from the average value (the mean). Text and logical values such as TRUE and FALSE are included in the calculation.

Syntax

STDEVA(value1,value2, ...)

Value1,value2, ...   are 1 to 30 values corresponding to a sample of a population. You can also use a single array or a reference to an array instead of arguments separated by commas.

Remarks

- STDEVA assumes that its arguments are a sample of the population. If your data represents the entire population, you must compute the standard deviation using STDEVPA.

- Arguments that contain TRUE evaluate as 1; arguments that contain text or FALSE evaluate as 0 (zero). If the calculation must not include text or logical values, use the STDEV worksheet function instead.

- The standard deviation is calculated using the "nonbiased" or "n-1" method.

- STDEVA uses the following formula:

$$\sqrt{\frac{n\sum x^2 - \left(\sum x\right)^2}{n(n-1)}}$$

Example

Suppose 10 tools stamped from the same machine during a production run are collected as a random sample and measured for breaking strength. The sample values (1345, 1301, 1368, 1322, 1310, 1370, 1318, 1350, 1303, 1299) are stored in A2:E3, respectively. STDEV estimates the standard deviation of breaking strengths for all the tools.

STDEV(A2:E3) equals 27.46

STDEVP

Calculates standard deviation based on the entire population given as arguments. The standard deviation is a measure of how widely values are dispersed from the average value (the mean).

Syntax

STDEVP(number1,number2, ...)

Number1,number2, ...   are 1 to 30 number arguments corresponding to a population. You can also use a single array or a reference to an array instead of arguments separated by commas.

Logical values such as TRUE and FALSE and text are ignored. If logical values and text must not be ignored, use the STDEVPA worksheet function.

Remarks

- STDEVP assumes that its arguments are the entire population. If your data represents a sample of the population, then compute the standard deviation using STDEV.

- For large sample sizes, STDEV and STDEVP return approximately equal values.

- The standard deviation is calculated using the "biased" or "n" method.

- STDEVP uses the following formula:

$$\sqrt{\frac{n\sum x^2 - \left(\sum x\right)^2}{n^2}}$$

Example

Using the same data from the STDEV example and assuming that only 10 tools are produced during the production run, STDEVP measures the standard deviation of breaking strengths for all the tools.

STDEVP(A2:E3) equals 26.05

STDEVPA

Calculates standard deviation based on the entire population given as arguments. The standard deviation is a measure of how widely values are dispersed from the average value (the mean).

Syntax

STDEVPA(value1,value2, ...)

Value1,value2, ...   are 1 to 30 values corresponding to a population. You can also use a single array or a reference to an array instead of arguments separated by commas.

Remarks

- STDEVPA assumes that its arguments are the entire population. If your data represents a sample of the population, you must compute the standard deviation using STDEVA.

- Arguments that contain TRUE evaluate as 1; arguments that contain text or FALSE evaluate as 0 (zero). If the calculation must not include text or logical values, use the STDEVP worksheet function instead.

- For large sample sizes, STDEVA and STDEVPA return approximately equal values.

- The standard deviation is calculated using the "biased" or "n" method.

- STDEVPA uses the following formula:

$$\sqrt{\frac{n\sum x^2 - \left(\sum x\right)^2}{n^2}}$$

Example

Using the same data from the STDEVA example and assuming that only 10 tools are produced during the production run, STDEVP measures the standard deviation of breaking strengths for all the tools.

`STDEVP(A2:E3)` equals 26.05

STEYX

Returns the standard error of the predicted y-value for each x in the regression. The standard error is a measure of the amount of error in the prediction of y for an individual x.

Syntax

STEYX(known_y's,known_x's)

Known_y's is an array or range of dependent data points.

Known_x's is an array or range of independent data points.

Remarks

- The arguments must be either numbers or names, arrays, or references that contain numbers.

- If an array or reference argument contains text, logical values, or empty cells, those values are ignored; however, cells with the value zero are included.

- If known_y's and known_x's are empty or have a different number of data points, STEYX returns the #N/A error value.

- The equation for the standard error of the predicted y is:

$$S_{y \cdot x} = \sqrt{\left[\frac{1}{n(n-2)}\right]\left[n\Sigma y^2 - (\Sigma y)^2 - \frac{[n\Sigma xy - (\Sigma x)(\Sigma y)]^2}{n\Sigma x^2 - (\Sigma x)^2}\right]}$$

Example

STEYX({2,3,9,1,8,7,5},{6,5,11,7,5,4,4}) equals 3.305719

SUBSTITUTE

Substitutes new_text for old_text in a text string. Use SUBSTITUTE when you want to replace specific text in a text string; use REPLACE when you want to replace any text that occurs in a specific location in a text string.

Syntax

SUBSTITUTE(text,old_text,new_text,instance_num)

Text is the text or the reference to a cell containing text for which you want to substitute characters.

Old_text is the text you want to replace.

New_text   is the text you want to replace old_text with.

Instance_num   specifies which occurrence of old_text you want to replace with new_text. If you specify instance_num, only that instance of old_text is replaced. Otherwise, every occurrence of old_text in text is changed to new_text.

Examples

SUBSTITUTE("Sales Data", "Sales", "Cost") equals "Cost Data"

SUBSTITUTE("Quarter 1, 1991", "1", "2", 1) equals "Quarter 2, 1991"

SUBSTITUTE("Quarter 1, 1991", "1", "2", 3) equals "Quarter 1, 1992"

To replace every occurrence of the text constant named Separator in the cell named CellCont2 with square brackets:

SUBSTITUTE(CellCont2, Separator, "] [")

SUBTOTAL

Returns a subtotal in a list or database. It is generally easier to create a list with subtotals using the **Subtotals** command (**Data** menu). Once the subtotal list is created, you can modify it by editing the SUBTOTAL function.

Syntax

SUBTOTAL(function_num,ref1,ref2, …)

Function_num   is the number 1 to 11 that specifies which function to use in calculating subtotals within a list.

Function_Num	Function
1	AVERAGE
2	COUNT
3	COUNTA
4	MAX
5	MIN
6	PRODUCT
7	STDEV
8	STDEVP
9	SUM
10	VAR
11	VARP

Ref1,ref2, …   are 1 to 29 ranges or references for which you want the subtotal.

Remarks

- If there are other subtotals within ref1,ref2, ... (or nested subtotals), these nested subtotals are ignored to avoid double counting.

- SUBTOTAL will ignore any hidden rows that result from a list being filtered. This is important when you want to subtotal only the visible data that results from a list that you have filtered.

- If any of the references are 3-D references, SUBTOTAL returns the #VALUE! error value.

Example

SUBTOTAL(9,C3:C5) will generate a subtotal of the cells C3:C5 using the SUM function

---

SUM

Adds all the numbers in a range of cells.

Syntax

SUM(number1,number2, ...)

Number1,number2, ...   are 1 to 30 arguments for which you want the total value or sum.

- Numbers, logical values, and text representations of numbers that you type directly into the list of arguments are counted. See the first and second examples following.

- If an argument is an array or reference, only numbers in that array or reference are counted. Empty cells, logical values, text, or error values in the array or reference are ignored. See the third example following.

- Arguments that are error values or text that cannot be translated into numbers cause errors.

Examples

SUM(3, 2) equals 5

SUM("3", 2, TRUE) equals 6 because the text values are translated into numbers, and the logical value TRUE is translated into the number 1.

Unlike the previous example, if A1 contains "3" and B1 contains TRUE, then:

SUM(A1, B1, 2) equals 2 because references to nonnumeric values in references are not translated.

If cells A2:E2 contain 5, 15, 30, 40, and 50:

SUM(A2:C2) equals 50

SUM(B2:E2, 15) equals 150

SUMIF

Adds the cells specified by a given criteria.

Syntax

SUMIF(range,criteria,sum_range)

Range   is the range of cells you want evaluated.

Criteria   is the criteria in the form of a number, expression, or text that defines which cells will be added. For example, criteria can be expressed as 32, "32", ">32", "apples".

Sum_range   are the actual cells to sum. The cells in sum_range are summed only if their corresponding cells in range match the criteria. If sum_range is omitted, the cells in range are summed.

Example

Suppose A1:A4 contain the following property values for four homes: $100,000, $200,000, $300,000, $400,000, respectively. B1:B4 contain the following sales commissions on each of the corresponding property values: $7,000, $14,000, $21,000, $28,000.

SUMIF(A1:A4,">160000",B1:B4) equals $63,000

SUMPRODUCT

Multiplies corresponding components in the given arrays, and returns the sum of those products.

Syntax

SUMPRODUCT(array1,array2,array3, ...)

Array1, **array2**, array3, ...   are 2 to 30 arrays whose components you want to multiply and then add.

- The array arguments must have the same dimensions. If they do not, SUMPRODUCT returns the #VALUE! error value.

- SUMPRODUCT treats array entries that are not numeric as if they were zeros.

Example

	A	B	C	D	E
1	3	4		2	7
2	8	6		6	7
3	1	9		5	3
4					

The following formula multiplies all the components of the two arrays on the preceding worksheet and then adds the products—that is, 3*2 + 4*7 + 8*6 + 6*7 + 1*5 + 9*3.

SUMPRODUCT({3,4;8,6;1,9}, {2,7;6,7;5,3}) equals 156

Remarks

The preceding example returns the same result as the formula SUM(A1:B3*D1:E3) entered as an array. Using arrays provides a more general solution for doing operations similar to SUMPRODUCT. For example, you can calculate the sum of the squares of the elements in A1:B3 by using the formula SUM(A1:B3^2) entered as an array.

SUMSQ

Returns the sum of the squares of the arguments.

Syntax

SUMSQ(number1,number2, ...)

Number1,number2, ...   are 1 to 30 arguments for which you want the sum of the squares. You can also use a single array or a reference to an array instead of arguments separated by commas.

Example

SUMSQ(3, 4) equals 25

SUMX2MY2

Returns the sum of the difference of squares of corresponding values in two arrays.

Syntax

SUMX2MY2(array_x,array_y)

Array_x   is the first array or range of values.

Array_y   is the second array or range of values.

Remarks

- The arguments should be either numbers or names, arrays, or references that contain numbers.

- If an array or reference argument contains text, logical values, or empty cells, those values are ignored; however, cells with the value zero are included.

- If array_x and array_y have a different number of values, SUMX2MY2 returns the #N/A error value.

- The equation for the sum of the difference of squares is:

$$\text{SUMX2MY2} = \sum (x^2 - y^2)$$

Example

SUMX2MY2({2, 3, 9, 1, 8, 7, 5}, {6, 5, 11, 7, 5, 4, 4}) equals -55

SUMX2PY2

Returns the sum of the sum of squares of corresponding values in two arrays. The sum of the sum of squares is a common term in many statistical calculations.

Syntax

SUMX2PY2(array_x,array_y)

Array_x   is the first array or range of values.

Array_y   is the second array or range of values.

Remarks

- The arguments should be either numbers or names, arrays, or references that contain numbers.

- If an array or reference argument contains text, logical values, or empty cells, those values are ignored; however, cells with the value zero are included.

- If array_x and array_y have a different number of values, SUMX2PY2 returns the #N/A error value.

- The equation for the sum of the sum of squares is:

$$\text{SUMX2PY2} = \sum (x^2 + y^2)$$

Example

SUMX2PY2({2, 3, 9, 1, 8, 7, 5}, {6, 5, 11, 7, 5, 4, 4}) equals 521

SUMXMY2

Returns the sum of squares of differences of corresponding values in two arrays.

Syntax

SUMXMY2(array_x,array_y)

Array_x is the first array or range of values.

Array_y is the second array or range of values.

Remarks

- The arguments should be either numbers or names, arrays, or references that contain numbers.

- If an array or reference argument contains text, logical values, or empty cells, those values are ignored; however, cells with the value zero are included.

- If array_x and array_y have a different number of values, SUMXMY2 returns the #N/A error value.

- The equation for the sum of squared differences is:

$$SUMXMY2 = \sum (x - y)^2$$

Example

SUMXMY2({2, 3, 9, 1, 8, 7, 5}, {6, 5, 11, 7, 5, 4, 4}) equals 79

SYD

Returns the sum-of-years' digits depreciation of an asset for a specified period.

Syntax

SYD(cost,salvage,life,per)

Cost is the initial cost of the asset.

Salvage is the value at the end of the depreciation (sometimes called the salvage value of the asset).

Life is the number of periods over which the asset is being depreciated (sometimes called the useful life of the asset).

Per is the period and must use the same units as life.

Remark

- SYD is calculated as follows:

$$SYD = \frac{(cost - salvage) * (life - per + 1) * 2}{(life)(life + 1)}$$

Examples

If you've bought a truck for $30,000 that has a useful life of 10 years and a salvage value of $7,500, the yearly depreciation allowance for the first year is:

SYD(30000,7500,10,1) equals $4,090.91

The yearly depreciation allowance for the tenth year is:

SYD(30000,7500,10,10) equals $409.09

T

Returns the text referred to by value.

Syntax

T(value)

Value   is the value you want to test. If value is or refers to text, T returns value. If value does not refer to text, T returns ""(empty text).

Remarks

You do not generally need to use the T function in a formula because Microsoft Excel automatically converts values as necessary. This function is provided for compatibility with other spreadsheet programs.

Examples

If B1 contains the text "Rainfall":

T(B1) equals "Rainfall"

If B2 contains the number 19:

T(B2) equals ""

T("True") equals "True"

T(TRUE) equals ""

TAN

Returns the tangent of the given angle.

Syntax

TAN(number)

Number   is the angle in radians for which you want the tangent. If your argument is in degrees, multiply it by PI()/180 to convert it to radians.

Examples

TAN(0.785) equals 0.99920

TAN(45*PI()/180) equals 1

TANH

Returns the hyperbolic tangent of a number.

Syntax

TANH(number)

Number   is any real number

The formula for the hyperbolic tangent is:

$$TANH(z) = \frac{SINH(z)}{COSH(z)}$$

Examples

TANH(-2) equals -0.96403

TANH(0) equals 0 (zero)

TANH(0.5) equals 0.462117

TBILLEQ

Returns the bond-equivalent yield for a treasury bill.

If this function is not available, run the Setup program to install the Analysis ToolPak. After you install the Analysis ToolPak, you must enable it by using the **Add-Ins** command on the **Tools** menu.

Syntax

TBILLEQ(settlement,maturity,discount)

Settlement   is the treasury bill's settlement date. The security settlement date is the date after the issue date when the treasury bill is traded to the buyer.

Maturity   is the treasury bill's maturity date. The maturity date is the date when the treasury bill expires.

Discount   is the treasury bill's discount rate.

Remarks

- Settlement and maturity are truncated to integers.

- If any argument is nonnumeric, TBILLEQ returns the #VALUE! error value.

- If settlement or maturity is not a valid date, TBILLEQ returns the #NUM! error value.

- If discount $\leq$ 0, TBILLEQ returns the #NUM! error value.

- If settlement > maturity, or if maturity is more than one year after settlement, TBILLEQ returns the #NUM! error value.

- TBILLEQ is calculated as TBILLEQ = (365 x rate)/360-(rate x DSM), where DSM is the number of days between settlement and maturity computed according to the 360 days per year basis.

Example

A treasury bill has the following terms:

March 31, 1993, settlement date
June 1, 1993, maturity date
9.14 percent discount rate

The bond equivalent yield for a treasury bill (in the 1900 date system) is:

TBILLEQ("3/31/93","6/1/93",0.0914) equals 0.094151 or 9.4151 percent

TBILLPRICE

Returns the price per $100 face value for a treasury bill.

If this function is not available, run the Setup program to install the Analysis ToolPak. After you install the Analysis ToolPak, you must enable it by using the **Add-Ins** command on the **Tools** menu.

Syntax

TBILLPRICE(settlement,maturity,discount)

Settlement   is the treasury bill's settlement date. The security settlement date is the date after the issue date when the treasury bill is traded to the buyer.

Maturity   is the treasury bill's maturity date. The maturity date is the date when the treasury bill expires.

Discount   is the treasury bill's discount rate.

Remarks

- Settlement and maturity are truncated to integers.

- If any argument is nonnumeric, TBILLPRICE returns the #VALUE! error value.

- If settlement or maturity is not a valid date, TBILLPRICE returns the #NUM! error value.

- If discount ≤ 0, TBILLPRICE returns the #NUM! error value.

- If settlement > maturity, or if maturity is more than one year after settlement, TBILLPRICE returns the #NUM! error value.

- TBILLPRICE is calculated as follows:

$$TBILLPRICE = 100 \times (1 - \frac{discount \times DSM}{360})$$

Where:

DSM = number of days from settlement to maturity, excluding any maturity date that is more than one calendar year after the settlement date.

Example

A treasury bill has the following terms:

March 31, 1993, settlement date
June 1, 1993, maturity date
9 percent discount rate

The treasury bill price (in the 1900 date system) is:

`TBILLPRICE("3/31/93","6/1/93",0.09)` equals 98.45

TBILLYIELD

Returns the yield for a treasury bill.

If this function is not available, run the Setup program to install the Analysis ToolPak. After you install the Analysis ToolPak, you must enable it by using the **Add-Ins** command on the **Tools** menu.

Syntax

TBILLYIELD(settlement,maturity,pr)

Settlement   is the treasury bill's settlement date. The security settlement date is the date after the issue date when the treasury bill is traded to the buyer.

Maturity   is the treasury bill's maturity date. The maturity date is the date when the treasury bill expires.

Pr   is the treasury bill's price per $100 face value.

Remarks

- Settlement and maturity are truncated to integers.

- If any argument is nonnumeric, TBILLYIELD returns the #VALUE! error value.

- If settlement or maturity is not a valid date, TBILLYIELD returns the #NUM! error value.

- If pr ≤ 0, TBILLYIELD returns the #NUM! error value.

- If settlement ≥ maturity, or if maturity is more than one year after settlement, TBILLYIELD returns the #NUM! error value.

- TBILLYIELD is calculated as follows:

$$TBILLYIELD = \frac{100 - par}{par} \times \frac{360}{DSM}$$

Where:

DSM = number of days from settlement to maturity, excluding any maturity date that is more than one calendar year after the settlement date.

Example

A treasury bill has the following terms:

March 31, 1993, settlement date
June 1, 1993, maturity date
98.45 price per $100 face value

The treasury bill yield (in the 1900 date system) is:

TBILLYIELD("3/31/93","6/1/93",98.45) equals 9.1417 percent

TDIST

Returns the Student's t-distribution. The t-distribution is used in the hypothesis testing of small sample data sets. Use this function in place of a table of critical values for the t-distribution.

Syntax

TDIST(x,degrees_freedom,tails)

X   is the numeric value at which to evaluate the distribution.

Degrees_freedom   is an integer indicating the number of degrees of freedom.

Tails   specifies the number of distribution tails to return. If tails = 1, TDIST returns the one-tailed distribution. If tails = 2, TDIST returns the two-tailed distribution.

Remarks

- If any argument is nonnumeric, TDIST returns the #VALUE! error value.

- If degrees_freedom < 1, TDIST returns the #NUM! error value.

- The degrees_freedom and tails arguments are truncated to integers.

- If tails is any value other than 1 or 2, TDIST returns the #NUM! error value.

- TDIST is calculated as TDIST = p(x<X), where X is a random variable that follows the t-distribution.

Example

TDIST(1.96,60,2) equals 0.054645

TEXT

Converts a value to text in a specific number format.

Syntax

TEXT(value,format_text)

Value   is a numeric value, a formula that evaluates to a numeric value, or a reference to a cell containing a numeric value.

Format_text   is a number format in text form from in the **Category** box on the **Number** tab in the **Format Cells** dialog box. Format_text cannot contain an asterisk (*) and cannot be the General number format.

Remarks

Formatting a cell with an option on the **Number** tab (**Cells** command, **Format** menu) changes only the format, not the value. Using the TEXT function converts a value to formatted text, and the result is no longer calculated as a number.

Examples

TEXT(2.715, "$0.00") equals "$2.72"

TEXT("4/15/91", "mmmm dd, yyyy") equals "April 15, 1991"

TIME

Returns the serial number of a particular time. The serial number returned by **TIME** is a decimal fraction ranging from 0 to 0.99999999, representing the times from 0:00:00 (12:00:00 A.M.) to 23:59:59 (11:59:59 P.M.).

Syntax

TIME(hour,minute,second)

Hour   is a number from 0 (zero) to 23 representing the hour.

Minute   is a number from 0 to 59 representing the minute.

Second   is a number from 0 to 59 representing the second.

Remarks

Microsoft Excel for Windows and Microsoft Excel for the Macintosh use different date systems as their default. For more information about date systems and serial numbers, see NOW.

Examples

TIME(12, 0, 0) equals the serial number 0.5, which is equivalent to 12:00:00 P.M.

TIME(16, 48, 10) equals the serial number 0.700115741, which is equivalent to 4:48:10 P.M.

TEXT(TIME(23, 18, 14), "h:mm:ss AM/PM") equals "11:18:14 PM"

TIMEVALUE

Returns the serial number of the time represented by time_text. The serial number is a decimal fraction ranging from 0 (zero) to 0.99999999, representing the times from 0:00:00 (12:00:00 A.M.) to 23:59:59 (11:59:59 P.M.). Use TIMEVALUE to convert a time represented as text into a serial number.

Syntax

TIMEVALUE(time_text)

Time_text   is a text string that gives a time in any one of the Microsoft Excel time formats. Date information in time_text is ignored.

Remarks

Microsoft Excel for Windows and Microsoft Excel for the Macintosh use different date systems as their default. For more information about date systems and serial numbers, see NOW.

Examples

TIMEVALUE("2:24 AM") equals 0.1

TIMEVALUE("22-Aug-55 6:35 AM") equals 0.274305556

TINV

Returns the inverse of the Student's t-distribution for the specified degrees of freedom.

Syntax

TINV(probability,degrees_freedom)

Probability   is the probability associated with the two-tailed Student's t-distribution.

Degrees_freedom   is the number of degrees of freedom to characterize the distribution.

Remarks

- If either argument is nonnumeric, TINV returns the #VALUE! error value.
- If probability < 0 or if probability > 1, TINV returns the #NUM! error value.
- If degrees_freedom is not an integer, it is truncated.
- If degrees_freedom < 1, TINV returns the #NUM! error value.
- TINV is calculated as TINV = p(t<X), where X is a random variable that follows the t-distribution.

TINV uses an iterative technique for calculating the function. Given a probability value, TINV iterates until the result is accurate to within $\pm 3\times10^{-7}$. If TINV does not converge after 100 iterations, the function returns the #N/A error value.

Example

TINV(0.054645,60) equals 1.96

TODAY

Returns the serial number of the current date. The serial number is the date-time code used by Microsoft Excel for date and time calculations. For more information about serial numbers, see NOW.

Syntax

TODAY( )

TRANSPOSE

Returns a vertical range of cells as a horizontal range, or vice versa. TRANSPOSE must be entered as an array formula in a range that has the same number of rows and columns, respectively, as array has columns and rows. Use TRANSPOSE to shift the vertical and horizontal orientation of an array on a worksheet. For example, some functions, such as LINEST, return horizontal arrays. LINEST returns a horizontal array of the slope and Y-intercept for a line. The following formula returns a vertical array of the slope and Y-intercept from LINEST:

```
TRANSPOSE(LINEST(Yvalues,Xvalues))
```

Syntax

TRANSPOSE(array)

Array   is an array or range of cells on a worksheet that you want to transpose. The transpose of an array is created by using the first row of the array as the first column of the new array, the second row of the array as the second column of the new array, and so on.

Example

Suppose A1:C1 contain 1, 2, 3, respectively. When the following formula is entered as an array into cells A3:A5:

```
TRANSPOSE($A$1:$C$1)
```
equals the same respective values in A3:A5

TREND

Returns values along a linear trend. Fits a straight line (using the method of least squares) to the arrays known_y's and known_x's. Returns the y-values along that line for the array of new_x's that you specify.

Syntax

TREND(known_y's,known_x's,new_x's,const)

Known_y's is the set of y-values you already know in the relationship $y = mx + b$.

- If the array known_y's is in a single column, then each column of known_x's is interpreted as a separate variable.

- If the array known_y's is in a single row, then each row of known_x's is interpreted as a separate variable.

Known_x's is an optional set of x-values that you may already know in the relationship $y = mx + b$.

- The array known_x's can include one or more sets of variables. If only one variable is used, known_y's and known_x's can be ranges of any shape, as long as they have equal dimensions. If more than one variable is used, known_y's must be a vector (that is, a range with a height of one row or a width of one column).

- If known_x's is omitted, it is assumed to be the array {1,2,3, ...} that is the same size as known_y's.

New_x's are new x-values for which you want TREND to return corresponding y-values.

- New_x's must include a column (or row) for each independent variable, just as known_x's does. So, if known_y's is in a single column, known_x's and new_x's must have the same number of columns. If known_y's is in a single row, known_x's and new_x's must have the same number of rows.

- If you omit new_x's, it is assumed to be the same as known_x's.

- If you omit both known_x's and new_x's, they are assumed to be the array {1,2,3, ...} that is the same size as known_y's.

Const is a logical value specifying whether to force the constant b to equal 0.

- If const is TRUE or omitted, b is calculated normally.

- If const is FALSE, b is set equal to 0 (zero), and the m-values are adjusted so that $y = mx$.

Remarks

- For information about how Microsoft Excel fits a line to data, see LINEST.

- You can use TREND for polynomial curve fitting by regressing against the same variable raised to different powers. For example, suppose column A contains y-values and column B contains x-values. You can enter x^2 in column C, x^3 in column D, and so on, and then regress columns B through D against column A.

- Formulas that return arrays must be entered as array formulas.

- When entering an array constant for an argument such as known_x's, use commas to separate values in the same row and semicolons to separate rows.

Example

Suppose a business wants to purchase a tract of land in July, the start of the next fiscal year. The business collects cost information that covers the most recent 12 months for a typical tract in the desired area. Known_y values are in cells B2:B13; the known_y values are $133,890, $135,000, $135,790, $137,300, $138,130, $139,100, $139,900, $141,120, $141,890, $143,230, $144,000, $145,290.

When entered as a vertical array in the range C2:C6, the following formula returns the predicted prices for March, April, May, June, and July:

TREND(B2:B13,,{13;14;15;16;17}) equals {146172;147190;148208;149226;150244}

The company can expect a typical tract of land to cost about $150,244 if it waits until July. The preceding formula uses the default array {1;2;3;4;5;6;7;8;9;10;11;12} for the known_x's argument, corresponding to the 12 months of sales data. The array {13;14;15;16;17} corresponds to the next five months.

TRIM

Removes all spaces from text except for single spaces between words. Use TRIM on text that you have received from another application that may have irregular spacing.

Syntax

TRIM(text)

Text   is the text from which you want spaces removed.

Example

TRIM(" First   Quarter   Earnings   ") equals "First Quarter Earnings"

TRIMMEAN

Returns the mean of the interior of a data set. TRIMMEAN calculates the mean taken by excluding a percentage of data points from the top and bottom tails of a data set. You can use this function when you wish to exclude outlying data from your analysis.

Syntax

TRIMMEAN(array,percent)

Array   is the array or range of values to trim and average.

Percent   is the fractional number of data points to exclude from the calculation. For example, if percent = 0.2, 4 points are trimmed from a data set of 20 points (20 x 0.2), 2 from the top and 2 from the bottom of the set.

Remarks

- If percent < 0 or percent > 1, TRIMMEAN returns the #NUM! error value.

- TRIMMEAN rounds the number of excluded data points down to the nearest multiple of 2. If percent = 0.1, 10 percent of 30 data points equals 3 points. For symmetry, TRIMMEAN excludes a single value from the top and bottom of the data set.

Example

`TRIMMEAN({4,5,6,7,2,3,4,5,1,2,3},0.2)` equals 3.777778

TRUE

Returns the logical value TRUE.

Syntax

TRUE( )

Remarks

You can enter the value TRUE directly into cells and formulas without using this function. The TRUE function is provided primarily for compatibility with other spreadsheet programs.

TRUNC

Truncates a number to an integer by removing the fractional part of the number.

Syntax

TRUNC(number,num_digits)

Number   is the number you want to truncate.

Num_digits   is a number specifying the precision of the truncation. The default value for num_digits is 0 (zero).

Remarks

TRUNC and INT are similar in that both return integers. TRUNC removes the fractional part of the number. INT rounds numbers down to the nearest integer based on the value of the fractional part of the number. INT and TRUNC are different only when using negative numbers: TRUNC(-4.3) returns -4, but INT(-4.3) returns -5 because -5 is the lower number.

Examples

TRUNC(8.9) equals 8

TRUNC(-8.9) equals -8

TRUNC(PI()) equals 3

TTEST

Returns the probability associated with a Student's t-Test. Use TTEST to determine whether two samples are likely to have come from the same two underlying populations that have the same mean.

Syntax

TTEST(array1,array2,tails,type)

Array1   is the first data set.

Array2   is the second data set.

Tails   specifies the number of distribution tails. If tails = 1, TTEST uses the one-tailed distribution. If tails = 2, TTEST uses the two-tailed distribution.

Type   is the kind of t-Test to perform.

If type equals	This test is performed
1	Paired
2	Two-sample equal variance (homoscedastic)
3	Two-sample unequal variance (heteroscedastic)

Remarks

- If array1 and array2 have a different number of data points, and type = 1 (paired), TTEST returns the #N/A error value.

- The tails and type arguments are truncated to integers.

- If tails or type is nonnumeric, TTEST returns the #VALUE! error value.

- If tails is any value other than 1 or 2, TTEST returns the #NUM! error value.

Example

TTEST({3,4,5,8,9,1,2,4,5},{6,19,3,2,14,4,5,17,1},2,1)
equals 0.196016

TYPE

Returns the type of value. Use TYPE when the behavior of another function depends on the type of value in a particular cell.

Syntax

TYPE(value)

Value   can be any Microsoft Excel value, such as a number, text, logical value, and so on.

If value is	TYPE returns
Number	1
Text	2
Logical value	4
Formula	8
Error value	16
Array	64

Remarks

TYPE is most useful when you are using functions that can accept different types of data, such as ARGUMENT and INPUT. Use TYPE to find out what type of data is returned by the function.

Examples

If A1 contains the text "Smith", then:

TYPE(A1) equals TYPE("Smith") equals 2

TYPE("MR. "&A1) equals 2

TYPE(2+A1) equals TYPE(#VALUE!) equals 16

TYPE({1,2;3,4}) equals 64

UPPER

Converts text to uppercase.

Syntax

UPPER(text)

Text is the text you want converted to uppercase. Text can be a reference or text string.

Examples

UPPER("total") equals "TOTAL"

If E5 contains "yield", then:

UPPER(E5) equals "YIELD"

CAESARENDOFDOC

VALUE

Converts a text string that represents a number to a number.

Syntax

VALUE(text)

Text is the text enclosed in quotation marks or a reference to a cell containing the text you want to convert. Text can be in any of the constant number, date, or time formats recognized by Microsoft Excel. If text is not in one of these formats, VALUE returns the #VALUE! error value.

Remarks

You do not generally need to use the VALUE function in a formula because Microsoft Excel automatically converts text to numbers as necessary. This function is provided for compatibility with other spreadsheet programs.

Examples

VALUE("$1,000") equals 1,000

VALUE("16:48:00")-VALUE("12:00:00") equals "16:48:00"-"12:00:00" equals 0.2, the serial number equivalent to 4 hours and 48 minutes.

VAR

Estimates variance based on a sample.

Syntax

VAR(number1,number2, ...)

Number1,number2, ...   are 1 to 30 number arguments corresponding to a sample of a population.

Remarks

- VAR assumes that its arguments are a sample of the population. If your data represents the entire population, then compute the variance using VARP.

- Logical values such as TRUE and FALSE and text are ignored. If logical values and text must not be ignored, use the VARA worksheet function.

- VAR uses the following formula:

$$\frac{n\sum x^2 - (\sum x)^2}{n(n-1)}$$

Example

Suppose 10 tools stamped from the same machine during a production run are collected as a random sample and measured for breaking strength. The sample values (1345, 1301, 1368, 1322, 1310, 1370, 1318, 1350, 1303, 1299) are stored in A2:E3, respectively. VAR estimates the variance for the breaking strength of the tools.

`VAR(A2:E3)` equals 754.3

VARA

Estimates variance based on a sample. In addition to numbers, text and logical values such as TRUE and FALSE are included in the calculation.

Syntax

VARA(value1,value2, ...)

Value1,value2, ...   are 1 to 30 value arguments corresponding to a sample of a population.

Remarks

- VARA assumes that its arguments are a sample of the population. If your data represents the entire population, you must compute the variance using VARPA.

- Arguments that contain TRUE evaluate as 1; arguments that contain text or FALSE evaluate as 0 (zero). If the calculation must not include text or logical values, use the VAR worksheet function instead.

- VARA uses the following formula:

$$\frac{n\Sigma x^2 - (\Sigma x)^2}{n(n-1)}$$

Example

Suppose 10 tools stamped from the same machine during a production run are collected as a random sample and measured for breaking strength. The sample values (1345, 1301, 1368, 1322, 1310, 1370, 1318, 1350, 1303, 1299) are stored in A2:E3, respectively. VARA estimates the variance for the breaking strength of the tools.

VARA(A2:E3) equals 754.3

VARP

Calculates variance based on the entire population.

Syntax

VARP(number1,number2, ...)

Number1,number2, ...   are 1 to 30 number arguments corresponding to a population.

Logical values such as TRUE and FALSE and text are ignored. If logical values and text must not be ignored, use the VARPA worksheet function.

Remarks

- VARP assumes that its arguments are the entire population. If your data represents a sample of the population, then compute the variance using VAR.

- The equation for VARP is:

$$\frac{n\sum x^2 - \left(\sum x\right)^2}{n^2}$$

Example

Using the data from the VAR example and assuming that only 10 tools are produced during the production run, VARP measures the variance of breaking strengths for all the tools.

VARP(A2:E3) equals 678.8

VARPA

Calculates variance based on the entire population. In addition to numbers, text and logical values such as TRUE and FALSE are included in the calculation.

Syntax

VARPA(**value1**,value2, ...)

Value1,value2, ...   are 1 to 30 value arguments corresponding to a population.

Remarks

- VARPA assumes that its arguments are the entire population. If your data represents a sample of the population, you must compute the variance using VARA.

- Arguments that contain TRUE evaluate as 1; arguments that contain text or FALSE evaluate as 0 (zero). If the calculation must not include text or logical values, use the VARP worksheet function instead.

- The equation for VARPA is:

$$\frac{n \sum x^2 - \left(\sum x \right)^2}{n^2}$$

Example

Using the data from the VARA example and assuming that only 10 tools are produced during the production run, VARPA measures the variance of breaking strengths for all the tools.

VARPA(A2:E3) equals 678.8

VDB

Returns the depreciation of an asset for any period you specify, including partial periods, using the double-declining balance method or some other method you specify. VDB stands for variable declining balance.

Syntax

VDB(**cost**,**salvage**,**life**,**start_period**,**end_period**,factor,no_switch)

Cost   is the initial cost of the asset.

Salvage   is the value at the end of the depreciation (sometimes called the salvage value of the asset).

Life   is the number of periods over which the asset is being depreciated (sometimes called the useful life of the asset).

Start_period   is the starting period for which you want to calculate the depreciation. Start_period must use the same units as life.

End_period   is the ending period for which you want to calculate the depreciation. End_period must use the same units as life.

Factor   is the rate at which the balance declines. If factor is omitted, it is assumed to be 2 (the double-declining balance method). Change factor if you do not want to use the double-declining balance method. For a description of the double-declining balance method, see DDB.

No_switch   is a logical value specifying whether to switch to straight-line depreciation when depreciation is greater than the declining balance calculation.

- If no_switch is TRUE, Microsoft Excel does not switch to straight-line depreciation even when the depreciation is greater than the declining balance calculation.

- If no_switch is FALSE or omitted, Microsoft Excel switches to straight-line depreciation when depreciation is greater than the declining balance calculation.

All arguments except no_switch must be positive numbers.

Examples

Suppose a factory purchases a new machine. The machine costs $2,400 and has a lifetime of 10 years. The salvage value of the machine is $300. The following examples show depreciation over several periods. The results are rounded to two decimal places.

VDB(2400, 300, 3650, 0, 1) equals $1.32, the first day's depreciation. Microsoft Excel automatically assumes that factor is 2.

VDB(2400, 300, 120, 0, 1) equals $40.00, the first month's depreciation.

VDB(2400, 300, 10, 0, 1) equals $480.00, the first year's depreciation.

VDB(2400, 300, 120, 6, 18) equals $396.31, the depreciation between the sixth month and the eighteenth month.

VDB(2400, 300, 120, 6, 18, 1.5) equals $311.81, the depreciation between the sixth month and the eighteenth month using a factor of 1.5 instead of the double-declining balance method.

Suppose instead that the $2,400 machine is purchased in the middle of the first quarter of the fiscal year. The following formula determines the amount of depreciation for the first fiscal year that you own the asset, assuming that tax laws limit you to 150-percent depreciation of the declining balance:

VDB(2400, 300, 10, 0, 0.875, 1.5) equals $315.00

VLOOKUP

Searches for a value in the leftmost column of a table, and then returns a value in the same row from a column you specify in the table. Use VLOOKUP instead of HLOOKUP when your comparison values are located in a column to the left of the data you want to find.

Syntax

VLOOKUP(lookup_value,table_array,col_index_num,range_lookup)

Lookup_value is the value to be found in the first column of the array. Lookup_value can be a value, a reference, or a text string.

Table_array is the table of information in which data is looked up. Use a reference to a range or a range name, such as Database or List.

- If range_lookup is TRUE, the values in the first column of table_array must be placed in ascending order: ..., -2, -1, 0, 1, 2, ..., A-Z, FALSE, TRUE; otherwise VLOOKUP may not give the correct value. If range_lookup is FALSE, table_array does not need to be sorted.

- You can put the values in ascending order by choosing the **Sort** command from the **Data** menu and selecting **Ascending.**

- The values in the first column of table_array can be text, numbers, or logical values.

- Uppercase and lowercase text are equivalent.

Col_index_num is the column number in table_array from which the matching value must be returned. A col_index_num of 1 returns the value in the first column in table_array; a col_index_num of 2 returns the value in the second column in table_array, and so on. If col_index_num is less than 1, VLOOKUP returns the #VALUE! error value; if col_index_num is greater than the number of columns in table_array, VLOOKUP returns the #REF! error value.

Range_lookup is a logical value that specifies whether you want VLOOKUP to find an exact match or an approximate match. If TRUE or omitted, an approximate match is returned. In other words, if an exact match is not found, the next largest value that is less than lookup_value is returned. If FALSE, VLOOKUP will find an exact match. If one is not found, the error value #N/A is returned.

Remarks

- If VLOOKUP can't find lookup_value, and range_lookup is TRUE, it uses the largest value that is less than or equal to lookup_value.

- If lookup_value is smaller than the smallest value in the first column of table_array, VLOOKUP returns the #N/A error value.

- If VLOOKUP can't find lookup_value, and range_lookup is FALSE, VLOOKUP returns the #N/A value.

Examples

	A	B	C	D
1	Air at 1 atm pressure			
2	Density	Viscosity	Temp	
3	(kg/cubic m)	(kg/m*s)*1E+05	(degrees C)	
4	0.457	3.55	500	
5	0.525	3.25	400	
6	0.616	2.93	300	
7	0.675	2.75	250	
8	0.746	2.57	200	
9	0.835	2.38	150	
10	0.946	2.17	100	
11	1.09	1.95	50	
12	1.29	1.71	0	

On the preceding worksheet, where the range A4:C12 is named Range:

VLOOKUP(1,Range,1,TRUE) equals 0.946

VLOOKUP(1,Range,2) equals 2.17

VLOOKUP(1,Range,3,TRUE) equals 100

VLOOKUP(.746,Range,3,FALSE) equals 200

VLOOKUP(0.1,Range,2,TRUE) equals #N/A, because 0.1 is less than the smallest value in column A

VLOOKUP(2,Range,2,TRUE) equals 1.71

WEEKDAY

Returns the day of the week corresponding to serial_number. The day is given as an integer, ranging from 1 (Sunday) to 7 (Saturday).

Syntax

WEEKDAY(serial_number,return_type)

Serial_number is the date-time code used by Microsoft Excel for date and time calculations. You can give serial_number as text, such as "15-Apr-1993" or "4-15-93", instead of as a number. The text is automatically converted to a serial number. For more information about serial_number, see NOW.

Return_type is a number that determines the type of return value.

Return_type	Number returned
1 or omitted	Numbers 1 (Sunday) through 7 (Saturday). Behaves like previous versions of Microsoft Excel.
2	Numbers 1 (Monday) through 7 (Sunday).
3	Numbers 0 (Monday) through 6 (Sunday).

Remarks

- Microsoft Excel for Windows and Microsoft Excel for the Macintosh use different date systems as their default. For more information, see NOW.

- You can also use the TEXT function to convert a value to a specified number format when using the 1900 date system:

  TEXT("4/16/90", "dddd") equals Monday

Examples

WEEKDAY("2/14/90") equals 4 (Wednesday)

If you are using the 1900 date system (the default in Microsoft Excel for Windows), then:

WEEKDAY(29747.007) equals 4 (Wednesday)

If you are using the 1904 date system (the default in Microsoft Excel for the Macintosh), then:

WEEKDAY(29747.007) equals 3 (Tuesday)

WEEKNUM

Returns a number that indicates where the week falls numerically within a year.

If this function is not available, run the Setup program to install the Analysis ToolPak. After you install the Analysis ToolPak, you must enable it by using the **Add-Ins** command on the **Tools** menu.

Syntax

WEEKNUM(serial_num,return_type)

Serial_num is a date within the week.

Return_type is a number that determines on what day the week begins. The default is 1.

Serial num	Week Begins
1	Week begins on Sunday. Weekdays are numbered 1 through 7.
2	Week begins on Monday. Weekdays are numbered 1 through 7.

Examples

If date is Sunday, January 9, 1994, then:

WEEKNUM("1/9/94", 1) equals 3

WEEKNUM("1/9/94", 2) equals 2

WEIBULL

Returns the Weibull distribution. Use this distribution in reliability analysis, such as calculating a device's mean time to failure.

Syntax

WEIBULL(x,alpha,beta,cumulative)

X   is the value at which to evaluate the function.

Alpha   is a parameter to the distribution.

Beta   is a parameter to the distribution.

Cumulative   determines the form of the function.

Remarks

- If x, alpha, or beta is nonnumeric, WEIBULL returns the #VALUE! error value.
- If x < 0, WEIBULL returns the #NUM! error value.
- If alpha ≤ 0 or if beta ≤ 0, WEIBULL returns the #NUM! error value.
- The equation for the Weibull cumulative distribution function is:

$$F(x;\alpha,\beta) = 1 - e^{-(x/\beta)^{\alpha}}$$

- The equation for the Weibull probability density function is:

$$f(x;\alpha,\beta) = \frac{\alpha}{\beta^{\alpha}} x^{\alpha-1} e^{-(x/\beta)^{\alpha}}$$

- When alpha = 1, WEIBULL returns the exponential distribution with:

$$\lambda = \frac{1}{\beta}$$

Examples

WEIBULL(105,20,100,TRUE) equals 0.929581

WEIBULL(105,20,100,FALSE) equals 0.035589

WORKDAY

Returns a number that represents a date that is the indicated number of working days before or after start_date. Working days exclude weekends and any dates identified as holidays. Use WORKDAY to exclude weekends or holidays when you calculate invoice due dates, expected delivery times, or the number of days of work performed. To view the number as a date, click **Cells** on the **Format** menu, click **Date** in the **Category** box, and then click a date format in the **Type** box.

If this function is not available, run the Setup program to install the Analysis ToolPak. After you install the Analysis ToolPak, you must enable it by using the **Add-Ins** command on the **Tools** menu.

Syntax

WORKDAY(start_date,days,holidays)

Start_date   is a date that represents the start date.

Days   is the number of nonweekend and nonholiday days before or after start_date. A positive value for days yields a future date; a negative value yields a past date.

Holidays   is an optional list of one or more dates to exclude from the working calendar, such as state and federal holidays and floating holidays. The list can be either a range of cells or an array constant of the numbers that represent the dates.

Remarks

- If any argument is nonnumeric, WORKDAY returns the #VALUE! error value.

- If start_date is not a valid date, WORKDAY returns the #NUM! error value.

- If start_date plus days yields an invalid date, WORKDAY returns the #NUM! error value.

- If days is not an integer, it is truncated.

Examples

WORKDAY(DATEVALUE("01/03/91"), 5) equals 33248 or 01/10/91

If January 7, 1991 and January 8, 1991 are holidays, then:
WORKDAY(DATEVALUE("01/03/91"), 5, {33245, 33246}) equals 33252 or 01/14/91

XIRR

Returns the internal rate of return for a schedule of cash flows that is not necessarily periodic. To calculate the internal rate of return for a series of periodic cash flows, use the IRR function.

If this function is not available, run the Setup program to install the Analysis ToolPak. After you install the Analysis ToolPak, you must enable it by using the **Add-Ins** command on the **Tools** menu.

Syntax

XIRR(**values**,**dates**,guess)

Values   is a series of cash flows that corresponds to a schedule of payments in dates. The first payment is optional and corresponds to a cost or payment that occurs at the beginning of the investment. All succeeding payments are discounted based on a 365-day year.

Dates   is a schedule of payment dates that corresponds to the cash flow payments. The first payment date indicates the beginning of the schedule of payments. All other dates must be later than this date, but they may occur in any order.

Guess   is a number that you guess is close to the result of XIRR.

Remarks

- Numbers in dates are truncated to integers.
- If any argument is nonnumeric, XIRR returns the #VALUE! error value.
- XIRR expects at least one positive cash flow and one negative cash flow; otherwise, XIRR returns the #NUM! error value.
- If any number in dates is not a valid date, XIRR returns the #NUM! error value.
- If any number in dates precedes the starting date, XIRR returns the #NUM! error value.
- If values and dates contain a different number of values, XIRR returns the #NUM! error value.
- In most cases you do not need to provide guess for the XIRR calculation. If omitted, guess is assumed to be 0.1 (10 percent).
- XIRR is closely related to XNPV, the net present value function. The rate of return calculated by XIRR is the interest rate corresponding to XNPV = 0.

- Microsoft Excel uses an iterative technique for calculating XIRR. Using a changing rate (starting with guess), XIRR cycles through the calculation until the result is accurate within 0.000001 percent. If XIRR can't find a result that works after 100 tries, the #NUM! error value is returned. The rate is changed until:

$$0 = \sum_{i=1}^{N} \frac{P_i}{(1 + rate)^{\frac{(d_i - d_1)}{365}}}$$

where:

di = the ith, or last, payment date.

d1 = the 0th payment date.

Pi = the ith, or last, payment.

Example

Consider an investment that requires a $10,000 cash payment on January 1, 1992, and returns $2,750 on March 1, 1992, $4,250 on October 30, 1992, $3,250 on February 15, 1993, and $2,750 on April 1, 1993. The internal rate of return (in the 1900 date system) is:

XIRR({-10000,2750,4250,3250,2750}, {"1/1/92","3/1/92","10/30/92","2/15/93","4/1/93"},0.1) equals 0.373363 or 37.3363 percent

XNPV

Returns the net present value for a schedule of cash flows that is not necessarily periodic. To calculate the net present value for a series of cash flows that is periodic, use the NPV function.

If this function is not available, run the Setup program to install the Analysis ToolPak. After you install the Analysis ToolPak, you must enable it by using the **Add-Ins** command on the **Tools** menu.

Syntax

XNPV(rate,values,dates)

Rate   is the discount rate to apply to the cash flows.

Values   is a series of cash flows that corresponds to a schedule of payments in dates. The first payment is optional and corresponds to a cost or payment that occurs at the beginning of the investment. All succeeding payments are discounted based on a 365-day year.

Dates   is a schedule of payment dates that corresponds to the cash flow payments. The first payment date indicates the beginning of the schedule of payments. All other dates must be later than this date, but they may occur in any order.

Remarks

- Numbers in dates are truncated to integers.

- If any argument is nonnumeric, XNPV returns the #VALUE! error value.

- If any number in dates is not a valid date, XNPV returns the #NUM! error value.

- If any number in dates precedes the starting date, XNPV returns the #NUM! error value.

- If values and dates contain a different number of values, XNPV returns the #NUM! error value.

- XNPV is calculated as follows:

$$XNPV = \sum_{i=1}^{N} \frac{P_i}{(1+rate)^{\frac{(d_i - d_1)}{365}}}$$

where:

d_i = the ith, or last, payment date.

d_1 = the 0th payment date.

P_i = the ith, or last, payment.

Example

Consider an investment that requires a $10,000 cash payment on January 1, 1992, and returns $2,750 on March 1, 1992, $4,250 on October 30, 1992, $3,250 on February 15, 1993, and $2,750 on April 1, 1993. Assume that the cash flows are discounted at 9 percent. The net present value is:

```
XNPV(0.09,{-10000,2750,4250,3250,2750},
{"1/1/92","3/1/92","10/30/92","2/15/93","4/1/93"}) equals
2086.647602
```

YEAR

Returns the year corresponding to serial_number. The year is given as an integer in the range 1900-9999.

Syntax

YEAR(serial_number)

Serial_number   is the date-time code used by Microsoft Excel for date and time calculations. You can give serial_number as text, such as "15-Apr-1993" or "4-15-93", instead of as a number. The text is automatically converted to a serial number. For more information about serial_number, see NOW.

Remarks

Microsoft Excel for Windows and Microsoft Excel for the Macintosh use different date systems as their default. For more information, see NOW.

Examples

YEAR("7/5/90") equals 1990

If you are using the 1900 date system (the default in Microsoft Excel for Windows), then:

YEAR(0.007) equals 1900

YEAR(29747.007) equals 1981

If you are using the 1904 date system (the default in Microsoft Excel for the Macintosh), then:

YEAR(0.007) equals 1904

YEAR(29747.007) equals 1985

YEARFRAC

Calculates the fraction of the year represented by the number of whole days between two dates (the start_date and the end_date). Use the YEARFRAC worksheet function to identify the proportion of a whole year's benefits or obligations to assign to a specific term.

If this function is not available, run the Setup program to install the Analysis ToolPak. After you install the Analysis ToolPak, you must enable it by using the **Add-Ins** command on the **Tools** menu.

Syntax

YEARFRAC(start_date,end_date,basis)

Start_date is a date that represents the start date.

End_date is a date that represents the end date.

Basis is the type of day count basis to use.

Basis	Day count basis
0 or omitted	US (NASD) 30/360
1	Actual/actual
2	Actual/360
3	Actual/365
4	European 30/360

Remarks

- All arguments are truncated to integers.

- If any argument is nonnumeric, YEARFRAC returns the #VALUE! error value.

- If start_date or end_date are not valid dates, YEARFRAC returns the #NUM! error value.

- If basis < 0 or if basis > 4, YEARFRAC returns the #NUM! error value.

Examples

YEARFRAC("01/01/93", "06/30/93",0) equals 0.5

YEARFRAC("01/01/93", "07/01/93",3) equals 0.49863

YIELD

Returns the yield on a security that pays periodic interest. Use YIELD to calculate bond yield.

If this function is not available, run the Setup program to install the Analysis ToolPak. After you install the Analysis ToolPak, you must enable it by using the **Add-Ins** command on the **Tools** menu.

Syntax

YIELD(settlement,maturity,rate,pr,redemption,frequency,basis)

Settlement   is the security's settlement date. The security settlement date is the date after the issue date when the security is traded to the buyer.

Maturity   is the security's maturity date. The maturity date is the date when the security expires.

Rate   is the security's annual coupon rate.

Pr   is the security's price per $100 face value.

Redemption   is the security's redemption value per $100 face value.

Frequency   is the number of coupon payments per year. For annual payments, frequency = 1; for semiannual, frequency = 2; for quarterly, frequency = 4.

Basis   is the type of day count basis to use.

Basis	Day count basis
0 or omitted	US (NASD) 30/360
1	Actual/actual
2	Actual/360
3	Actual/365
4	European 30/360

Remarks

- The settlement date is the date a buyer purchases a coupon, such as a bond. The maturity date is the date when a coupon expires. For example, suppose a 30-year bond is issued on January 1, 1996, and is purchased by a buyer six months later. The issue date would be January 1, 1996, the settlement date would be July 1, 1996, and the maturity date would be January 1, 2026, which is 30 years after the January 1, 1996, issue date.

- Settlement, maturity, frequency, and basis are truncated to integers.

- If any argument is nonnumeric, YIELD returns the #VALUE! error value.

- If settlement or maturity is not a valid date, YIELD returns the #NUM! error value.

- If rate < 0, YIELD returns the #NUM! error value.

- If pr ≤ 0 or if redemption ≤ 0, YIELD returns the #NUM! error value.

- If frequency is any number other than 1, 2, or 4, YIELD returns the #NUM! error value.

- If basis < 0 or if basis > 4, YIELD returns the #NUM! error value.

- If settlement ≥ maturity, YIELD returns the #NUM! error value.

- If there is one coupon period or less until redemption, YIELD is calculated as follows:

$$YIELD = \frac{(\frac{redemption}{100} + \frac{rate}{frequency}) - (\frac{par}{100} + (\frac{A}{E} \times \frac{rate}{frequency}))}{\frac{par}{100} + (\frac{A}{E} \times \frac{rate}{frequency})} \times \frac{frequency \times E}{DSR}$$

where:

A = number of days from the beginning of the coupon period to the settlement date (accrued days).

DSR = number of days from the settlement date to the redemption date.

E = number of days in the coupon period.

- If there is more than one coupon period until redemption, YIELD is calculated through a hundred iterations. The resolution uses the Newton method, based on the formula used for the function PRICE. The yield is changed until the estimated price given the yield is close to price.

Example

A bond has the following terms:

February 15, 1991, settlement date
November 15, 1999, maturity date
5.75 percent coupon
95.04287 price
$100 redemption value
Frequency is semiannual
30/360 basis

The bond yield (in the 1900 date system) is:

`YIELD("2/15/91","11/15/99",0.0575,95.04287,100,2,0)` equals 0.065 or
6.5 percent

YIELDDISC

Returns the annual yield for a discounted security.

If this function is not available, run the Setup program to install the Analysis ToolPak. After you install the Analysis ToolPak, you must enable it by using the **Add-Ins** command on the **Tools** menu.

Syntax

YIELDDISC(settlement,maturity,pr,redemption,basis)

Settlement   is the security's settlement date. The security settlement date is the date after the issue date when the security is traded to the buyer.

Maturity   is the security's maturity date. The maturity date is the date when the security expires.

Pr   is the security's price per $100 face value.

Redemption   is the security's redemption value per $100 face value.

Basis   is the type of day count basis to use.

Basis	Day count basis
0 or omitted	US (NASD) 30/360
1	Actual/actual
2	Actual/360
3	Actual/365
4	European 30/360

Remarks

- The settlement date is the date a buyer purchases a coupon, such as a bond. The maturity date is the date when a coupon expires. For example, suppose a 30-year bond is issued on January 1, 1996, and is purchased by a buyer six months later. The issue date would be January 1, 1996, the settlement date would be July 1, 1996, and the maturity date would be January 1, 2026, which is 30 years after the January 1, 1996, issue date.

- Settlement, maturity, and basis are truncated to integers.

- If any argument is nonnumeric, YIELDDISC returns the #VALUE! error value.

- If settlement or maturity is not a valid date, YIELDDISC returns the #NUM! error value.

- If pr ≤ 0 or if redemption ≤ 0, YIELDDISC returns the #NUM! error value.

- If basis < 0 or if basis > 4, YIELDDISC returns the #NUM! error value.

- If settlement ≥ maturity, YIELDDISC returns the #NUM! error value.

Example

A bond has the following terms:

February 15, 1993, settlement date
March 1, 1993, maturity date
99.795 price
$100 redemption value
Actual/360 basis

The bond yield (in the 1900 date system) is:

`YIELDDISC("2/15/93","3/1/93",99.795,100,2)` equals 5.2823 percent

YIELDMAT

Returns the annual yield of a security that pays interest at maturity.

If this function is not available, run the Setup program to install the Analysis ToolPak. After you install the Analysis ToolPak, you must enable it by using the **Add-Ins** command on the **Tools** menu.

Syntax

YIELDMAT(settlement,maturity,issue,rate,pr,basis)

Settlement   is the security's settlement date. The security settlement date is the date after the issue date when the security is traded to the buyer.

Maturity   is the security's maturity date. The maturity date is the date when the security expires.

Issue   is the security's issue date, expressed as a serial date number.

Rate is the security's interest rate at date of issue.

Pr is the security's price per $100 face value.

Basis is the type of day count basis to use.

Basis	Day count basis
0 or omitted	US (NASD) 30/360
1	Actual/actual
2	Actual/360
3	Actual/365
4	European 30/360

Remarks

- The settlement date is the date a buyer purchases a coupon, such as a bond. The maturity date is the date when a coupon expires. For example, suppose a 30-year bond is issued on January 1, 1996, and is purchased by a buyer six months later. The issue date would be January 1, 1996, the settlement date would be July 1, 1996, and the maturity date would be January 1, 2026, which is 30 years after the January 1, 1996, issue date.

- Settlement, maturity, issue, and basis are truncated to integers.

- If any argument is nonnumeric, YIELDMAT returns the #VALUE! error value.

- If settlement, maturity, or issue is not a valid date, YIELDMAT returns the #NUM! error value.

- If rate < 0 or if pr ≤ 0, YIELDMAT returns the #NUM! error value.

- If basis < 0 or if basis > 4, YIELDMAT returns the #NUM! error value.

- If settlement ≥ maturity, YIELDMAT returns the #NUM! error value.

Example

A bond has the following terms:

March 15, 1993, settlement date
November 3, 1993, maturity date
November 8, 1992, issue date
6.25 percent semiannual coupon
100.0123 price
30/360 basis

The yield (in the 1900 date system) is:

`YIELDMAT("3/15/93","11/3/93","11/8/92",0.0625,100.0123,0)` equals 0.060954 or 6.0954 percent

ZTEST

Returns the two-tailed P-value of a z-test. The z-test generates a standard score for x with respect to the data set, array, and returns the two-tailed probability for the normal distribution. You can use this function to assess the likelihood that a particular observation is drawn from a particular population.

Syntax

ZTEST(array,x,sigma)

Array   is the array or range of data against which to test x.

X   is the value to test.

Sigma   is the population (known) standard deviation. If omitted, the sample standard deviation is used.

Remarks

- If array is empty, ZTEST returns the #N/A error value.

- ZTEST is calculated as follows:

$$ZTEST(array, x) = 1 - NORMSDIST\left(\frac{\mu - x}{\sigma \div \sqrt{n}}\right)$$

Example

ZTEST({3,6,7,8,6,5,4,2,1,9},4) equals 0.090574

Using the CALL and REGISTER Functions

The following describes the argument and return value data types used by the CALL, REGISTER, and REGISTER.ID functions. Arguments and return values differ slightly depending on your operating environment, and these differences are noted in the data type table.

The *Microsoft Excel 97 Developer's Kit* contains detailed information about dynamic link libraries (DLLs) and code resources, the Microsoft Excel application programming interface (API), file formats, and many other technical aspects of Microsoft Excel. It also contains code samples and programming tools that you can use to develop custom applications. To obtain a copy of the *Microsoft Excel 97 Developer's Kit,* contact your software supplier or Microsoft Press®. In the United States, contact Microsoft Press at (800) 677-7377.

Data Types

In the CALL, REGISTER, and REGISTER.ID functions, the type_text argument specifies the data type of the return value and the data types of all arguments to the DLL function or code resource. The first character of type_text specifies the data type of the return value. The remaining characters indicate the data types of all the arguments. For example, a DLL function that returns a floating-point number and takes an integer and a floating-point number as arguments would require "BIB" for the type_text argument.

The following table contains a complete list of the data type codes that Microsoft Excel recognizes, a description of each data type, how the argument or return value is passed, and a typical declaration for the data type in the C programming language.

Code	Description	Pass by	C Declaration
A	Logical (FALSE = 0), TRUE = 1)	Value	short int
B	IEEE 8-byte floating-point number	Value (Windows) Reference (Macintosh)	double (Windows) double * (Macintosh)

Code	Description	Pass by	C Declaration
C	Null-terminated string (maximum string length = 255)	Reference	char *
D	Byte-counted string (first byte contains length of string, maximum string length = 255 characters)	Reference	Unsigned char *
E	IEEE 8-byte floating-point number	Reference	double *
F	Null-terminated string (maximum string length = 255 characters)	Reference (modify in place)	char *
G	Byte-counted string (first byte contains length of string, maximum string length = 255 characters)	Reference (modify in place)	unsigned char *
H	Unsigned 2-byte integer	Value	unsigned short int
I	Signed 2-byte integer	Value	short int
J	Signed 4-byte integer	Value	long int
K	Array	Reference	FP *
L	Logical (FALSE = 0, TRUE = 1)	Reference	short int *
M	Signed 2-byte integer	Reference	short int *
N	Signed 4-byte integer	Reference	long int *
O	Array	Reference	Three arguments are passed: unsigned short int * unsigned short int * double [ ]
P	Microsoft Excel OPER data structure	Reference	OPER *
R	Microsoft Excel XLOPER data structure	Reference	XLOPER *

Remarks

- The C-language declarations are based on the assumption that your compiler defaults to 8-byte doubles, 2-byte short integers, and 4-byte long integers.

- In the Microsoft Windows programming environment, all pointers are far pointers. For example, you must declare the D data type code as `unsigned char far *` in Microsoft Windows.

- All functions in DLLs and code resources are called using the Pascal calling convention. Most C compilers allow you to use the Pascal calling convention by adding the Pascal keyword to the function declaration, as shown in the following example:

```
pascal void main (rows,columns,a)
```

- If a function uses a pass-by-reference data type for its return value, you can pass a null pointer as the return value. Microsoft Excel will interpret the null pointer as the #NUM! error value.

Additional Data Type Information

This section contains detailed information about the F, G, K, O, P, and R data types and other information about the type_text argument.

F and G Data Types

With the F and G data types, a function can modify a string buffer that is allocated by Microsoft Excel. If the return value type code is F or G, then Microsoft Excel ignores the value returned by the function. Instead, Microsoft Excel searches the list of function arguments for the first corresponding data type (F or G) and then takes the current contents of the allocated string buffer as the return value. Microsoft Excel allocates 256 bytes for the argument, so the function may return a larger string than it received.

K Data Type

The K data type uses a pointer to a variable-size FP structure. You must define this structure in the DLL or code resource as follows:

```
typedef struct _FP
{
   unsigned short int rows;
   unsigned short int columns;
   double array[1];      /* Actually, array[rows][columns] */
} FP;
```

The declaration double array[1] allocates storage for only a single-element array. The number of elements in the actual array equals the number of rows multiplied by the number of columns.

O Data Type

The O data type can be used only as an argument, not as a return value. It passes three items: a pointer to the number of rows in an array, a pointer to the number of columns in an array, and a pointer to a two-dimensional array of floating-point numbers.

Instead of returning a value, a function can modify an array passed by the O data type. To do this, you can use ">O" as the type_text argument. For more information, see "Modifying in Place—Functions Declared as Void" below.

The O data type was created for direct compatibility with Fortran DLLs, which pass arguments by reference.

P Data Type

The P data type is a pointer to an OPER structure. The OPER structure contains 8 bytes of data, followed by a 2-byte identifier that specifies the type of data. With the P data type, a DLL function or code resource can take and return any Microsoft Excel data type.

The OPER structure is defined as follows:

```
typedef struct _oper

{
    union
    {
        double num;
        unsigned char *str;
        unsigned short int bool;
        unsigned short int err;
        struct
        {
            struct _oper *lparray;
            unsigned short int rows;
            unsigned short int columns;
        } array;
    } val;
    unsigned short int type;
} OPER;
```

The type field contains one of these values.

Type	Description	Val field to use
1	Numeric	num
2	String (first byte contains length of string)	str
4	Boolean (logical)	bool
16	Error: the error values are:	err
	0 #NULL!	
	7 #DIV/0!	
	15 #Value!	
	23 #REF!	
	29 #NAME?	
	36 #NUM!	
	42 #N/A	
64	Array	array
128	Missing argument	
256	Empty cell	

The last two values can be used only as arguments, not return values. The missing argument value (128) is passed when the caller omits an argument. The empty cell value (256) is passed when the caller passes a reference to an empty cell.

R Data Type—Calling Microsoft Excel Functions from DLLs

The R data type is a pointer to an XLOPER structure, which is an enhanced version of the OPER structure. In Microsoft Excel version 4.0 and later, you can use the R data type to write DLLs and code resources that call Microsoft Excel functions. With the XLOPER structure, a DLL function can pass sheet references and implement flow control, in addition to passing data. A complete description of the R data type and the Microsoft Excel application programming interface (API) is beyond the scope of this topic. The *Microsoft Excel Developer's Kit* contains detailed information about the R data type, the Microsoft Excel API, and many other technical aspects of Microsoft Excel.

Volatile Functions and Recalculation

Microsoft Excel usually calculates a DLL function (or a code resource) only when it is entered into a cell, when one of its precedents changes, or when the cell is calculated during a macro. On a worksheet, you can make a DLL function or code resource volatile, which means that it recalculates every time the worksheet recalculates. To make a function volatile, add an exclamation point (!) as the last character in the type_text argument.

For example, in Microsoft Excel for Windows 95 and Microsoft Excel for Windows NT, the following worksheet formula recalculates every time the worksheet recalculates:

```
CALL("Kernel32","GetTickCount","J!")
```

Modifying in Place—Functions Declared as Void

You can use a single digit n for the return type code in type_text, where n is a number from 1 to 9. This tells Microsoft Excel to modify the variable in the location pointed to by the nth argument in type_text, instead of returning a value. This is also known as modifying in place. The nth argument must be a pass-by-reference data type (C, D, E, F, G, K, L, M, N, O, P, or R). The DLL function or code resource must also be declared with the void keyword in the C language (or the procedure keyword in the Pascal language).

For example, a DLL function that takes a null-terminated string and two pointers to integers as arguments can modify the string in place. Use "1FMM" as the type_text argument, and declare the function as void.

Versions prior to Microsoft Excel 4.0 used the > character to modify the first argument in place; there was no way to modify any argument other than the first. The > character is equivalent to n = 1 in Microsoft Excel version 4.0 and later.

For more information

The following books provide detailed information on financial, statistical, and engineering methods.

Abramowitz, Milton, and Irene A. Stegun. Handbook of Mathematical Functions with Formulas, Graphs, and Mathematical Tables. 10th ed. Washington, D.C.: U.S. Government Printing Office, 1972.

Devore, Jay L. Probability and Statistics for Engineering and the Sciences. 4th ed. Belmont, Calif.: Wadsworth, 1991.

Fabozzi, Frank J. The Handbook of Fixed-Income Securities. 3rd ed. Homewood, Ill.: Irwin Professional, 1990.

Hewlett-Packard, HP-12C Owner's Handbook and Problem-Solving Guide. N.p.: Hewlett-Packard, 1981.

Lynch, John J., Jr., and Jan H. Mayle. Standard Securities Calculation Methods, Fixed Income Securities Formulas. New York: Securities Industry Association, 1994.

McCall, Robert B. Fundamental Statistics for the Behavioral Sciences. 6th ed. Belmont, Calif.: Wadsworth, 1994.

Press, W. H., B. P. Flannery, S. A. Teukolsky, and W. T. Vetterling. Numerical Recipes in C: The Art of Scientific Computing. 2nd ed. New York: Cambridge University Press, 1992.

Sokal, Robert R., and F. James Rohlf. Biometry: The Principles and Practice of Statistics in Biological Research. 2nd ed. New York: W. H. Freeman, 1995.

Stigum, Marcia, and John Mann. Money Market Calculations: Yields, Break-Evens, & Arbitrage. 2nd ed. Homewood, Ill.: Irwin Professional, 1989.

Monks, Joseph G. Operations Management: Theory and Problems. 3rd ed. New York: McGraw-Hill, 1987.

Get quick, easy answers—anywhere!

Microsoft® Excel 97 Field Guide
Stephen L. Nelson
U.S.A. **$9.95** ($12.95 Canada)
ISBN: 1-57231-326-9

Microsoft® Word 97 Field Guide
Stephen L. Nelson
U.S.A. **$9.95** ($12.95 Canada)
ISBN: 1-57231-325-0

Microsoft® PowerPoint® 97 Field Guide
Stephen L. Nelson
U.S.A. **$9.95** ($12.95 Canada)
ISBN: 1-57231-327-7

Microsoft® Outlook™ 97 Field Guide
Stephen L. Nelson
U.S.A. **$9.99** ($12.99 Canada)
ISBN: 1-57231-383-8

Microsoft® Access 97 Field Guide
Stephen L. Nelson
U.S.A. **$9.95** ($12.95 Canada)
ISBN: 1-57231-328-5

Microsoft Press® Field Guides are a quick, accurate source of information about Microsoft® Office 97 applications. In no time, you'll have the lay of the land, identify toolbar buttons and commands, stay safely out of danger, and have all the tools you need for survival!

Microsoft Press® products are available worldwide wherever quality computer books are sold. For more information, contact your book retailer, computer reseller, or local Microsoft Sales Office.

To locate your nearest source for Microsoft Press products, reach us at www.microsoft.com/mspress/, or call 1-800-MSPRESS in the U.S. (in Canada: 1-800-667-1115 or 416-293-8464).

To order Microsoft Press products, call 1-800-MSPRESS in the U.S. (in Canada: 1-800-667-1115 or 416-293-8464).

Prices and availability dates are subject to change.

Keep things **running** smoothly around the **Office.**

These are *the* answer books for business users of Microsoft® Office 97 applications. They are packed with everything from quick, clear instructions for new users to comprehensive answers for power users. The Microsoft Press® *Running* series features authoritative handbooks you'll keep by your computer and use every day.

Running Microsoft® Excel 97
Mark Dodge, Chris Kinata, and Craig Stinson
U.S.A. $39.95   ($54.95 Canada)
ISBN: 1-57231-321-8

Running Microsoft® Office 97
Michael Halvorson and Michael Young
U.S.A. $39.95   ($54.95 Canada)
ISBN: 1-57231-322-6

Running Microsoft® Word 97
Russell Borland
U.S.A. $39.95   ($54.95 Canada)
ISBN: 1-57231-320-X

Running Microsoft® PowerPoint® 97
Stephen W. Sagman
U.S.A. $29.95   ($39.95 Canada)
ISBN: 1-57231-324-2

Running Microsoft® Access 97
John Viescas
U.S.A. $39.95   ($54.95 Canada)
ISBN: 1-57231-323-4

Microsoft Press® products are available worldwide wherever quality computer books are sold. For more information, contact your book retailer, computer reseller, or local Microsoft Sales Office.

To locate your nearest source for Microsoft Press products, reach us at www.microsoft.com/mspress/, or call 1-800-MSPRESS in the U.S. (in Canada: 1-800-667-1115 or 416-293-8464).

To order Microsoft Press products, call 1-800-MSPRESS in the U.S. (in Canada: 1-800-667-1115 or 416-293-8464).

Prices and availability dates are subject to change.

Take
productivity
in **stride.**

Microsoft Press® *Step by Step* books provide quick and easy self-paced training that will help you learn to use the powerful word processor, spreadsheet, database, and presentation applications of Microsoft® Office 97, both individually and together. In approximately eight hours of instruction prepared by the professional trainers at Catapult, Inc., the easy-to-follow lessons present clear objectives and real-world business examples, with numerous screen shots and illustrations. Put Microsoft's Office 97 applications to work today, *Step by Step*.

Microsoft® Excel 97 Step by Step
U.S.A. $29.99   ($39.99 Canada)
ISBN: 1-57231-314-5

Microsoft® Word 97 Step by Step
U.S.A. $29.99   ($39.99 Canada)
ISBN: 1-57231-313-7

**Microsoft® PowerPoint® 97
 Step by Step**
U.S.A. $29.95   ($39.95 Canada)
ISBN: 1-57231-315-3

Microsoft® Outlook™ 97 Step by Step
U.S.A. $29.99   ($39.99 Canada)
ISBN: 1-57231-382-X

Microsoft® Access 97 Step by Step
U.S.A. $29.95   ($39.95 Canada)
ISBN: 1-57231-316-1

**Microsoft® Office 97 Integration
 Step by Step**
U.S.A. $29.95   ($39.95 Canada)
ISBN: 1-57231-317-X

Microsoft Press® products are available worldwide wherever quality computer books are sold. For more information, contact your book retailer, computer reseller, or local Microsoft Sales Office.

To locate your nearest source for Microsoft Press products, reach us at www.microsoft.com/mspress/, or call 1-800-MSPRESS in the U.S. (in Canada: 1-800-667-1115 or 416-293-8464).

To order Microsoft Press products, call 1-800-MSPRESS in the U.S. (in Canada: 1-800-667-1115 or 416-293-8464).

Prices and availability dates are subject to change.

Microsoft Press

Register Today!

Return this
Microsoft® Excel 97
Worksheet Function Reference
registration card for
a Microsoft Press® catalog

U.S. and Canada addresses only. Fill in information below and mail postage-free. Please mail only the bottom half of this page.

1-57231-341-2A

MICROSOFT® EXCEL 97
WORKSHEET FUNCTION REFERENCE

Owner Registration Card

NAME

INSTITUTION OR COMPANY NAME

ADDRESS

CITY   STATE   ZIP

Microsoft *Press*
Quality Computer Books

For a free catalog of
Microsoft Press® products, call
1-800-MSPRESS

BUSINESS REPLY MAIL
FIRST-CLASS MAIL   PERMIT NO. 53   BOTHELL, WA

POSTAGE WILL BE PAID BY ADDRESSEE

MICROSOFT PRESS REGISTRATION
MICROSOFT® EXCEL 97
WORKSHEET FUNCTION REFERENCE
PO BOX 3019
BOTHELL WA   98041-9946